Strategic Pragmatism

Organization Studies
John Van Maanen, general editor

1. *Competition and Control at Work: A New Industrial Sociology,* Stephen Hill, 1982.

2. *Strategies for Change: The Future of French Society,* Michael Crozier, translated by William R. Beer, 1982

3. *Control in the Police Organization,* edited by Maurice Punch, 1983

4. *Disorganized Crime: The Economics of the Visible Hand,* Peter Reuter, 1983

5. *Industrial Democracy at Sea,* edited by Robert Shrank, 1983

6. *The Mediators,* Deborah M. Kolb, 1983

7. *Sons of the Machine: Case Studies of Social Change in the Workplace,* Charles H. Savage, Jr., and George F. F. Lombard, 1986

8. *The Workplace Within: Psychodynamics of Organizational Life,* Larry Hirschhorn, 1988

9. *Symbolic Communication: Signifying Calls and the Police Response,* Peter K. Manning, 1988

10. *Front Stage, Backstage: The Dramatic Structure of Labor Negotiations,* Raymond A. Friedman, 1994

11. *Strategic Pragmatism: The Culture of Singapore's Economic Development Board,* Edgar H. Schein, 1996

Strategic Pragmatism

The Culture of Singapore's Economic Development Board

Edgar H. Schein

The MIT Press
Cambridge, Massachusetts
London, England

Fourth printing, 2001

This book was set in Melior by Wellington Graphics.

Printed and bound in the United States of America.

Library of Congress Cataloging-in-Publication Data

Schein, Edgar H.
  Strategic pragmatism : the culture of Singapore's Economic Development Board / Edgar H. Schein.
      p.   cm. — (Organization studies ; 11)
  Includes bibliographical references and index.
  ISBN 0-262-19367-1 (alk. paper)
  1. Singapore. Economic Development Board. 2. Singapore—Economic policy. I. Title. II. Series: Organization studies (Cambridge, Mass.) ; 11.
  HC445.8.S15 1996
  338.95957—dc20   95-26598
                                                                         CIP

Contents

Foreword
Lester Thurow

In thirty years Singapore has gone from being a third world country with a per capita GDP of $500 to having a per capita GDP of $15,000 and being on the edge of the rich industrial world. No country has ever developed faster. When Singapore began its economic journey, it was commonly believed that one had to be part of a large internal market to develop. Following conventional wisdom, it started its journey with a strategy of import substitution in a much larger Malaysian Federation. Based on experience and necessity, it shifted to an export-led strategy and a commitment to becoming the world's best place for offshore manufacturing as a city-state with a very small market. During the course of its journey, it proved that city-states could not only prosper but could get rich faster than those with the largest internal markets. The ability to adjust rapidly was more important than economies of scale.

A wide variety of factors contribute to Singapore's success. No nation saves and invests more; people even argue as to whether it is investing too much. No nation has invested more resources in the skills and education of its people. Its goal is to have the world's best-educated labor force, from top to bottom. No one has ever started substantial investments in R & D at an earlier state of economic development. Singapore knew early that it would have to go upscale in technology and could not for long make it as a low-wage country. If its development strategy was successful, as it was, it would quickly have to compete with countries with lower wages. No one on the Pacific is better prepared to build and operate high-technology companies.

Singapore took advantage of what few advantages it had. Its geographic location made it potentially one of the world's great seaports.

But to realize that potential it had to spend lavishly on infrastructure, and then combine that infrastructure with a management drive that would give it the ability to load and unload ships faster than anyone else in the world. A vision of development springing from world-class infrastructure initially developed around the seaport and was later extended to the airport and telecommunications. The world's first electronic library may well be in Singapore. Singapore was both willing to copy others' successes and committed to being the world's best—take what others have done and build on it. All were part of an overall strategy of making Singapore a global city and a regional headquarters location for Southeast Asia.

Singapore paid its civil servants very well and held them to rigid standards of honesty seen in few other countries. Everything was on the table and potential investors got what they saw. Private investors were treated as valued clients when most of the third world was still suspicious of them—if not outright hostile.

In an era in which many countries are dividing into smaller countries, Singapore now seems like the leading edge of the future. Singapore has proved to other nations that it is possible to be both small and rich.

Nothing is ever completely transferable without modification from one part of the world or one culture to another, but Singapore has much to teach the rest of the world both in terms of substance and process. It benchmarks against the very best, it commits to being world-class, and it borrows whatever is best—but with the understanding that it must adapt whatever it has borrowed to local circumstances and culture.

Singapore is an interesting test case, perhaps the prototypical test case, of whether there is something unique about Asian values when it comes to economic development. And if there is something unique, why did that uniqueness not show itself until the last three decades? Singapore is not a conventional Western liberal democracy, but it is uniquely economically successful.

Given the success and the unique environment, it is fitting that one of the world's great experts on corporate cultures, Edgar H. Schein, decided to look at the economic culture of Singapore and its Economic Development Board. No country comes closer to having a corporate culture and to being run as a corporation where economic growth replaces profits as the explicitly defined goal. As Professor

Schein makes evident, Singapore's culture is just as intrinsic a part of its success story as its high level of investment or any of the other more tangible factors. Nor did it happen to grow by accident.

The two questions Professor Schein asks are straightforward but nonetheless difficult to answer. What is the nature of the corporate culture in the Economic Development Board in Singapore, and how did Singapore build an economic culture that works?

His story begins with a shared vision and a desire to build. The goal of "The Next Lap" in Singapore's journey is "To Develop Singapore into a Global City with Total Business Capabilities." Putting flesh on that vision is the job of the Economic Development Board (EDB). The EDB is neither the head nor the heart of the system, but best thought of as its energizer. The EDB has developed a unique system of working with the companies of Singapore (both local and foreign) that is intimate without being intrusive. It pushes firms hard to go upscale in technology—but does not try to run them.

Perhaps the most interesting of the announced cultural imperatives of the EDB is the "mental toughness and ability to absorb failure." One cannot know what is possible unless one tests the system, and if the system is being tested, some failures will result. One learns from examining airline crashes, not from looking at successful flights. The issue is to avoid punishing those who fail in the course of testing the limits of the system, but instead to punish those who are incompetent and those who do not learn from failure. Identify failure; change what does not work; create a learning environment! Easy advice—but hard to do unless one builds the corporate culture that supports such attitudes.

The EDB's other cultural imperatives are equally interesting. Create a long-range vision, build a team, draw out the best in team members. Demand total loyalty to the mission and a 120 percent commitment from everyone. Provide one-stop shopping for the clients from a totally professional organization devoted to teamwork, open communications, and a borderless organization. The rules are clear, there is no corruption, and integrity is total.

Being willing to copy to catch up, being willing to learn from others, and rejecting the "not invented here" syndrome are central to success, but are very difficult attitudes to instill in human beings. This is one of the places where it is important to learn how the Singapore culture was built. How does one build a spirit where one can be very proud of what one has done but still be willing to adopt anything found useful in the rest of the world?

Charting the cultural side of Singapore's success provides a unique window onto economic development. Professor Schein charts it well. The journey through his book will give you new insights into Singapore's journey into development.

Preface

Origin of the Project

Most studies of economic development begin with an analysis of the environment of the country, its resources, its internal structures, and its institutions. In this kind of institutional analysis, attention is given to the political climate, the prevailing economic philosophy, and the basic structures of government and industry. Too little attention is paid to the human dynamic that drives a particular country to develop and to the organizational structures that are evolved to make the human vision come to fruition.

These human factors are especially relevant if one examines the case of Singapore, which has experienced dramatic economic growth over the last thirty-five years. This book focuses on the leaders that created Singapore's Economic Development Board (EDB), the organization that became the instrument for developing an economic strategy and putting it into practice. The board is an international organization headquartered in Singapore and is viewed by many as primarily responsible for creating and implementing the various economic development programs that have propelled Singapore's rapid growth and modernization.

In telling the story of the EDB it is not my intention to provide a general model of economic development, but rather to analyze a case of organizational and cultural dynamics that illustrates the unique aspects of a given country's economic development. Lessons can be drawn about the complexity of the development process and about the managerial principles that make an organization particularly effective.

The project began in 1991 when a former EDB chairman asked me to be a consultant to a business writer who had been hired to write about the "corporate culture" of the EDB. Singapore's Nanyang Technological University was in the process of creating a number of joint programs with MIT's Sloan School of Management, so it was natural for the EDB to consult our dean, Lester Thurow, about locating a professor working on organizational culture. Dean Thurow suggested me because of my interest in that field.

Why focus on the EDB culture? Many of the EDB's past and present leaders believe that the EDB's culture was and is the key to understanding how the EDB had been able not only to stimulate Singapore's development but had, in that process, created a cadre of leaders who were now in senior government and private sector jobs espousing similar cultural values. Because many of these leaders believe that the culture of the EDB is partially responsible for Singapore's success, they felt that it needed to be described, analyzed, and documented.

The initial plan to serve as a consultant to the business writer fell through because he was unable to take on the project. I heard nothing more from the EDB that year, but I was recruited to give a management seminar to Singapore's Civil Service Institute in the spring of 1992. This two-week experience provided some familiarity with Singapore and made it quite obvious that, as many travelers are wont to say, "Things work in Singapore." I was approached at the end of the seminar by two senior members of the EDB with a request to help find a new writer or take on the project myself. In the meantime, the initial decision to have the story written by a business writer had also been rethought by the EDB and its alumni group, the EDB Society, in the direction of having the book be more analytical and oriented toward lessons that might be learned about economic development in a small country. A stimulus to this view was the increasing number of requests by less developed countries to get help from Singapore in planning their own development efforts. As noted, such requests did not imply that these countries wanted to imitate Singapore, which was recognized to be in a unique situation, but it was felt that Singapore's experience would provide perspective on development processes that could be useful to other countries.

The EDB Society, which ultimately sponsored this project, was formed in 1991 by former members of the EDB who had gone on to various high positions in industry and government and who believed that their EDB experience had been particularly valuable in their career development. It was their idea to commission a book on the EDB culture to commemorate the thirty-five years of economic success that Singapore had enjoyed and to which the EDB had contributed. Given that The EDB Society now wanted a more academic and critical analysis, I was approached to take on the project and, if willing, to write a proposal and timetable; these plans were accepted in the fall of 1992.

A few words are in order on why I chose to do this research. I was between writing projects and needed a new focus for my interest in organizational culture. I have always been interested in the problems of obtaining understanding across cultural boundaries, so a project in Singapore would not only be stimulating but would also be a major learning experience. I had worked in European companies for many years and had some feel for those cultures, but had hardly any Asian experience. I had been in Singapore briefly in 1980 and found the contrast between then and 1991 dramatic. Things were clearly happening there. But perhaps most important of all was that the Singaporeans I met were all articulate, enthusiastic, stimulating, highly motivated, and very persuasive. Singapore had adopted English as its primary language, so communication would not be major problem as I interviewed and observed people in action.

How to Present the Story

The organization of this book provided some unusual challenges because I was writing to several audiences with different needs and expectations. The sponsor of the project wanted a book that would explain the EDB to its current and future members and would make them understand the power and reach of the EDB culture. They did not want, as they put it, "a coffee-table book" but rather one that would educate. The former chairmen and some of the current leaders of the EDB had a grand vision of a book that would explain some of the psychosocial subtleties of economic development and would therefore appeal to organizations such as the World Bank. Their view was that too much was written about economics in economic development and not enough about how change is actually effected.

Potential publishers and my colleagues wanted a book that would appeal to a broad managerial audience in showing how a particular organization illustrated important general management principles. And of course, I wanted a book that would permit me to articulate my own insights in a way that would satisfy my analytical as well as aesthetic criteria. The ultimate criterion that dictated what made it into print was what I could, in the end, articulate to my own level of satisfaction. I would have to take my chances with the various audiences.

A major dilemma surrounding the organization of the material was how to present the positive picture of the EDB that emerged in the data within the sociopolitical context of Singapore as a nation that many Western academics regard as politically less developed. This dilemma was heightened by the controversy that surrounds Singapore's political system, fanned especially by the case of the caning of a U.S. teenager in May 1994. When I talked to various Western audiences about the EDB as an organization, inevitably the skeptical response would be, "But what about Singapore's political system, their repression of free speech and a free press, their one-party system, their suppression of political dissidents, their extensive and detailed laws about spitting, gum chewing, urinating in elevators, and their excessive levels of punishment for what seem to Westerners minor infractions?"

It became obvious to me that once people had made up their minds about Singapore and its seeming violation of certain Western-defined human rights, it was very difficult to get them to look at any of this in a historical or cultural context. I had to go through my own transition of overcoming an initial stereotype of Singapore to begin to understand how the Singaporean worldview evolved. The story of the EDB is particularly helpful here because it illustrates many elements of Singaporean society and culture that are not at all consistent with the stereotype, and forces us to look more deeply into both the phenomenon of organizational culture and the cultural contexts within with organizations exist.

In particular, the manner in which power and hierarchy function within the EDB requires us to reexamine many Western conceptions of power, authority, and the role of hierarchy in systems of governance. How can a leader be an autocrat yet make people feel empowered, and how can subordinates be both autonomous and subservient? How can organizational communication be "open," an ideal found in many Western management theories, yet be carefully screened to protect status, face, and confidential information about clients of the organization? In other words, what we have in the EDB is an organization that was able to actualize much of what organization theory defines as "ideal" and yet to do that in a cultural context that appears on the surface to be quite inimical to such an organizational form. It is in the unraveling of such paradoxes that I found the most fruitful insights on management, organization, and economic development.

Organization of the Book

In the end I decided to tell several stories. In chapter 1 I foreshadow the basic organization of the book in presenting the EDB from three perspectives—its own perspective, the perspective of its investor clients, and my own analytical perspective. Part I, comprising chapters 2 to 7, presents a historical retrospective of the key leaders of the EDB through the decades. These chapters elaborate the EDB's perspective on itself. Part II, comprising chapters 8 and 9, presents first U.S. investor perceptions and then some data from European, Asian, and local investors and managers. These chapters provide the perspective of the EDB's clients and Singapore's foreign investors. Part III shifts to my own analytical perspective and presents the culture in terms of a contextual and operational paradigm in chapters 10 and 11. In Part IV, I review problems and issues in chapter 12 and 13, and lessons and conclusions in chapter 14.

Acknowledgments

This book would not have been possible without the help of a great many people. The members of the EDB itself, past and present, were consistently supportive and worked hard to set up my visits, gather information that I needed, and provide firsthand accounts to bring the culture of the organization to life. Lam Yeen Lan, the secretary of the EDB, acted as project manager and worked diligently to bring all of the pieces into alignment. My wife and I especially appreciated her generosity and hospitality during our visits to Singapore, and her hard work in providing various kinds of information. Also most helpful in providing information and conceptual guidance were Chan Chin Bock, who originally recruited me to do the project, and Shirley Chen, the EDB's director of corporate services. Special thanks go to the executive committee of the EDB Society for their financial and intellectual support of the project and their continued feedback as the project evolved.

No study like this could succeed without the cooperation of the many informants who were interviewed, sometimes repeatedly. I cannot single them out here, but they are listed in the appropriate appendixes. Also of great importance in gaining some objectivity were my colleagues who read early versions of chapters, especially Don Michael and John Van Maanen. Both were highly influential in guiding my thinking of how one can present material like this in a credible fashion. Some seminal discussions with Lucian Pye helped to put all of this into a broader cultural perspective. The referees who read the manuscript for The MIT Press were also most helpful in suggesting improvements to the text, especially John Van Maanen, who is editor of the series in which this book appears.

Most important, I could not have done this project without the active participation and support of my wife at all stages. She participated in all the visits to Singapore, attended the many group lunches and dinners at which vital information was obtained, helped me to sort out what I was observing and what it meant, and edited the final manuscript. She was especially helpful in keeping the writing from getting too abstract and irrelevant. Throughout the whole project she was a true colleague, confidante, and highly effective critic.

1

Singapore's Economic Development Board— Three Perspectives

This book is about the culture of Singapore's Economic Development Board (EDB), a quasi-governmental agency set up in 1961 by Singapore's leaders to implement a plan to attract foreign investment. Singapore was a British colony that achieved self-rule in 1958. It joined the Malaysian Federation in 1963 and achieved full independence in 1965 when it left the federation. The EDB had been set up well before full independence on the assumption that Singapore would need rapid economic development once it achieved self-rule and would have to get along without the British naval bases that contributed heavily to its economy. It is widely asserted that the EDB was a crucial element in the economic growth that Singapore achieved and that the success of the EDB is largely a function of the culture that this organization created.

The story of the EDB and its organizational culture is therefore important for several reasons:

1. It sheds light on how Singapore, in the space of thirty-five years, could be transformed from a fairly impoverished underdeveloped former colony into a modern city-state that today aspires to be in the top ranks of developed economies.

2. It illustrates the importance of noneconomic factors in the analysis of economic development. In particular, it clarifies some of the issues between "Asian" and "Western" concepts of organization and management in that Singapore turns out to be a genuine East-West hybrid.

3. It sheds light on why the World Bank and other organizations are urging developing countries to look to Singapore for guidance and help on how to manage their own development. This assistance is forthcoming through a consulting organization that the Economic Development Board has set up, which has attracted requests for help

from countries as widely dispersed as Cambodia, Ghana, Indonesia, and Oman.

This account does not attempt to evaluate or judge Singapore's economic strategy or political system, nor do I propose to compare Singapore's economic development to that of other rapidly growing economies. Rather, I am attempting to show how the managerial processes and cultural assumptions of one key organization, the Economic Development Board, contributed to the creation and implementation of Singapore's economic growth. What is to be learned from this story has more to do with the processes of economic development than the actual content of a given strategy of growth. What these processes reveal is the importance of the human factor at many levels, not just at the leadership level.

In other words, if one is to understand some of the actual mechanisms by which Singapore's "economic miracle" took place and appreciate why other developing countries are seeking Singapore's advice, one must look beyond the actions of the leadership of the society and the particular economic conditions that prevailed at the time. In addition, one must focus on the organization that helped create an economic strategy and was responsible for its subsequent implementation—the Economic Development Board.

As we will see, what is remarkable about this organization is not only its ability to change and grow as Singapore's economic and political circumstances changed, but its ability to develop a cadre of leaders who became influential in Singapore's government and private industry. The EDB was thus an agent and catalyst of the development of a broader set of capabilities that Singapore has displayed over the decades. It is those organizational capabilities that attract other developing nations and need, therefore, to be better understood.

By using a variety of data I will attempt to show how the EDB came to be, how it operated in the past and operates today, how its management style and culture were responsible for developing leaders for the society as a whole, and how the EDB through its various operations was consistently successful in solving the problems of Singapore's foreign investors. At the same time, in analyzing the culture of the EDB, I will attempt to show how some of the cultural elements that have strong historical roots may be dysfunctional in today's political and economic climate and may be creating problems for Singapore and the EDB. Those problems will need to be addressed if Singapore's further economic aspirations are to be achieved.

A Note on Research Method

The deciphering of an organization's culture requires an interactive process between the researcher and the members of the organization, because the description of the culture must make sense to the insiders even though the analysis creates categories and levels of abstraction that the insiders may find novel and sometimes even disturbing (Schein 1992). A cultural analysis is likely to uncover themes that have been held in the organization's "unconscious," not all of which are likely to be perceived as positive elements in the organization. I made this point clear before undertaking the research, and I felt that the leaders of the EDB and the EDB Society understood and accepted it.

From the beginning it was obvious that I was dealing with a spirited, proud, high-morale organization that believed in itself completely yet wanted to find a way to become more conscious of its vulnerabilities and shortcomings. The EDB leaders I encountered were both optimistic and concerned about the future, and wondered whether the EDB could maintain its track record of success in the face of a more turbulent world.

My mandate then was complicated. I had to describe the strength of this organization (the culture that its members believed to be the source of its success), and yet identify the "weaknesses" in that culture and do a critical analysis that would help the organization improve itself. I had to get into the culture enough to get a feel for why the EDB worked as well as it did without losing my critical capacity to see how those very organizational processes might become dysfunctional in the future. I had to accurately depict the positive self-image of the EDB without, however, losing sight of the problems and issues mentioned by many informants.

Problems and issues in Singapore and in the EDB were identified by my informants throughout the study, but invariably within the context of an overwhelmingly positive view of how the EDB operated. This positive view was especially evident among the current members of the EDB in that problems were invariably cast as opportunities to do even better. Such a positive self-image notwith-standing, to fulfill the expectation that this study would identify weaknesses and enable the EDB to improve itself, I decided to pull all the problems, issues, and criticisms into two chapters at the end of the book rather than scattering them throughout the text. This point needs to be understood by the reader lest it appear that I have presented an idealized version of the EDB. How an organization looks at itself is, however, an essential element of its culture, hence a positive optimistic self-presentation—if based on a track record of success and on current observable realities—is an accurate view of its current culture.

I also decided that it was important for the reader to be able to tell from what point of reference a problem or issue was identified. But given the sensitivities to criticism that were culturally very obvious in many of my informants, I decided to identify the sources of criticism only by title and role, not by name.

My prior experience as a consultant and clinical researcher helped in conducting this somewhat complex kind of research project. As a process consultant working in organizations, I had learned that one can take an objective clinical stance toward the client system and that such a stance is, in fact, the essence of both ethnography and effective consultation (Schein 1987a, 1987b). The consultant must get into the culture of the organization sufficiently to identify what kinds of interventions will be genuinely helpful; the ethnographer has to learn to be helpful in order to get access to the kinds of information that will ultimately permit the detailed sort of descrip-tion that he or she is after. The most effective stance toward this kind of fieldwork is therefore a combination of ethnography, participant observation, data gathering by means of interviews and question-naires as appropriate, and occasionally more confrontational inter-ventions into the system to observe and analyze responses.

I defined the project as a two-year action research endeavor involv-ing several kinds of basic data:

1. Observation of EDB meetings to get a feel for how day-to-day work was actually done;
2. Interviews of Singaporean government officials who had been instrumental in creating and maintaining the EDB;
3. Interviews of current members of the EDB at all levels of the organization;

4. Interviews of EDB "alumni" who had spent formative years in the EDB and then gone on to other careers in industry or government;

5. Interviews of business executives who had made the decision to invest in Singapore by placing their operations there (questionnaires where needed);

6. Interviews of current managers who had day-to-day dealings with the EDB in maintaining and enlarging their operations;

7. Interviews of local Singaporean businessmen who had dealings with the EDB;

8. Analysis of written historical accounts, current and past literature by the EDB such as annual reports and promotional materials of various sorts;

9. Information gleaned from miscellaneous accounts of Singapore, its history, and its current mode of operation.

Interviews in Singapore were conducted during two visits of several weeks' duration in the spring of 1993 and 1994. Because the EDB operates worldwide, interviews in the international offices were conducted in San Francisco, Chicago, Washington, Boston, and New York. Some EDB members from Europe and Asia were interviewed in Hong Kong and in meetings they attended in various U.S. locations. Business executives from a dozen or more companies were interviewed in person or by phone, and those that could not be reached were given brief questionnaires.

Efforts were made to reach managers who had decided not to invest in Singapore, and all interviewees were asked to provide both the pros and cons of investing in Singapore. Some additional critical data were obtained by this means, but it must be stated at the outset that this kind of cultural analysis based on "action research" cannot be likened to more traditional comparative studies. Instead of focusing on a few variables that are observable in several kinds of organizations or countries, the emphasis here is on a comprehensive analysis of a single case that reveals a variety of themes and variables that may or may not be found in other organizations or that may have different meanings in different cultural contexts.

The intention is to increase in-depth understanding of how the economic development process worked in Singapore, not to develop a general model of economic development. It is for this reason that no explicit comparisons are made to other rapidly developing economies such as Hong Kong. If anything, the case of Singapore reveals how idiosyncratic the dynamics of economic development really are and argues therefore for more detailed analyses rather than broad comparative studies. Members of the EDB who have worked with other countries are the first to point out Singapore's historically unique situation. They feel that the only kind of help they can offer to other countries is to analyze what may be the unique factors operating in these countries at a particular time in history.

What then permits one to be analytical and critical in this kind of inquiry? To make sense of a mass of case detail, the clinical researcher must fall back on theory, in this case organization theory and cross-cultural theory, and on the diversity of his or her own experience. As one analyzes a case, one inevitably sees elements that resemble other cases and can draw potential inferences. At the same time, the clinical researcher approaches all cases with a set of theoretical tools that have been tested against observed cases and therefore permit extrapolation and hypothesis formation (Schein 1987a, 1987b, 1992).

A check on one's reasoning is provided by the functional equivalent of the clinical case conference, during which others who are knowledgeable in the field listen to the case presentation and make analytical and critical comments. That function has been fulfilled by presenting portions of my analysis to experts on Southeast Asia, on economic development, and on organizational culture to obtain feedback and further data or suggestions. In getting comments from these various perspectives, I look for coherence and consistency. If some of the results are questioned or are inconsistent with other results, it is necessary to review the raw interview data and the logic by which the result was arrived at.

This process is to some degree subjective and must be acknowledged as such. In the end, this story is my own construction, and I do not claim that I can surmount all of my biases. Such biases inevitably show up in my choice of what to present and how to present it. The historical analysis is geared to highlighting how the EDB culture came to be and, as with all history, much detail is omitted. To a considerable degree this study depends on oral history, based on the perceptions of key actors in the drama as to how they came to be where they are. It is not a history based on formal documentation and records. The description of the culture is based on my own definitions of "organizational culture" and my own method of analyzing cultural phenomena (Schein 1992).

As many have recently pointed out, knowledge in the social and organizational domain cannot be objectified in terms of traditional concepts of natural science (Van Maanen 1988). In the end, even the physicist is only telling a story, and the validity of a given story can be judged only by its capacity to explain something that was not understood before, by its ability to make something coherent, and ultimately, by its capacity to be useful to others. The concept of validity itself is a social construction defined by a given community of researchers, so we should have no illusions that one account is more valid than another in some absolute philosophical or epistemological sense.

For me the relevant community that must make this judgment is the organization that is being described here and my fellow social scientists whose model of how to obtain knowledge accepts the assumption that we are all looking at the world through our own lenses, and that objectivity is at best a relative phenomenon. In the last analysis, I must gamble on the fact that another observer going to Singapore and becoming acquainted with the EDB would see similar things to those that I observed and, although he or she might interpret or judge them differently, would reach similar conclusions to those I have reported here.

The Need for Multiple Perspectives

To understand the EDB and its role in Singapore, one must view it from several perspectives. One perspective is that of the present and past members of the EDB itself, as articulated in my interviews and enhanced by my observations of the EDB in meetings of various sorts. A second perspective is that of the past and current "clients" of the EDB, the managers and entrepreneurs who decided to invest in Singapore and build manufacturing and other facilities there. A third perspective that I will intersperse throughout the story is my own analysis of the organization and its culture, based on my direct observations and experiences with the EDB, reading, interviews with other Singaporeans not directly involved with the EDB, and reflection on all of the above. I make no claim that any one of these perspectives is in some absolute sense more valid than any other but, by presenting the EDB from several perspectives, I hope to provide the reader with a feeling for the EDB and the complexity of the economic development process.

The multiple perspectives also help to frame why this kind of single case analysis is important and what is to be learned from it. From the point of view of the EDB, it is important to gain insight into itself and to have a vehicle for perpetuating the best elements of its culture. It is important for present and future members of the EDB to understand some of the core assumptions and beliefs that govern its behavior. Unless they are made explicit, one cannot really evaluate how functional they are as one looks to Singapore's future.

From the point of view of the present and future clients of the EDB, the foreign and local investors, it is important to communicate what it is that past clients have found to be particularly effective in how the EDB conducts its business, to provide feedback to the EDB and, most important, to educate potential future investors to the pros and cons of dealing with Singapore. The lessons learned by the EDB can potentially be useful to other economic development organizations in other countries even though the cultural, political, and economic conditions will in every case be different and may require another kind of response. Nevertheless, what investors look for, want, and need, as well as how the EDB has dealt with them, is important to understand.

My own analytical perspective will focus on the implications of the EDB culture for management and organization theory in general. As I will articulate, the way the EDB operates simultaneously illustrates and contradicts some of the most salient organization theories of the day. As we are being told how organizations are reducing or even abandoning hierarchies and creating flat networks, we find in the EDB—and to some extent in other parts of the Singapore establishment—both a fairly steep hierarchy and a very flat and very effective network that is able to coordinate rapidly.

We are told in many theories that organizational effectiveness hinges on high levels of employee involvement and delegation of decisions to the lowest possible level, and we find in the EDB culture that indeed the first-line level of the organization feels very empowered, yet decisions are made by a fairly formal hierarchical process that, at times, reflects extreme centralization. Current management theory emphasizes the importance of effective communication and open, truthful transmission of information, and indeed one finds a high level of openness in the EDB. But at the same time, the nature of the task, that is, working with clients whose own plans must be kept highly confidential, requires difficult judgments of when to enter what data into the total organization's information system. Furthermore, operating in an Asian context requires high levels of interpersonal sensitivity when it comes to approving or disapproving projects, providing performance appraisals, and building teams from among potentially competing individuals. In the end, the EDB is a set of paradoxes that illustrates how oversimplified much of our contemporary organization and management theory is.

The EDB Perspective on Itself

Structure, Strategy, and Operations

The EDB is a global organization that includes 236 managers and senior officers and a support staff of 183 junior officers, clerks, secretaries, drivers, and other support personnel. It was created as a "statutory board" by the Singapore Parliament in 1961. The EDB's basic structure consists of a government-appointed twelve-member board, a chairman who functions as the chief executive, a managing director who functions as the chief operating officer, and a group of operating units under directors. The basic organization of the EDB is shown in table 1.1.

As a statutory board, the EDB possesses the status of a government corporation and therefore enjoys greater administrative flexibility than other government agencies. It has some freedom to go outside the civil service structure with its own salary scales and can carry out various business dealings without having to follow all government procedures. The board meets monthly to review, comment on, and ratify the decisions proposed by the organization.

The EDB's headquarters are currently housed in several floors of one of Singapore's centrally located ultramodern office buildings. It also has offices in New York, San Francisco, Los Angeles, Chicago, Washington, Boston, London, Paris, Frankfurt, Milan, Stockholm, Hong Kong, Tokyo, Osaka, and Jakarta. Each office is staffed by one or more directors and support staff.

Table 1.1
The organization of the EDB

1. International Operations Division
2. Operations Division
   a. Enterprise Development Division devoted to the stimulation of entrepreneurship and the development of local small and medium-size enterprises
   b. Services Development Division devoted to the development of the service sector
   c. Industry Development Division devoted to the development of selected cluster of companies in selected strategically relevant industries
   d. Manpower and Capability Development Division devoted to developing the capability of local and overseas enterprises to support the industry clusters, and to attract foreign talent needed to support evolving industry
   e. International Business Development to spearhead the regionalization initiatives
3. Strategic Business Units
   a. National Biotechnology Program
   b. China Focus Unit to monitor and advise on China policy
   c. EDB Consulting Group
4. Services
   a. Planning Division
   b. Human Resources Division
   c. Corporate Services Division
   d. Internal Audit Unit

The EDB presents itself today through a wide variety of brochures, reports, and promotional materials that highlight its current mission: *"To Develop Singapore into a Global City with Total Business Capabilities"* (1992–1993 Annual Report, p. 1).

For a number of years the symbol was "Singapore, Inc.," reflecting Singapore's efforts to run the country much like a business. Today that symbol has been replaced by the even more ambitious "Singapore Unlimited," reflecting a number of strategic thrusts that go well beyond attracting foreign investments for manufacturing. There is growing emphasis on promoting services (particularly those relating to manufacturing), on further encouraging the entry of higher technology enterprises that would provide training and upward mobility for Singaporeans, and on building clusters of industries that reflect common technologies, raw material sources, and marketing opportunities. Such clusters would aid in stimulating local enterprises, which could become sole-source suppliers and thereby build up local industries into units large enough to become multinationals themselves.

To overcome its physical size limitations, lack of raw materials, lack of a home market, and labor shortages, Singapore has launched a strategy of regionalization in which it works with its immediate neighbors to create attractive low-cost manufacturing opportunities for investors. To build its home base, Singapore is making an effort to get more value-added activities such as marketing, research, and development, and to encourage the regional headquarters of multinational organizations to locate in Singapore. At the same time, more of an effort is being made to stimulate entrepreneurial activity within Singapore, and Singaporean industries are encouraged to invest more in ventures outside of Singapore. The EDB itself has a large fund for investment in joint ventures of various sorts and for the encouragement of clusters of industries that fit into its own long-range strategy. Underlying these initiatives is Singapore's desire to serve as the business hub for Southeast Asia by becoming the regional leader in information and manufacturing technology.

The basic work of the EDB is carried out through its first-line senior officers who are assigned a technical area to develop by becoming familiar with the area, the major companies worldwide operating in that area, and the prospects for recruiting those companies to develop a project in Singapore. As projects are developed, the proposing officers recruit from among their peers the necessary additional people they will need. Teams are thus formed, and officers often end up "matrixed" across several divisions, reporting to several bosses simultaneously. This way of working internally mirrors Singapore's overall manner of operation, in that most senior civil servants or private sector executives have as many as five different jobs in different organizations at the same time. Such "multitasking" reflects a scarcity of sufficiently trained people in Singapore, but it has the benefit of creating networks and building trust across a wide range of government units and private companies.

Much of the critical work of the organization takes place in the field, as described by one of the directors.

The general career path for an overseas director is to start out as an industry specialist in one of the operational divisions in Singapore where you learn the workings of an industry in depth. If you have the desire and are viewed to have the talent, you get recruited to be an international director, usually with six months' or less notice. During that six months you not only have to train your replacement in Singapore, but use whatever little extra time you have to learn about the other industry sectors that will be involved in your overseas assignment. So being sent overseas is an instant training course in moving from being a specialist to being a generalist.

Once you are in an international office, roughly three-quarters of your time may be used maintaining contact and building relationships with organizations that are already working in Singapore, developing repeat business and generating new ideas that might produce new value-added kinds of business with the same organizations. This means regularly visiting as many as fifty companies a year in your geographical area and building contacts that may not lead to anything immediately, but that will eventually lead to new concepts and new investments.

To do this job well requires three kinds of knowledge. You have to have knowledge of the industries involved, much of which you get from journals and from the direct contact with executives from the companies with which you are dealing. Second, you have to know a lot about the specific companies with which you are dealing, including their strategies and their issues. Third, you have to have a knowledge of Singapore's strategy and its situation. The job then is to integrate these three sets of knowledge into a coherent idea or project that will be a success for the company as well as for Singapore.

On a day-to-day basis the work is making calls and sending reports back to Singapore on each and every call. The format for these reports is built into the software that each director has on his PC and now his laptop, and it includes nuts and bolts such as who was visited when and so on, a summary of no more than four lines (enforced by the software), a discussion that can be as long as the person wants it to be identifying the issues, the officer's assessment of the situation, and the implications in terms of actions to be pursued.

The director also decides which other officers are involved with that particular company and therefore should see the report, and it is then entered directly into the system and sent electronically to Singapore where it can be accessed by everyone who needs to know about that industry or that particular company.

The training for this kind of work comes from several sources. First of all, industry specialists in the headquarters organization are constantly passing knowledge to the field, while the field generalists are constantly informing the headquarters specialists about situations in particular companies. There is a good two-way flow of information there.

Second, a lot of information is gathered from monthly board reports, which are the papers deriving from a monthly presentation that one of the industry segments is required to make to the EDB board. Over the years a fairly specific format has been learned for making these kinds of reports. The industry group will work up the essence of it, it is then reviewed by various supervisory levels, and finally endorsed by senior management so that by the time it gets to the board it will be a fairly thoroughly digested document that reflects a great many points of view.

This director noted how the process leads to useful learning:

In that process, of course, we learn a great deal from our colleagues and from our supervisors on how to approach problems and how to present points. The actual presentation to the board is prime training for communication and presentation skills.

If, during the board meeting, new and interesting questions come up that are pertinent to the particular issues being discussed, that will be noted in the minutes of the meetings and those minutes will then be circulated to all the officers in the following month so that if new ideas are surfaced, they will not be lost.

In addition, all the officers get the minutes of the weekly operations committee meetings and selected items of information from the monthly meeting of the executive committee. We also get extensive briefings from the various industry groups during periodic home visits, and have a chance to visit local organizations. Beyond that, we avidly read industry journals and learn a tremendous amount from the company executives with whom we deal.

For example, while still an industry officer in Singapore, a young person will be allowed to visit the briefing meetings with senior executives from some of the companies and learn first hand from those senior managers what some of the issues in the company and in that industry are. *The prime source of learning is the contact with operating managers in the various companies.*

The strategic issues for Singapore itself are generally surfaced initially through the annual strategic planning meeting, which occurs early in the year and which will highlight issues that have been gathered over the year through the information that all the directors have surfaced and sent into headquarters, based on all their visits to companies and their observations of what is going on. The management committee and other task forces that may be formed then cull these issues and create out of that the agenda for the annual meeting.

If issues are identified that require more intensive investigation, a senior-level interorganizational committee will be formed. It in turn will generate a group of task forces of university people, private sector people, and civil servants reflecting all the possible issues that can come up. The EDB will often be instrumental in picking the people for these task forces and inviting them. Those groups may meet for anywhere from six months to two years and come up with major reports and recommendations dealing with Singapore's overall economic strategy.

Tan Chin Nam, the managing director of the EDB, described the organization as "very flat," which meant that "the directors and chairman all deal directly with the officers and go around the hierarchy whenever that is necessary." He also described the EDB as a "learning organization" that depends on multilateral dialogue, and he emphasized that the EDB is internally a "boundaryless organization." Tan chairs the weekly "operations meeting," which involves some thirty-five directors and officers; he described this meeting as "an opportunity to capitalize on the collective wisdom of members." It is "a synthesis session regarding opportunities and clients." He is in charge of the agenda, which involves getting progress reviews of all the major projects plus any additional items that he or anyone else contributes by telephoning the secretary. The secretary of the meeting is always a senior officer, and the position rotates every month. The meeting is a forum for discussion but not necessarily a place where anything is decided, because only the directors and officers are formally empowered to make decisions. On the other hand, the concepts and ideas that form the basis of decisions bubble up through the system.

An important mechanism of coordination is the work pattern of the current chairman, Philip Yeo, who travels frequently to various international sites to help to promote projects, to maintain relationships with companies that have invested in Singapore, and to sensitize himself to global trends. He reviews all projects in a single large "float file" and makes comments when he feels it is appropriate. These comments are then circulated back to the senior officers and/or directors and thus become part of the knowledge pool of the entire organization. Staff from each major international region (United States, Europe, Asia) meet twice annually, once for strategy and planning and once for operational review, and the entire organization meets once a year to set strategy and revitalize itself.

Decisions are made in the management structure through a process of proposal, review, and approval. If a decision is initiated at the top, such as a major shift in strategy, it is communicated intensively and extensively throughout the organization on paper, electronically, in meetings, and through any other media needed to get the message across. Most strategic and operational decisions, however, begin down in the organization with a proposal from a first-line officer in an industry segment, or a director in a geographical region, or from a working group or task force assigned to look into some particular issue.

Climate and Values

The EDB has a distinct "climate." When one first encounters members of the EDB, one is immediately struck by their energy, intensity, enthusiasm, positive attitude, willingness to tackle whatever problem is at hand, speed of response, and thoroughness of preparation for whatever event is taking place. Both formal protocol (doing things correctly) and efficiency (identifying and solving problems in a timely manner) are obviously important values. Insiders, as well as managers, who have dealt with the EDB regularly refer to its "can-do" attitude and its willingness to solve problems immediately and efficiently. The can-do spirit has become a mythical symbol of the EDB, to the extent that it is even embodied in a cartoon version of the work of the EDB with the officers depicted as supermen and superwomen flying around solving difficult problems.

One group of first-line officers described the situation this way: "EDB officers are expected to be supermen. There is a thirty-year tradition to be upheld and even though the job is now harder and requires longer hours, the tradition of getting everything done, doing it efficiently, and doing it on a lean basis and resolving all problems as they arise is still very strong" (1993 interview).

They pointed out that one of the keys to understanding the EDB is that one has to take a longer-range orientation and at the same time be very opportunistic and pragmatic. One makes errors but turns them into benefits as quickly as possible. I asked for some detail on past errors and found that the group was unwilling to provide any. When challenged, they explained that there were very strong written and unwritten rules about not violating the confidence of any of their clients. So even though they share information inside the organization both verbally and in writing, they clearly did not feel comfortable in revealing details to an outsider.

When one begins to probe just how all of this works, a set of beliefs and values emerges that one former EDB official, who is now the president of a large firm, characterized as a set of "cultural imperatives." By this he meant a set of imperatives that the EDB lives by and that are taught to new members as necessary to survival and effective work in the EDB. These imperatives are shown in table 1.2.

It is important to note the spirit and ambition that these imperatives embody. The EDB sees itself as an organization that provides total service to its investor clients—the "one-stop" concept that is mentioned frequently—and it provides this service with absolute integrity and professionalism. If a request comes from a present or future client company, the officer working with that company will

Table 1.2
The "cultural imperatives" of the EDB

1. A special brand of leadership that has
   - strategic long-range vision,
   - the ability to build a team, and
   - the ability to draw out the best in team members.
2. Total loyalty to the mission of building the nation.
3. 120 percent commitment from all.
4. Absolute professionalism with clients.
5. Total integrity in all dealings with clients.
6. Clear rules and absence of corruption.
7. Mental toughness and ability to absorb failure.
8. An internally boundaryless organization.
9. Teamwork and openness of communication.
10. "One-stop service" for the clients.

do whatever is needed to get it processed appropriately and quickly. The group cited one example of a company that had at one point been told they did not have to pay for any of its tax stamps. But after ten years of tax relief, they were informed by the internal revenue service that not only did they have to pay for ten years worth of tax stamps, but they had to pay additional penalties for not having previously paid. The EDB officer then went to the internal revenue department and various other agencies to see what kinds of compromises could be reached. Eventually the situation was resolved with the company paying for the stamps but not the penalties.

Even though the number of officers is quite large, they are still able to get to know each other through joint work on projects, operations committee meetings, Friday recreational club teas, E-mail, and country desk programs where they work together on projects pertaining to a particular geography. Most are required to become members and officers of the various recreation clubs, to attend training courses together, and generally to do a lot of informal networking including traveling together abroad on various assignments. A small Christian group also gets together informally at lunch time. Teamwork is further enhanced by deliberately hiring in cohorts of ten or so and putting them through a common induction program. During meetings and in joint work on task forces, EDB officers will of course get acquainted with people from other government departments. This stimulates intersector trust and makes it easier for government agencies to work together as future problems arise.

The EDB enhances its view of itself as a close-knit community by frequently giving awards to publicize special accomplishments, printing an in-house publication called *Network* that carries personal news about all employees, supporting the use of first names across many levels of the hierarchy, and encouraging informal rituals such as giving all your colleagues in a department a piece of cake on the occasion of a promotion, transfer, or even departure from the EDB. Friendships and marriages among employees are valued and publicized, and are limited only to the extent that spouses cannot work for each other and neither spouse can work in the personnel function because of access to confidential personnel records.

Although the EDB has had some ups and downs in its thirty-three-year history, it is today a high-morale organization that presents itself as confident and successful, as well as the key element in Singapore's economic scene. Even though it is acknowledged that the EDB is not the sole source of Singapore's economic success, the EDB credits itself for being the critical integrating element, the forward-looking entrepreneurial driving force, the basic sales and marketing arm of Singapore, and the organization that managed, through its culture, to train a cadre of Singapore's leaders.

Because of its history of success there is also a sense of elitism and a feeling that, of all of the various government agencies, the EDB is the most important one as reflected in its having more autonomy and status, as well as somewhat higher pay. Being offered a job in the EDB was viewed by most young university graduates as a great honor and opportunity. In recent years, however, there has been a tendency to make it clear during performance reviews that an officer was not expected to spend his or her entire career at the EDB. This comment is not an invitation to leave but a reminder that the "old system" of being totally loyal to the organization for a lifetime was no longer necessary or always the best way to be. Once the EDB sense of mission of working for the country has been thoroughly absorbed, it was thought to be highly desirable to transport this sense of mission into other organizations.

The EDB promotes itself and its various programs by publishing a great deal of material to market Singapore and to document its accomplishments and future strategies. Much of this material is inspirational in nature and reflects once again the enthusiasm, energy, spirit, and pride of the organization. At its annual "staff day" for all Singapore members of the EDB, original songs, skits, videotapes, and inspirational speeches by leaders were followed by an elaborate tea at which employees of all levels mingled with management and invited guests. In many ways the EDB has elements of a typical sales organization of a large consumer-oriented corporation, only in this case what is being sold is a country and the EDB mission goes beyond marketing into entrepreneurial and venture capital activities.

In summary, the EDB tries to embody in its own operations the very things that it claims for Singapore and that are its basis for attracting investors. The cultural imperatives shown in table 1.2 are not merely a statement of espoused values but an operational philosophy that permeates all aspects of EDB operations.

The Perspective of Investors

From the very beginning in 1961, EDB's leaders defined their job as having to persuade Singaporean and foreign investors to invest in desired projects. They knew that the essence of this job was, first of all, to find out what potential investors would need—land, buildings, a motivated and skilled labor pool, tax breaks and other financial incentives, a stable political environment, and a sympathetic government. They then had to develop the resources and capability to fulfill these needs and convince investors to visit and see for themselves what Singapore could do for them. Hewlett-Packard's initial entry into Singapore in the late 1960s as recalled by Clyde Coombs, a retired manufacturing manager, illustrates this process very well.

Hewlett-Packard

The Hewlett-Packard Company (HP) began to manufacture computers in the mid-1960s. Having made the decision to go into computers, the question arose whether the manufacturing function could make a contribution to the profitability of the computer line. It was decided that core-memory production might be the one area where they could do their own manufacturing instead of buying the component. Clyde Coombs was given the assignment of figuring out if this could work by building a manufacturing facility somewhere outside the United States where labor costs would be low and employees would be available to do the skilled but highly repetitive, routinized work.

I identified thirteen possible countries and after investigating various formal materials, boiled things down to Taiwan, Japan, Hong Kong, and Singapore. Taiwan was an early favorite, but was eliminated because it looked like there were too many political problems, too many rules, and potentially too much graft and corruption. Japan was not seriously considered at this point because of labor costs. Hong Kong looked feasible for short-run investments but, because of potential future political instability vis-à-vis the People's Republic of China, it would not be a good place for a long-range investment. So things began to point to Singapore.

I then telephoned Eric Goh, who headed the San Francisco office of the EDB. The minute I told him what we were thinking about, he was all over me; he was really a salesman who just wouldn't quit. If I needed any information he would get it immediately, and he just wouldn't give up until we had at least agreed to visit Singapore and see for ourselves. (1993 interview)

The enthusiasm and tenacity of the EDB representative in San Francisco became one of the major forces that pushed them forward. HP already knew something about Singapore because they had a sales office there and had obtained information about the success of Texas Instruments (TI) in building a factory there in a very short time—an effort that in a 1969 story in the *Straits Times* was labeled TI's "Fifty-Day Miracle." But Eric Goh's determined effort to get HP to visit Singapore was the deciding factor in pursuing the Singapore possibility.

When HP executives made their first visit and met with I. F. Tang, the chairman of the EDB, Coombs was immediately impressed with his high energy, his clear sense of Singapore's strategy, and his clarity about the rules and what HP could expect from Singapore. "They seemed to know what they were trying to achieve, and, if one wanted to work with them, one knew from the outset what the legitimate expectations and rules really were. They had clear rules and they kept their promises" (1993 interview).

Once they had met the senior EDB person, the HP delegation was assigned a project officer who "made things pleasant and feasible because he had all his bases covered very well." By this Coombs meant that the EDB would provide one-stop service in making available appropriate tax incentives, land, facilities, labor, training support, financial aid if needed, and whatever relevant information was required. "If you asked them about something, it would be on your desk the next day; if other government agencies were involved, they would do all of the negotiating and problem solving for you."

After they negotiated to acquire the land, but before their own factory was built, they leased the top two floors of a six-story building, the only space left that suited their needs. To prepare the building for occupancy, they needed working elevators and electricity, among other things—all of which required the installation of a big transformer for the building. The transformer had been ordered and was en route, but it would not arrive for several weeks. In the meantime, William Hewlett had decided to visit the Singapore facility and panic spread that the power might not be on by the time of his visit, which meant that the elevator might not work. Coombs said that "the one thing they were *not* going to have happen is to have Mr. Hewlett walk up six flights of stairs."

Coombs presented the problem to his EDB liaison officer who promptly took it to the Jurong Town Corporation (JTC), an offshoot of the EDB that was in charge of the land development and the building of the manufacturing facilities. They immediately understood the problem and got everything in working order, but because the transformer probably was not going to be installed in time for the visit, they had to do something else about the power supply. They decided to string a gigantic cable extension cord from a neighboring building to the building housing HP's offices. So on the day of the visit, the elevator and the lights actually worked and Hewlett had an impressive tour of the facility. Coombs learned later that this was the only time for the next six weeks that the elevator was actually used because it was taking so much power from the adjacent building. But the willingness and ability to solve the problem impressed Coombs immensely.

In the next two decades HP expanded its various manufacturing facilities, set up design centers, R & D facilities, and a software development center. From a small factory employing 62 people, HP operations in Singapore have grown to a fixed investment of over $300 million and a staff of more than 6,000 managed primarily by Singaporeans. Both HP and the EDB would say that they had a genuinely symbiotic collaborative relationship that benefits both the company and the country.

What this example highlights is that many of the elements of the "cultural imperatives" came into play in fulfilling HP's needs without, however, compromising Singapore's own strategy of developing partnerships only with those companies who would, in the long run, help to train and develop its own people. HP came to understand that from Singapore's point of view, not all companies were equally acceptable as potential investors—they had to have a long-range strategy, they had to be involved in technologies that would ultimately be of value to Singapore, and they had to value human resources.

Coombs noted that the companies coming into Singapore were characterized either as "cowboys" who had a short-run orientation and wanted some quick unskilled labor, and would then take their profits and move on, or as "settlers," as represented by companies such as HP, who had a long-range desire to remain and enter into a symbiotic relationship with Singapore. HP was impressed that the EDB was committed to training its own people and therefore clearly preferred the settlers. Because labor was often recruited from the countryside and from other nonindustrial areas, the EDB ran a one-week induction program for newly hired people to teach them how to keep good hours, maintain discipline, and in other ways learn to work in a modern industrial corporation.

If this were an isolated case one might just note HP's good fortune, but tales of mutual help and symbiotic relationships between Singapore and various multinational companies (MNCs) abound and, in most of those cases, a key variable appears to be the manner in which the EDB recruited, persuaded, and subsequently supported the companies who chose to invest there. For example, Alan Murray, chairman and CEO of the Mobil Corporation, said in a phone interview in 1993:

Though the general climate in Singapore was good for business, it was really the EDB that created the specific economic incentives, provided what was needed like pioneer status (tax relief for five years), investment tax credits, and so on that made us choose Singapore as a place to make these big investments rather than some of the other countries in the region. We do have operations in all those other countries, but Singapore provided the best economic climate for the big investment and was the best locale for exporting.

More detail of this kind will be presented in chapters 8 and 9, but for now I can summarize the main reasons that executives from overseas companies gave for investing in Singapore:

1. One-stop service that allows the investor to deal with only one person in the government in the event of a problem;

2. Political stability and absence of corruption in the government;

3. Clarity of Singapore's rules and the fact that the government keeps its promises;

4. A commitment to solving whatever problems come up in a timely and efficient manner (reflecting efficient internal communications);

5. The pro-business attitude of the government and the professionalism of the EDB project officers ("they know more about my business than I do");

6. The high quality of the labor pool in terms of both technical aptitude and work motivation.

The EDB from an Analytic Perspective: Paradoxes and Puzzles

1. *Strategic pragmatism.* The EDB's own aspirations and the views of many outside investors seem to mesh very well. But a number of points must be raised if one is to fully understand how and why this is working as well as it is. First of all, Singapore has always had a clear and well-articulated strategy of economic development. The nuances of this strategy have changed over the years, but what strikes especially the foreign investors is that Singapore only wants certain kinds of companies as investors and that it never compromised its own values and rules just to "make a sale."

At the same time, once Singapore committed to a company, it pulled out all the stops to make the relationship work. One can think of this as a kind of "strategic pragmatism" in the sense that the EDB was very clear about its long-range goals but, at the same time, remained tactically very flexible in working toward these goals and nimble in solving the day-to-day problems of their clients. One of the analytical questions that will have to be addressed then is how the EDB was able to do this, and especially to maintain this posture as strategic priorities changed over the decades.

2. *Government intervention in private enterprise.* The EDB is an agency of the Singapore government and the economic strategy it pursues is ultimately influenced to a degree by the senior minister (Lee Kuan Yew), prime minister, deputy prime minister, the minister of trade and industry, the minister of finance, and key leaders in other government agencies. At the same time, the EDB is expected to be in touch with global economic trends and to provide feedback to the ministries and statutory boards to help shape economic policy.

Several questions arise. First, how can a government working through a statutory board and a set of civil servants provide the necessary incentives to stimulate economic activity over a long period of time? Second, how can a government integrate its economic strategies appropriately with pure market forces? And, third, how can a government agency like the EDB avoid formalization and bureaucratization?

3. *Participatory autocracy/nonhierarchic hierarchy.* To Westerners one of the most puzzling aspects of how the EDB conducts itself is its ability to maintain simultaneously a strong hierarchy and a high

level of involvement at all levels of the organization. The strong spirit and commitment noted earlier can be observed throughout the organization, yet the decision-making process seems to be skewed toward a top-down "command and control" model. Western organization theories tend to view "command and control" versus "high involvement" as alternatives, but the way the EDB works suggests that both models can coexist and that an organization's effectiveness increases to the extent that it can integrate the two models. How does the EDB manage this? How does this large internationally decentralized organization manage to tightly coordinate all of its projects, yet give freedom to solve problems locally to all of its first-line officers?

4. *Individualistic groupism.* Teamwork and an internally boundaryless organization are virtually sacred cows in the EDB, but the reward and promotion system emphasizes individual accomplishment. Leaders are those who can get things done and who have political savvy, yet a central aspect of leadership in the EDB is the ability to build teams, to convince others by persuasion instead of using position power. In this context, how do EDB members balance their need for individual accomplishment with their need to be effective team players, or to put it another way, how do EDB officers balance individualistic competitiveness with collaborative teamwork? How do individual officers of the EDB avoid role overload and conflict given that they are "multitasked," simultaneously managing their own projects and being recruited for other projects by fellow officers and managers?

5. *Distributed centralism.* The EDB from the beginning has thought of itself as a global organization differentiated not only geographically but also by industry and function. First-line officers have to be industry experts to manage their sales and client service roles, yet the organization must have a way of centralizing and coordinating all of the information it collects about potential projects to make decisions that fit the overall strategy. Furthermore, as the client companies themselves become more global, the EDB encounters a given company in many countries and many settings. If that company is a potential investor, how does the EDB collect all of the relevant information about the company so that the proper approach can be made? If all encounters with current and future potential companies are communicated upward and laterally because of inter-

nal boundarylessness, how can the organization absorb this mass of information and maintain coordination among its various projects?

6. *Modulated openness.* Perhaps the most puzzling aspect of all to a Western observer is how, in an internally boundaryless hierarchic organization that exists in an Asian context and is influenced by Chinese culture, does a given member of the organization figure out how to be appropriately "open?" How do EDB officers learn what to put into the written information system, what to discuss over the telephone, what to mention only in a face-to-face context, and what kind of information not to mention at all? And what kinds of informal rules about openness help to maintain organizational effectiveness?

Reflecting on such questions, one should note how much the United States takes for granted certain Western ideas of individualism, competition, hierarchy, unity of command, individual accountability, the primacy of tasks over relationships, and the necessity for adversarial relationships among labor, management, and government. As we get deeper into the EDB story and the Singaporean context within which the EDB exists, it will become evident that the EDB works as well as it does because it starts with some very different assumptions about the nature of economic activity; the role of government in society; the relationship of government, business, and labor; the nature of human relationships; and how people should be recruited, developed, and managed for optimal organizational performance. Having articulated these assumptions, we then also have to ask what their costs and benefits are as one looks ahead.

7. *Unqualified positive perfectionism?* The reader will already have noticed that both the EDB's view of itself and the perspective of its industrial clients is very positive. All indications are that the EDB is a highly effective organization that has succeeded admirably in helping Singapore to fulfill its mission to become a developed modern city-state. With this positive attitude one finds as well a level of perfectionism that shows up most in unwillingness to expose "work in progress." The external image must be as nearly perfect as one can make it, and one must always put a very positive face on everything. The EDB, and for that matter Singapore as a whole, does not take criticism easily, and it is not easy to get EDBers to be self-critical when talking to outsiders. But with probing and prodding, some of the weaknesses begin to reveal themselves, and para-

doxically one of the greatest weaknesses may well be the unwillingness to be self-critical in public.

What this reluctance suggests is that the unqualified positive "cando" attitude not only reflects a genuine track record of accomplishment, but also masks a fear of discovering a lack of depth, as if a true self-examination might reveal some real weaknesses. Such a defensive attitude might also be the product of a very young organization being given very difficult and challenging tasks that stretch everyone to the limit. In such a context one must be completely self-confident or one cannot do the job at all, a pattern that is often seen in young consultants who are thrown into the trenches by the senior partners.

My interviews with alumni, older members of the EDB, and non-EDBers reinforced all the positive elements we will discuss, but also balanced these with some concerns. These concerns will be collected in chapters 12 and 13 as part of the analysis of the strengths and weaknesses of the EDB culture. Until then I will reflect the positive tone that all of the observations, interviews, and questionnaires exhibited, and in that sense try to mirror accurately how the organization presents itself publically.

To enrich the picture we must look next at the EDB's view of itself by examining some retrospective accounts of how the EDB came to be. One of the best ways to understand an organizational culture is by studying some of its roots and by looking at the personalities of its founders and key leaders.

I

The EDB's Perspective on Itself: Historical and Cultural Legacies

The purpose of part I is to provide a historical context for the evolution of the EDB. The alumni and older members of the EDB feel strongly that the culture of the organization is, to a large measure, the cause of its success. In an effort to describe that culture and analyze it, the best approach is historical. The actual experiences of an organization and the style of its early leaders create and sustain a given organizational culture. Therefore in the next six chapters I will present the EDB through the eyes of its founders and early leaders and, in that process, try to bring the culture to life. This is the culture as presented to me by the members of the organization. In part II, I will present the perspective of the investor clients of the EDB, and in parts III and IV, I will take a more analytical outsider perspective toward the EDB culture.

2

Some Historical Roots of the EDB Culture

The quality of a people determines the outcome of a nation. It is how you select your people, how you train them, how you organize them, and ultimately how you manage them that makes the difference. (Lee Kuan Yew interview, 1993)

Our job as a government is to set out our objective, direction, and modus operandi clearly and unequivocally and lead. The rest is up to Singaporeans to achieve and excel. (Prime Minister Goh Chok Tong, then the Minister of Trade and Industry, 1980 speech)

Given the sociopolitical and economic conditions before and after the Malaysian episode, the EDB simply had no choice but to ride on the backs of the MNC (multinational corporations) investment just as the PAP (People's Action Party) government rode on the communist tiger to wrangle independence from the British. (Toh Mun Heng, 1993)[1]

The EDB culture evolved through the actions and beliefs of its early leaders. To get a full appreciation of that culture, it is therefore necessary to reconstruct some aspects of the history of Singapore, especially that pertaining to these early leaders.[2] The account below is based entirely on the recollections of people who were present at various stages in that historical evolution. Unavoidably these recollections will be biased to some degree, but the purpose here is not to depict history accurately so much as to build a context that enables us to understand how the EDB came to be the kind of organization that it is. Where I can quote or paraphrase directly I will do so, but much of the picture is my own reconstruction based on the accounts of a dozen or more people interviewed, my own reading, and a review of early drafts by several people who lived through this period.

We begin by analyzing the factors that influenced the early leaders' basic beliefs about the role of government in economic affairs. Their own experiences, especially in coping with communist activities in Malaya and Singapore in the 1950s, strongly influenced those beliefs.

The Historical Origins of State Intervention in Economic Affairs

The People's Action Party (PAP), which has ruled Singapore for more than a quarter century, has a firm faith in technocracy. It believes that rationalism and technical expertise are the best way to solve the country's social and economic problems. Socio-economic development and nation-building, it is assumed, occur when the economic system and the government work closely together under the guidance of a rigorously selected and well trained "meritocratic elite." (Bellows 1989)[3]

One of the central assumptions driving Singapore's approach to economic development was that the government could and should manage this process through a statutory board, the EDB. This assumption was developed within a network of friendships that existed prior to and during the formation of the EDB. The network starts with Lee Kuan Yew and a close friend from his student days, Goh Keng Swee. Both men received their education in the United Kingdom and were part of a Singaporean community who had suffered with their families through the Japanese occupation during World War II. Lee formed the People's Action Party in 1954 and the Party won a majority in the general elections in 1959.[4] He had been a lawyer for various labor groups, and in the 1950s he was a politician who worked primarily to achieve independence for Singapore. Although he was greatly influenced by his British education, he realized that ultimately Singapore had to "throw off the colonial yoke."

Throughout the 1950s, Singapore found itself in political turmoil because of its own postwar conflicts, poverty, and the rapid growth of communism in China. The Chinese population of Singapore consisted of two very distinct segments with different backgrounds, educational levels, and attitudes. A large segment had grown up under the British, spoke primarily English, and had an elite who had been educated overseas. Both Lee and Goh came from that segment. Another segment, which had migrated more recently to Singapore, identified with mainland China, spoke only Chinese dialects, and was more receptive to chauvinist and communist appeals because they believed that the communists could best guarantee that the

Chinese cultural heritage would not be lost. Lee Kuan Yew knew that if he was to be politically successful, he had to have the support of both segments.

As Singapore's leaders saw it, communist tactics during the 1950s were heavily dominated by the principle that the end justifies the means, which resulted in a variety of subversive activities and the fomenting of violence. Their fear of communism was exacerbated throughout Malaya and Singapore because of their belief in the domino theory, the success of communism in mainland China, and Indonesia's leaning toward the left under Sukarno. Communists had infiltrated the labor unions in Singapore and were regularly calling for strikes.

In spite of the fact that the Singaporean unions and other labor groups all had communist elements, Lee Kuan Yew had to work with them to convince the Chinese community that he was not selling out to British culture. In the process he obtained an important political education, especially as it pertained to communist willingness to use any means—fair or foul—to achieve its ends. The level of infiltration and violence was such that the British had created fairly strong internal security agencies both in Malaya and Singapore. When Lee Kuan Yew came into power, it was both natural and convenient for him to perceive the need to continue such internal security measures and to root out the communist elements as much as possible to assure some measure of political stability. As Lee himself put it during our interview in May 1993, he had learned that "one cannot deal with the communists by arguing ideology with them." Instead, he came to believe strongly that "the best way to fight communism was by providing people jobs and housing." Economic development would be the answer to Singapore's future, but this required political stability as Lee Kuan Yew saw it, and that in turn required a strong controlling government.

Learning from Others

In the late 1950s it was fashionable among developing countries to invite the United Nations (UN) and the World Bank to do studies of what a given underdeveloped country needed and to seek financial and technical support from them. The World Bank had done such a study for Malaya and concluded that the best approach was "import substitution" by developing the manufacturing sector and producing locally many of the goods that the country had been importing. In 1960 Goh Keng Swee invited a UN team to look at Singapore.

Albert Winsemius, a successful businessman from the Dutch shipping industry and a former director-general for industrialization in the Netherlands, was recruited to head the team. He had established a foundation for promoting foreign investment in the Netherlands that enabled him "to act relatively freely without the cumbersome procedures and regulations of the bureaucracy. It was quite successful; in 5 years' time we attracted some 400 foreign firms."[5] Winsemius was obviously familiar with the problems of a nation that was sophisticated in trading and commercial activities but had no manufacturing experience. It was speculated that the UN asked him to be the leader of the mission because it recognized this similarity of circumstances that Singapore and the Netherlands shared.

I. F. Tang, an expatriate Chinese educated in mainland China and the West, was a key member of the mission. He was taken from the UN Economic Commission for Asia and the Far East (ECAFE) to become the substantive secretary of the mission. He later became the EDB's second chairman. Other members included a number of Westerners who were experts on specific industries and technical areas.

A key theme that illustrates Singapore's mentality at the time is evident in a quote from a senior EDB official who joined the board in 1964: "We knew only what we were and what we had been." But, by virtue of having been a successful trading center, a successful urban economy, and a successful port and shipbuilding center under British rule, Singapore's leaders knew that they were starting well ahead of other developing world countries, and this knowledge allowed them to focus on the manufacturing sector. In their specifications to the UN for a mission, they emphasized that they wanted to learn how to add the manufacturing sector to the commerce function.

The UN report strongly supported Prime Minister Lee and Goh's view that unemployment was the primary problem and recommended that investors be attracted to create a labor-intensive manufacturing industry that would provide jobs and training for Singaporeans. Some excerpts from the original UN report give a flavor of the situation.

Singapore is and will continue to be a leading world trading center centered around its port activities. Entrepôt trade and banking have in the past developed favorably. However the normal expansion of these activities will not be sufficient to keep pace with the rapid increase of population—about 4% a year. For that reason the government of Singapore has launched a program to expand manufacturing industries. With a view to speeding up this program it has—following consultations with the United Nations Economic Commission for Asia and the Far East—requested the United Nations Bureau of Technical Assistance Operations to assign an industrial survey mission to undertake the necessary investigations. The mission was 1) to undertake economic investigations, 2) to draw up a list of economically feasible industries in the fields of ship building and repair, metal and engineering (except steel industry), chemicals, and electrical equipment and appliances, 3) to prepare an outline plan for the development of industrial estates and 4) to advise on the necessary economic organizational and operational measures for promoting sound and speedy development of manufacturing industries.

In our preliminary report we gave some recommendations on the proposed Economic Development Board. They were mainly 1) that the Economic Development Board should be a non-political body; 2) that it should be many sided, having on the board representatives of all economic sectors of Singapore. The reason for these recommendations was that economic expansion should be a common goal of everybody, regardless of political attachments. These recommendations were accepted. We further recommend the establishment of the following divisions: financial, industrial facilities, projects, technical consulting service and promotion.

On the operation of each of these departments we recommend 1) that eventually the board delegates the responsibility for financing to the Singapore Industrial Development Bank which will enable the bank at a later stage to attract capital from others; 2) that the department of industrial facilities which has to coordinate the expansion programs for such facilities delegate its work as much as possible to existing governmental organizations; 3) that the projects division especially concentrates on preparing a set of brochures on specific possibilities in Singapore, which can serve as a basis for the work of the promotion division; 4) that the most important part of the Economic Development Board is the promotion division.[6]

The report was very precise in its analysis and recommendations, and according to Goh, it confirmed much of what he already knew. Singapore had formed an Industrial Promotion Board five years earlier and had accumulated important experience of its own. In addition, the economic development division of the ministry of finance had been working on a five-year plan that emphasized industry development. Goh, however, was most impressed with Winsemius and kept him on as a consultant after the UN mission had finished its work. This relationship lasted until the late 1980s, and throughout this period Winsemius was influential in the development and implementation of a number of key strategic decisions.

For example, when the EDB decided in 1966 to open a separate international operations division under Chan Chin Bock, Winsemius recommended not only that it be located in New York—because of its access to U.S. multinationals—but that J. P. Bourdrez be asked to serve as its first director. Bourdrez had helped the Dutch Economic Development Board to internationalize and had relevant experience to share with Chan. He had retired in New York but was willing to come out of retirement to provide whatever assistance was needed to make the EDB's New York office successful.

Goh also remembered that the prospect of creating an economic development program built around manufacturing would represent a new departure and noted that "if one is going to try something new, one had better get the help of someone who has gone through something similar."[7] Where in the world had there been a somewhat comparable experience? The model that seemed to fit best was Israel because it had been able to industrialize under conditions somewhat similar to Singapore's. So in 1958 Goh set off on a trip around the world to educate himself for his future political responsibilities.

In Israel he met E. J. Mayer, who was the director of the industrial planning department at Israel's ministry of commerce and industry. Mayer remembers Goh introducing himself more or less as follows: "I am a member of the People's Action Party and we are going to fight an election shortly, at which my party will sweep the board. I will then have to carry some responsibility in the government and, to prepare myself for this task, my party sent me on a round-the-world trip to get information about the best methods for industrial development." Mayer was very impressed with Goh and spent some time with him. On this visit Goh also met the late J. Cahen, professor of industrial management at the Haifa Technion. Both Mayer and Cahen subsequently became involved with the EDB, the former as its first managing director and the latter as an occasional consultant.

Mayer also had an impact on Lee Kuan Yew. In thinking back over their early history, now Senior Minister Lee recalled in his 1993 interview what he considered to be a very fateful meeting with Mayer. The British were going to pull out their naval bases and take 25 percent of Singapore's gross national produce with them, leaving Lee feeling very discouraged about its economic future given that

Singapore had no natural resources of its own. Senior Minister Lee recalled that on one of his trips to Africa he was visited by Mayer. They spent a long evening together discussing Singapore's situation and the problems of economic development, leading to two great insights that Lee said he has never forgotten. "If you are surrounded by neighbors who don't want or need your products (the situation both in Israel and in Singapore at that time), you must 'leapfrog' them economically so that they will come to need your products." By this he meant that one must skip one or more steps in the economic development chain to get ahead of other countries that are following a more traditional path. The emphasis on high-tech and knowledge-based industries was no doubt partially influenced by this advice.

Lee also recalled the insight that economic development was not just the creation of any industrial activity to generate income, but required that the activity would be relevant to the world. He told another story about the time the British were proposing to leave. At one point, he was in London asking them to slow down their departure so that Singapore would not be left too destitute. He appeared on British television to discuss the issues and the implications for Singapore. The head of Marks and Spencer, a London department store, saw Lee on television and was so moved with compassion that he went to Lee and said sympathetically, "I tell you, if your people can make fish hooks with feathers on them, we'll be glad to sell them." This made Lee feel that at least someone understood in principle Singapore's plight.

Lee also recalled Mayer saying, "Recognize that the only resource you have is your people, their brains, and their skills. Sort them and pick the best." Lee recognized the wisdom in this and noted that "the quality of a people determines the outcome of a nation." This insight crystallized for him what he called "the basics": it is how you select your people, how you train them, how you organize them, and ultimately how you manage them that makes the difference. I asked him why more countries and organizations do not follow such good advice, to which he replied, "Well, they either get enamored of various theories or they don't want to do the difficult parts of that prescription." As an example, what was most difficult for him in Singapore was the reform of the education system. He inherited four different education systems based on the needs of four different ethnic and language groups and wanted to find a way to bring them all into a single English-based system. Even within the Chinese community of Singapore there were so many dialects and so few people who spoke Mandarin that the Chinese could do better speaking English to each other.

Lee said that it took him some time to recognize the importance of unifying the educational system and then, "It still took twenty years to build a common educational system and many, many different efforts and programs, but you have to integrate the educational system no matter how long it takes." One step was to require English as either a first or a second language in all of Singapore's schools and then "let the market show that kids who know English very well will get the better jobs." That did happen and gradually people got the message, so English increasingly became the language of choice.

Cooperation with the Labor Sector

The industrial relations situation referred to above was also commented on in some detail in the 1961 report of the UN Mission:

If Singapore wants to industrialize, the community as a whole and almost every section of it has to face the responsibility which will fall upon them. This will not prove to be easy in every respect. One of the main complications in Singapore's economic development is that part of her economic life is highly developed—port activities and entrepôt trade—the remainder in certain aspects is far underdeveloped. Income, profits, wages in the former sections are high. The tendency to push up wages of the less sheltered industries and of undertakings which have to compete with firms abroad has had a disastrous effect. Manufacturing industry has in a few years' time decreased its employment by thousands of workers almost by 20%.

This has been caused primarily by unsatisfactory industrial relations resulting in unrest, low productivity and irrational wage demands. In some quarters expectations are high for the rapid development of modern manufacturing industries, but existing manufacturing industries decreased during the last few years by some 20%, partly due to contraction of export markets for Singapore, but by far the greater part due to unfavorable industrial relations, and consequently a weakening of their competitive position through union demands. In a sincere and realistic cooperation between government, employers and unions, great things can be achieved but the reality is that for the moment this sincere cooperation is far off. Some of the trade unions may be irresponsible now and again. But what can we expect from a young organization? And are all employers really up to date in their thinking and approach to management labor relations? Both are in the same boat. Start rowing, would seem the best advice. Today's situation is no basis for an economic expansion program. And it will have to change quickly if Singapore is to catch up with the need for additional employment. . . .

In our opinion Singapore has the basic assets for industrialization. With the resourcefulness of her people, an active industrial promotion program by the government, and—this is the main point—close cooperation between employers and labor, Singapore can successfully carry out the expansion programs proposed in this report to achieve their basic objectives. Her greatest asset is the high aptitude of her people to work in manufacturing industries. They can rank among the best factory workers in the world, but for that they need expansion possibilities, jobs. The cooperation between employers and labor must come about.

If not, labor will suffer for it. Capital can go to other countries. Enterprise can quiet down or escape. Labor has no escape possibilities. It needs employment here and has no time to wait.[8]

Lee could see that labor and management fighting each other would not solve any problems, so he worked closely with the militant union leaders to create a kind of code of cooperation. At the same time, he realized that the best way for the unions to be collaborative was to have something important to do in their own right other than fighting management. So he eventually invested union funds in an insurance business and in one of Singapore's taxi companies. He felt that by giving them the experience of being owners and running these businesses, he in effect could force them to learn the management point of view. They had to hire professional managers and they now have boards of governors to help run what have become successful businesses. We can see in these decisions the evolution of the assumption that all sectors of Singaporean society had to work together for economic development to succeed, and that the government had to play a strong role in making that collaboration happen.

The EDB Is Created

When the EDB was established in 1961, the initial strategy was to create jobs through attracting labor-intensive manufacturing companies and to develop a climate of collaboration between labor and management that would be attractive to foreign investors. The name Economic Development Board was chosen by Finance Minister Goh Keng Swee, as was the idea of making it a statutory board, which would permit the government to intervene but at the same time provide some independence to the economic development activity. He asked S. Dhanabalan, his assistant, to draft a three-page paper for the cabinet to approve a draft law to be sent to parliament to establish the EDB and took it forward to fund the EDB with an initial budget of S$100 million (roughly U.S.$25 million at the 1960s rate of exchange).

The original goals and organizational structure of the EDB were spelled out in its first annual report (1961): "The primary function of the Board is to promote the establishment of new industries in Singapore and to accelerate the growth of existing ones." The EDB structure was modeled on the European system of an active board, whose chairman functions as the chief executive officer, and a managing director who functions more as a chief operating officer. The original organizational structure and mandate of the divisions is shown in table 2.1.

The *Investment Promotion Division* is concerned with one of the most important activities of the Economic Development Board, namely, the promotion of industrial investment. Great efforts would have to be made to attract local and foreign entrepreneurs and to establish co-operation between domestic and foreign industries specifically in the field of know-how. This program would consist of mainly two parts:

(1) Spreading information to interested circles about the advantages of locating manufacturing industries in Singapore.

(2) Giving information and assistance to specific manufacturers either by receiving them in Singapore or endeavoring to reach them in their own countries. (1961 Annual Report, p. 4)

Table 2.1
1961 organization of the EDB

Chairman and Board Members
Director
Secretariat
Legal Adviser   Industrial Economist
Promotion Division
Finance Division
Projects Division and Technical Consultant Service
Industrial Facilities Division

The *Finance Division* is responsible in general for the financial activities of the Board. This applies to dealing with the Board's funds, their investments, lending, preparation of its annual budget, appropriate procedures for disbursements and budgetary control. (Ibid., p. 6)

The *Projects Division* and Technical Consultant Service constitutes within the Economic Development Board the body responsible for the technical and economic evaluation of projects. . . . With regard to its Technical Consultant Service functions, in order to serve as a central clearing house and repository of technical and economic information, the Division began to build up and retain a body of technical and economic documentation which should enable it to provide ad hoc information to the Board and to the Board's clients as and when required. (Ibid., p. 6–7)

The *Industrial Facilities Division* has been constituted to ensure the adequate provision of suitable land together with all ancillary services such as electricity, water and roads and other communications. (Ibid., p. 10)

The first chairman of the EDB was Hon Sui Sen, a senior civil servant who had worked his way to the top of the civil service ladder as the permanent secretary of the Economic Development Division. He had also been land commissioner; but, more important, he was seen in all of his prior jobs as a superb administrator. Hon, Lee, and Goh and their families were well acquainted with one other, having survived the Japanese occupation together. Hon was appointed by Goh, the finance minister, and before taking on the job he was sent to the World Bank for six months of training.

The board met monthly to approve the various projects and schemes that were developed by the officers in the trenches, but one gets the impression from how people talk about the EDB that this approval function pretty much rubber stamped what the line organization, the chairman, and the managing director wanted to do.

The appointment of Hon Sui Sen as the EDB's first chairman reflects some of the attitudes toward people that came to play a major role in how the EDB culture evolved. First of all, Lee recalled that Hon was one of the very few Singaporeans whom the British had allowed to climb to the higher administrative levels of the civil service. In describing the formation of the EDB, Lee said that "I gave my best man to Dr. Goh to do with whatever he needed," a philosophy of human resource management that foreshadowed most of the selection and development policies of the future—a reliance on excellent people and an assumption that they could learn whatever the job required even if they had not been specifically trained for it. These "excellent people" would then be put into whatever jobs most needed their skills and attention.

It was significant that Hon had the reputation of being a man of integrity and wisdom, traits that not only explained his rise in the civil service but that were obviously important if the intention was to display to the world a noncorrupt, principled government. The fact that Hon Sui Sen was also a close and trusted friend of then Prime Minister Lee not only made it easier to coordinate activities, but represented the first step in building the network of collaboration among government agencies that would later make one-stop service feasible.

In 1961 Lee and Goh had in mind a clear strategy for the EDB and had appointed a trustworthy and competent core staff; but in addition, they needed an experienced managing director to help it really take off. The chairman and his staff had all the right motivations, but very little practical experience in how to promote foreign investment. Winsemius had become acquainted with E. J. Mayer and considered him to have the requisite experience to undertake the directorship on a temporary basis until a local candidate could be found. Mayer had been working for the Israelis on economic development as the director of the Industrial Planning Development Board and as adviser to the ministry of commerce and industry. He was successfully recruited by Goh to become the EDB's first managing director, and his appointment along with a job description was announced on 2 November 1961 in the *Straits Times:*

ISRAELI EXPERT COMES TO HEAD $100 MILLION INDUSTRY BOARD

The Director is expected:

a) to assist in the formulation of economic policy with particular reference to development in the industrial sector of the economy, and when necessary to advise the Government on the direction of policy,

b) to liaise with Government Ministries and statutory boards such as the proposed Port Authority, Public Utility Departments, Housing and Development Board and Singapore Telephone Board, in matters relating to policy and details of economic development,

c) to follow up the recommendations of the United Nations Industrial Survey Mission to Singapore 1960–1961 and organize and direct a comprehensive industrial promotion programme,

d) to organize and direct the operation of an Industrial Financing Service in the Economic Development Board which will operate as an industrial development bank,

e) to organize and direct a Technical Consultant Service in the Board to serve industries in Singapore, and,

f) to co-ordinate with other competent authorities of Government in the planning of physical facilities for industries and port facilities, particularly the development of the Jurong Industrial Area.

In subsequent interviews Mayer told reporters in 1961 that Singapore had all it needed for successful industrialization—idle capital, purchasing power, labor, brain power, communications, etc.[9] On the trade union movement, he remarked: "Singapore cannot claim a monopoly in industrial actions. Strikes happen everywhere, even in highly industrialized countries." He said it was natural that management and unions could not always see eye to eye on a subject and suggested extensive education in industrial management for both management personnel and trade unionists. Mayer noted that the most effective way to educate these two classes of people representing conflicting interests was to get them to attend the same course and seminar on industrial management to narrow their differences for the good of the state.

From Mayer's point of view, his new appointment represented an unusual challenge. His diagnosis of the situation as he looked back on it is as follows:

At the time, nobody in Singapore had any experience in formulating and executing an interventionist economic policy. This was only to be expected in a country with such a strong free-trade tradition. They were looking for a model. They felt that without government intervention to help with the finance and incentives of various kinds, there would not be sufficient entrepreneurship coming forward and growth would be too slow. A very small country, without natural resources or much of a home market and without a skilled industrial labor force was not thought to be too attractive as a location for foreign investors, nor were local businessmen too keen to enter industry. At the same time, Singapore was unwilling, and rightly so, to give up its status of a free port and adopt a system of high protective tariffs behind which local industry could develop.

Singapore's assets were:

• An incorruptible and stable government.

• An efficient civil service on the British model, personified by Mr. Hon Sui Sen, with some elements of the Mandarin tradition thrown in.

• Adequate finance to support its industrial initiatives.

• One of the few truly multi-racial societies in the world.
• A population which is traditionally hard working. (According to Lee Kuan Yew, Singapore is the only country in S. E. Asia where people don't have a siesta after lunch).
• A population where education is held in the highest regard.
• An excellent geographic location.

Within these parameters I had the task of formulating policies, nursing staff, promoting Singapore, formulating projects, getting them off the ground, finding investors, and a lot more.[10]

The work of implementing the master plan fell to half a dozen young officers including S. Dhanabalan, Ngiam Tong Dow, and Joseph Pillay—all of whom later became prominent in politics and industry. They were given line authority and a broad mandate in order to help build their confidence and to provide them experience in dealing with experts and foreigners. At the same time, it was important to have Asian frontline people because many of the early investors were coming from Hong Kong and Taiwan. Foreign technical experts were available to be used in an advisory capacity and Mayer could help in structuring the process, but the main work of promoting foreign investment fell to the Singaporean senior officers. Efforts were also made to involve I. F. Tang, who had been secretary of the UN Mission and was its only Asian member, but he was not able to contribute in more than an advisory capacity until several years later when his commitments to the UN to create a major conference in the Philippines and to organize a mission to Burma had been fulfilled.

To recap, the EDB was to become a *"One-Stop" government agency to promote the establishment of new industries in Singapore and accelerate the growth of existing ones"* (1961 Annual Report p. 1).

Operationally this meant that the EDB should locate foreign investors, sell them on coming to Singapore, help them to find land and facilities for building their factories, assist them in recruiting and training a labor pool at the required skill level, provide whatever infrastructure was needed, offer whatever financial incentives or tax breaks were necessary, even make investments if necessary, and solve all problems that might arise subsequently as the manufacturing operation expanded without, however, compromising any of its own strategies, rules, and principles. Within six months of its formation, the EDB had hired thirteen senior officers of whom ten were local and three expatriate, thirty-five junior officers, and thirty-three additional support staff. The EDB was off and running.

Analytical Summary

The accounts given by Lee Kuan Yew, Goh Keng Swee, and others who remembered the early 1960s are of course retrospective reconstructions and not therefore necessarily accurate as to specific dates and events. But those specifics are not the primary goal of this analysis. What we are after is some understanding of the attitudes and beliefs of the leaders who created both the context of the EDB and the EDB itself. From that perspective what is striking in these accounts is:

1. the willingness to learn from others and to accept help;
2. the intense focus on people and their particular talents;
3. the commitment to education and training;
4. the single-minded pursuit of the mission to develop Singapore economically and the willingness to do politically whatever was necessary to accomplish it;
5. the building of a network of relationships to sustain the elements of the economic strategy;
6. the willingness to make long-range plans and the patience to stick to them, while at the same time pragmatically doing whatever was necessary in the short run;
7. the commitment to globalism by adopting English as the working language.

Whatever one may think about the degree of regimentation that was imposed on Singapore, the striking thing is that it was all part of a master plan of economic development that hinged on political stability. The prior circumstances were such that political stability was not only necessary to attract foreign investment but was, according to most of the people interviewed, a welcome change that was accepted because it produced almost immediate positive results in terms of economic improvement. Jobs, housing, education, and training all became available.

What is also apparent is that, although Lee Kuan Yew was a strong autocratic and paternalistic leader, he did not act alone in choosing this political and economic strategy. Singapore's economic development must be viewed as the result of the efforts of a whole network of young foreign-educated Singaporeans who worked together to create these strategies. It was the combined wisdom and energy of this group that created the various components of the economic strategy, and it was their personal skills that caused it to be implemented successfully.

A final point that should be noted is that at this juncture, although Singapore was primarily Chinese in terms of ethnic origins, it was trying to take advantage of and blend several very different cultural traditions—the Greco-Christian via the British and Dutch connections, the Confucian via their Chinese ethnic origins, and the Singaporean via their own multicultural experiences (Malay, Indian, British, and Chinese). Particularly significant in this mix is the role of British culture in that Singapore was not only a British colony, but so many of its leaders were educated in the United Kingdom or in Commonwealth universities under the Colombo Plan.[11]

The recollections highlight the degree to which political, economic, and social circumstances dictated the choices that Singapore's leaders made and show that the long-range strategy around which most decisions were taken was to make Singapore a politically stable, cosmopolitan, safe, and clean place so that foreign investment could be attracted. Given this overall strategy, let us look next at how it was articulated into specific strategic elements and programs as Singapore evolved.

3

Variations on a Theme: The Major Strategic Eras

In the initial years, the EDB started as a pseudo "ministry of foreign affairs" to foster external investment and business links. Over time, it has evolved into a super hospitality agency for foreign MNCs, a paternal promotion agency for local enterprises as well as an agency devoted to economic development. . . . the EDB has over time metamorphosed from a conventional statutory board to a dynamic public agency with a distinctive corporate management culture and style. (Low 1993)[1]

The EDB culture is ultimately the product of the interaction of several factors:

1. the personalities and styles of the founders, especially the EDB's first chairman, Hon Sui Sen;

2. the mentalities and personal styles of its initial members, especially the first group of officers who were assigned to the EDB and were charged with getting the promotion program going (e.g., Joe Pillay, S. Dhanabalan, Ngiam Tong Dow);

3. the strategic priorities as interpreted by the leaders and officers, and as experienced by them in their early efforts to promote foreign investments;

4. their actual experiences of success and failure; and

5. the personalities and styles of later leaders who arrived with different strategic priorities and mandates.

To present this culture in a historical context therefore requires analyzing the impact of individual personalities, strategic priorities, and experiences of success and failure. What such an analysis reveals is that the EDB had to change its emphasis dramatically as Singapore's economic circumstances changed, yet many elements of the EDB culture that had been formed in its first decade of existence and under its founder remained very stable. The ability to retain its core values and operational philosophy while altering its capabilities and practices to accommodate a rapidly changing world is, in fact, one of the main continuing characteristics of this organization.

I have chosen to begin the discussion with an overview of the strategic eras to give the reader a broad sense of the evolution of Singapore's thirty-five-year economic history. The intention is to show the ability of the EDB to decipher the political-economic context in which Singapore had to operate and its capacity to adapt to that context. One of the striking themes that surfaces in the analysis is Singapore's constant ability to take a longer-range point of view. Although Singapore faced an immediate crisis with the arrival of independence, the economic strategies that emerged all had in common a longer-range component leading ultimately to a very different kind of society than that of the other Asian NICs (newly industrialized countries). And as I will argue repeatedly, one of the most salient characteristics of the EDB in particular and Singapore in general is this "strategic pragmatism," the ability to simultaneously solve immediate problems and to fit the solutions into a longer-range plan.

Major Strategic Eras

There are many ways in retrospect to categorize the various economic strategies that Singapore employed from 1960 on. Singapore's own published analyses are constructed around the major thrusts of each decade.[2] When one listens to the various alumni and former chairmen, however, more complex themes surface and it becomes evident that the various strategies overlap and build on each other. My categorization tries to reflect these overlaps and is therefore less tied to decades or particular dates, except where one can identify clear beginning or endings. I also try to articulate the major problems or issues that the strategies were attempting to address.

Curing Unemployment through Import Substitution (1961–1965)

In the early 1960s the paramount goal was the creation of labor-intensive industries to create full employment in relatively low-value-added factories that produced such items as nails, textiles, footwear, paint, polo shirts, and plastic flowers. Singapore knew that it had a strategic advantage for trade and that its location was favorable as a place for distribution. Oil companies such as Shell and British Petroleum had already invested in Singapore because they realized that it was the perfect place to store and distribute products and to build and maintain ships. But to deal with unemployment, Singapore needed to build up its manufacturing base.

The operational economic philosophy was "import substitution" and the desirability of this philosophy was supported not only by prevailing policies in the World Bank but also by the anticipation of a large common market that would result when Singapore joined the Malaysian Federation in 1963. When the common market failed to materialize, when Singapore lost its membership in the Federation in 1965, and when the British decided to close their naval bases in the late 1960s, not only was an immediate crisis of economic survival created, but also a fundamental question was raised about the viability of import substitution as a development philosophy. From 1965 on, a major reexamination of how to proceed was therefore launched.

Shift to Export Orientation and Internationalization (1965)

The realization that Singapore had to do it on its own led not only to a reorientation toward manufacturing for *export* but, simultaneously, to a stronger emphasis on internationalization and the attraction of foreign investment from the West. A major effort would have to be made to identify companies in America, Europe, and the rest of Asia that would be willing to locate their manufacturing facilities in Singapore and export components or total products from there. This effort paid off eventually with the creation of a number of multiplant projects by U.S. companies such as General Electric (GE), Hewlett-Packard, American Optical, Timex, Bethlehem Steel, GTE, Grumman, and Lockheed; European companies such as Philips, Siemens, Olivetti, and Beecham; and Japanese companies such as Seiko, Sumitomo, and Yamazaki. In retrospect, this strategy differentiated Singapore markedly from other Asian NICs and led ultimately to over 50 percent of its labor force working for foreign MNCs.

However, as unemployment and housing problems waned, it became apparent that if the EDB continued to be successful in attracting the MNCs there would, in fact, soon be a *labor shortage,* requiring a more liberal attitude toward the use of immigrant foreign labor, new assumptions about what kind of industry to attract, and new attitudes toward the education and training of Singaporeans. Specifically, this redirection highlighted the need for Singapore to upgrade and train its own labor force, because it was recognized that the companies who would be most desirable would be the higher-technology companies that would require fairly highly trained but low-cost labor. Under this scenario, Singapore would eventually seek out the more capital-intensive and higher value-added industries like electronics, petrochemicals, and pharmaceuticals. This would lead to a third and overlapping strategic thrust.

Shift from Labor-Intensive Industries to Training Labor for Capital-Intensive and Higher-Tech Industries (1968–)

To become attractive to the various higher-tech industries, Singapore now had to become the "precision engineering shop" of Asia and therefore had to develop crash programs to upgrade its labor force. This need, combined with the continuing emphasis on internationalization, led to highly innovative joint deals between the EDB and MNCs like Rollei of Germany and Philips of Holland, and eventually to the creation of joint institutes between Singapore and Germany, France, and Japan. By working with organizations that already had the skills that Singaporeans needed, they were able to speed up the training and move workers more directly into apprenticeships and regular jobs. Many of the MNCs were specifically selected as targets by the EDB because of their willingness to enter into jointly sponsored training programs that would quickly enhance the skill levels of Singaporeans in specific targeted areas. At the same time, young Singaporeans were sent abroad as apprentices to selected companies in Germany and Switzerland.

A new reality emerged with the economic success of the late 1960s and early 1970s—rising wages that would make Singapore less attractive to the traditional manufacturer, especially at a time when other countries in Europe and Asia were becoming more competitive on labor costs. Once again Singapore had to reexamine the basis of its strength and develop a strategic thrust that could take advantage of it.

From Skill-Based Industries to Knowledge-Based Industries and Services (Evolved through the 1970s, Articulated in the 1980s)

The EDB recognized that not only would it become less competitive in the traditional low-value-added manufacturing areas because of rising wages and labor shortages, but manufacturing itself was evolving toward more automation and robotics, where knowledge of the process and skills in maintenance would be the critical labor resource. This is not to say that this strategic initiative displaced earlier ones, but rather that the EDB leaders and planners could foresee that they needed even higher levels of training and development to be able to attract what increasingly came to be labeled as the manufacturing *service* sector.

The "second industrial revolution" (SIR), as spelled out by the minister of trade and industry, Goh Chok Tong, in his 1981 budget presentation was to replace labor-intensive with knowledge-based industries and services connected with manufacturing, tourism, and finance. "Textiles, shoes, furniture—these are subject to high tariffs and import quotas beyond our control. The prime objective of the plan is to develop Singapore into a modern industrial economy based on science, technology, skills and knowledge." In a similar vein, Prime Minister Lee Kuan Yew said: "All sectors of the economy have to mechanize, automate, computerize, and improve management; or relocate their factories" (Singapore, *The Mirror*, 15 January, 1982, p. 1).

The focus now shifted to attracting those high-tech industries that were willing to pay higher wages and that were less labor intensive. These included: computers, integrated circuits, specialty chemical products, and industrial electronic equipment. The emphasis on education and training shifted from training skilled technicians to increasing the number of graduate engineers and expanding the whole technical education sector.

The next major shift was connected to the negative impact of the 1985 global recession and the recognition that the EDB needed some "revitalization" and a reorganization to remove what some perceived as its more complacent and reactive elements. The Singapore economy was caught in the grip of the mid-1980s' world recession and, after two decades of consistent growth, actually shrank by 1.8 percent in 1985.

An economic committee headed by Brigadier General Lee Hsien Loong, the minister of trade and industry, was set up to determine the cause of the local recession and to review economic prospects for the future. The committee drew on various task forces and study groups that represented all sectors of the Singapore economy and reached the conclusion that the cost of doing business in Singapore had become too high and that a variety of drastic measures would have to be taken to contain costs as well as to redefine the basic economic strategy. To increase productivity, the government mandated a variety of remedies including an across-the-board 12 percent pay cut, reduced property taxes, and a "flexi-wage" system that would tie wage increases to a company's profitability. At the same time it mandated that Singapore's basic growth strategy should be reexamined.

Within the EDB several decades of success built on earlier strategies had led to some complacency and some bureaucratization in the form of functional compartmentalization. During the 1960s the EDB had to be quite entrepreneurial to get the right kind of foreign investment and to build up the infrastructure, but during the 1970s and early 1980s so many MNCs came into Singapore that the EDB ended up playing mostly the role of host and problem solver, and in the process lost some of its entrepreneurial edge. The appointment of Philip Yeo as chairman in 1986 was accompanied by a mandate to revitalize the EDB, to reposition its strategy in the new economic context, and to bring back more of the old entrepreneurial spirit. This repositioning led to the evolution of a number of new strategic elements.

Regionalization, the Growth Triangle, and the Development of Local Industry (1986—)

Efforts to develop local industry had of course been part of the original mandate of the EDB, but in the intense internationalization effort a number of practices evolved that actually made it harder for local companies, particularly entrepreneurial ones, to find the support they needed. For example, although there were financial support packages available from the EDB and later from the Development Bank of Singapore, they were not well marketed. There was much more focus on the MNC projects because of their significantly larger investments and the opportunities for technology transfer that they offered. Thus locals often got less attention and help. But there was a growing recognition that local industries should be encouraged to become the primary suppliers of the MNCs, to think more actively about the service quality of products, and to expand their own businesses overseas. New programs to upgrade and support local suppliers and other industries were launched and old programs were revived and enhanced.

It also became apparent that Singapore's geographic location, its strength as a trading hub, and its excellent infrastructure would make it an attractive site for regional headquarters, R & D facilities, marketing centers, and other higher value-added service-oriented activities. If such centers could be created in Singapore, it would further upgrade the jobs available to Singaporeans and thereby increase Singapore's overall standard of living.

At the same time, the EDB did not want to lose MNCs that would begin to seek the lower-cost manufacturing operations that had become available in Malaysia, Thailand, and Indonesia. The EDB therefore evolved the concept of regionalization and the growth triangle to allow Singapore to become the developer and deal maker between its neighbors and the MNCs. By helping to develop industrial parks in both the neighboring Indonesian islands and the Malaysian state of Johor, Singapore could help a company place its low-cost manufacturing into one of those sites while keeping the headquarters, R & D, distribution, and marketing in Singapore.

The MNCs themselves were becoming more global in their operations. Instead of the EDB doing their promoting primarily in the home country of the MNC or with the subsidiary in Singapore, they might now be dealing with a subsidiary in Japan or in Thailand, a regional headquarters in Singapore, and a joint venture or two anywhere in the region and still be dealing with the same company. They would not only have to coordinate their information laterally, but would also have to develop strategies for partnering with a company that would involve much more complex projects and financial arrangements. Singapore as a hub would be the beachhead, broker, and coordination center, and the EDB would become the "business architect" for a company, helping to open channels to new markets like China and even participating as equity partners in complex joint ventures. The concept of real "partnering" with their foreign investors was part of the original long-range strategy, partly to obtain stability and security in the region, but it now escalated to new levels in a variety of highly innovative projects.

An important element in this new strategy was the development of projects in other parts of Asia, especially in China. In a 1993 speech Senior Minister Lee Kuan Yew described this aspect of the strategy as Singapore exporting its "software" its know-how in building, promoting, and managing industrial parks, and developing foreign investments. If Singapore could get the contract to develop such projects in China, India, and other countries, it would provide economic space for Singapore-linked projects and would also provide potential markets for local Singaporean companies to begin to invest more actively outside of Singapore. The goal here was to stimulate entrepreneurship and the evolution of local companies into MNCs and to provide a second wing for Singapore as an external economy.

These strategic eras reflect, according to Chan Chin Bock, the EDB's third chairman and currently head of the new EDB consulting venture, a deeper underlying reality that must be understood. In the first decade Singapore had to be both the salesperson/marketer and the entrepreneur because one could not convince companies to invest in Singapore without Singapore being willing to share some of the risks. If Singapore put up its own development funds in support of various activities or actually acted as an equity partner, it not only increased the confidence of the overseas investor, but it committed the EDB to supporting the project and making it a success.

In the period roughly from 1970 to 1985 the EDB became more of a "host" to the MNCs, supporting them and solving their various problems, but there was less need for entrepreneurial activity. The EDB functioned more as a technocrat and became more reactive as the various MNCs pursued their own strategies in Singapore. When the economic crisis of the mid-1980s hit, it was apparent that the new thrust under Philip Yeo would require the EDB to once again become much more entrepreneurial.

What made this possible was that Singapore's earlier success had created financial reserves that could now be used for investment. Instead of investing in overseas real estate as a major option, the ministry of finance and the ministry of trade and industry, working with the EDB, eventually allocated S$1 billion to the EDB for investments in projects. The EDB's investment philosophy, however, was not to invest for profit, but rather to invest for a limited time to get the project off the ground and to build the confidence of the other investors. If after some years the project could stand on its own, the EDB planned for its partners to buy it out so that it could recycle its capital into other projects. The ultimate purpose of its investment was not to make money per se but to stimulate projects and to ensure their success.

But this meant that the EDB's task was once again the complex blending of marketing and selling Singapore while at the same time figuring out what to invest in, with whom to form partnerships, and how to structure those relationships. One of the recent examples that illustrates this complexity was to bring together in 1994 Hewlett-Packard, Texas Instruments, Canon, and the EDB into TECH SEMICONDUCTOR, a U.S.$300 million joint venture to build semiconductors in Singapore, with the EDB owning 26 percent of the new enterprise. Two other examples include EDB's formation of a separate stategic business unit to explore investments in biotechnology and a separate unit to concentrate on developing projects within China.

In sum, it is not easy to discern how accomplishments thus far blend into visions of the future, but one can review a few of the projects that are already in the works to provide some flavor of the level of Singapore's industrialization. These examples are only a smattering of what is going on.

• plans to launch a communications satellite into space by 1999 as part of the development of a telecommunications infrastructure.

• the building of a S$65 million telecommunications R & D park to permit companies interested in this area to do research.

• S$500 million committed for new precision-engineering projects.

• design centers set up locally by Hewlett-Packard, Texas Instruments, Thomson, Matsushita (MESA), Motorola, Apple, Philips, AT & T, Seagate, Murata, Siemens, etc. HP wins an award in the United States for a printer designed by a local team.

• a regional headquarters and three new plants set up by Motorola.

• plans for an educational theme park in the Science Center to promote "edutainment" (science education presented in an entertaining way).

• plans for a S$3.4 billion petrochemical project extension on the island of Pulau Ayer Merbau.

• a S$50 million center for German industry to help small- and medium-sized firms to enter Asia.

• help Takashimaya to open its largest shopping center outside of Japan in the Ngee Ann City commercial complex.

• creation of Tang Village, a replica of a traditional Chinese village inside Singapore.

• plans for film, video, and television production.

Many other examples could be provided from the oil industry, the food industry, information technology, banking, financial and venture capital services, aerospace, defense and weapons technology, and so on. But how does all this fit into some kind of vision of the future?

Recent Trends in Singapore's Internal Evolution—From "Singapore, Inc.," to "Singapore, Unlimited," "The Next Lap," and Now "The Learning Nation" (1990s—)

Plans for Singapore's further development are summarized in the 1991 Strategic Economic Plan (SEP) put out by the government as a guideline and summary of the plans formulated by the EDB and other government agencies. In the executive summary the goals and main strategic thrusts are outlined and elaborated as follows:

. . . to attain the status and characteristics of a first league developed country within the next 30 to 40 years. Based on certain optimistic and pessimistic scenarios Singapore aims to catch up with—on a moving-target basis—the GNP per capita of the United States by 2030 or the Netherlands by 2020. . . .
Key facets of the Vision are economic dynamism, a high quality of life, a strong national identity and the configuration of a global city. . .
To achieve this vision, eight strategic thrusts were identified:

• Enhancing human resources
• Promoting national teamwork
• Becoming internationally oriented
• Creating a conducive climate for innovation
• Developing manufacturing and service clusters
• Spearheading economic redevelopment
• Maintaining international competitiveness
• Reducing vulnerability

The major constraints to achieving these ambitious goals are full employment and present limits set on the foreign worker population; Singapore has reached the limits of sea-front land and sea space. In order to continue to grow at relatively high rates, it is necessary to reorganize the way human and physical resources are managed. (SEP)[3]

To achieve elements of this vision, the growth triangle initiative will be further expanded by encouraging companies to undertake distributed processing further afield and by establishing business ventures with indigenous companies in these areas. The broader concept of regionalization also has implicit in it the notion that if Singapore can establish enough joint ventures with its neighbors and in other less developed countries, it not only creates business opportunities for its own development, but enhances its security as well by becoming more and more indispensable to the whole region.

One element of this strategy is to develop Singapore's role as a hub for tourism by developing joint venture resorts and hotels, by building up the infrastructures in less developed countries that are not ready to tackle the complexity of manufacturing, and by training the personnel in these countries to Singapore's standards of safety, cleanliness, efficiency, and service. Implicit in this notion is the marketing advantage of showing the tourist or other investor that going into less developed areas does not require compromising these standards. Joint venturing of this sort not only guarantees a marketing advantage but also ensures that Singaporean companies will be "on the hook" to make the ventures succeed.

On the internal front the goal is to continue to upgrade the kinds of manufacturing and services that are promoted in order to provide higher-grade employment for Singaporeans and to stimulate local industry and entrepreneurship to create Singapore-based MNCs. Because the cost of labor relative to other developing countries will continue to increase, Singapore has to figure out what would continue to attract MNCs and on what dimensions to emulate other highly developed countries. That means "Singapore needs to identify and cultivate the right kinds of niches and within these niches, move as close to the level of developed countries as it is possible to achieve" (SEP 1991, p. 7). That, in turn, means more regional headquarters, an information and possibly a financial hub, and limited basic R & D (but at a high level of technical expertise in the design and development end of R & D).

In the human resource area the goals are:

- A high standard of competence
- A high level of basic education
- A high degree of industry relevance in training programmes
- Effective programmes for mid-career training
- Nurturing important human resource qualities, such as the work ethic and creativity.

This requires what is called *"A Soft Infrastructure:"*

- A technological infrastructure, comprising a pool of trained manpower in key technologies as well as a network of technical competence centres and research institutes which enable companies to be effective in design and innovation
- A social climate and institutional structure which supports innovation
- A national system which encourages a high degree of cooperation among labour, business and government

Singapore must become *A Global City:*

To overcome size limitation Singapore must tap global opportunities by adopting a more liberal immigration policy for highly skilled and professional people, Singapore companies must be encouraged to set up operations outside their own borders (learn to live overseas and like it), and Singapore must provide support through EDB for local companies to invest overseas.

Economic Resilience must be created through anticipating various contingencies. Singapore must create a Scenario Analysis Group, have good economic indicators to identify danger signals, and limit high degrees of dependency on any one country or type of industry.[4]

For each of the various strategic thrusts, the annual corporate planning conference held by the EDB in 1991, 1992, and 1993 identified a series of specific initiatives, schemes, and programs to ensure implementation. For example, to stimulate local industry, over twenty-five different schemes were put in place as shown in table 3.1. What these programs illustrate is the aggressive effort made by the EDB to solve whatever problems are identified and the ability to invent and implement vehicles to solve the problems. Within the EDB a major program of organizational development and organizational learning has been launched and the concept has now evolved of trying to stimulate Singapore to see itself as a "learning nation."

Summary

I have reviewed the major strategic eras in the EDB's thirty-five-year history, noting that they built on each other and evolved in response to the economic circumstances that the EDB identified. The theme

Table 3.1
Small and medium-size business assistance schemes and programs for every stage of growth

Start-up	Growth	Expansion	Going Overseas
Local Enterprise Computerization Program	Iso 9000 Certification	Automation Leasing Scheme	Business Development Scheme
Local Enterprise Finance Scheme	Local Enterprise Computerization Program	Brand Development Assistance Scheme	Double Deduction for Overseas Investment Development Expenditure
Product Development Assistance Scheme	Local Enterprise Finance Scheme	Business Development Scheme	Franchise Development Assistance Scheme
R & D Incubator Program	Local Enterprise Technical Assistance Scheme	Franchise Development Assistance Scheme	Local Enterprise Finance Scheme (Overseas)
Skills Development Fund	Local Industry Upgrading Program	Iso 9000 Certification	Local Industry Upgrading Program
Venture Capital	Market and Investment Development Assistance Scheme	Local Enterprise Computerization Program	Market and Investment Development Assistance Scheme
	Product Development Assistance Scheme	Local Enterprise Finance Scheme	Overseas Enterprise Incentive/Overseas Investment Incentive
	Pioneer Status/Investment Allowance	Local Enterprise Technical Assistance Scheme	
	Skills Development Fund	Local Industry Upgrading Program	
	Software Development Assistance Scheme	Market and Investment Development Assistance Scheme	
	Venture Capital	Pioneer Status/Investment Allowance	
		Product Development Assistance Scheme	
		Skills Development Fund	
		Software Development Assistance Scheme	
		Total Business Plan	
		Venture Capital	

Source: *Growing with Enterprise: A National Report,* Singapore, EDB, 1993, p. 23.

of strategic pragmatism comes to mind again in that Singapore displayed throughout this period a remarkable adaptive and learning capability without, however, sacrificing short-run problem solving. And throughout these periods of strategic change, the EDB as an organization maintained a certain basic character and style, even as it evolved under the leadership of different chairmen. To understand the bases of such stability it is necessary to examine the character of the different chairmen.

4

The Founding Chairman: Hon Sui Sen (1961–1968)

The task was to develop virtually from scratch an organization that would
be the chief instrument and prime mover not only of Singapore's industrialization but also because industry was to be a leading sector of Singapore's
economy, of Singapore's rapid economic growth (Hon Sui Sen [1981], EDB,
Thirty Years of Economic Development, 1991, p. 13)

Hon Sui Sen was universally acknowledged to have been a perfect
choice as the founding chairman of the EDB.[1] His successors considered him to be a wise, kind, and persuasive man, highly regarded by
fellow politicians and extremely technically competent. His immediate successor, I. F. Tang, saw him as a man of humility and yet great
spirit and "a master of economic development." Almost all of the
elements that the EDB had to work on were enhanced by his background, skill set, personality, and managerial style. During his seven-
year tenure he made the EDB into a virtual economic czar.

Background

Hon Sui Sen was born in Penang, Malaysia, and received his primary
school education there. He won a scholarship to Raffles College in
Singapore, where he studied physics. During his college years he
became a close friend of Goh Keng Swee. He did very well in college
and was accepted into the Straits Settlements civil service in 1939,
serving first as a magistrate and then as a collector of land revenue.
After World War II he became land commissioner in 1957. He then
went on to the ministry of finance, where he became permanent
secretary in 1959.

Getting Started

Although Hon had all the right instincts and was a good strategist, he lacked knowledge of how to do the day-to-day work of promotion. It is for this reason that E. J. Mayer was hired as the temporary managing director to set up the organization. Ngiam Tong Dow, who was one of the original group of civil servants assigned to the EDB and later became its fourth chairman, described the average day as "all legwork." "The goal was to create jobs, more jobs, and still more jobs, and the system was to make calls on any and all companies who could be contacted—high tech, low tech, whatever tech. . . . For every one hundred calls you might get ten responses, and from those ten responses you might get two visits, and from those two visits you might get one 'yes'" (1994 interview).

Early investors were mostly local Singaporean companies, companies from Hong Kong and Taiwan, and Chinese-run companies from Thailand and Indonesia. For example, the first factory was National Iron and Steel, a local company in the business of converting the scrap metal from the breaking up of ships into bars for construction. The EDB was a part investor. Primary incentives were extensive tax breaks for companies who were awarded "Pioneer certificates." The Royal Dutch Shell Company, which had decided back in the late 1950s to build a refinery in Singapore, was awarded the first such certificate in 1961. The flavor of the occasion when the refinery opened is captured in Shell's own account:

The evening of the 26 July 1961 was one of the finest that month. For over a week the rain had been falling, but this day, even the weather seemed to respect the occasion. On Pulau Bukom, 500 guests, including Singapore's Finance Minister, Assemblymen, Consular and Commonwealth representatives, religious, community and business leaders, as well as trade unionists, gazed at the vast structure that reared before them—an intricate silvery network of pipes from which columns of steel rose tall and resplendent.

At half past seven Finance Minister Dr. Goh Keng Swee, the guest of honor, stood on the speaker's platform which overlooked the structure. A year ago, this very site was but a huge pile of earth with a scattering of trees and scrubs. Dr. Goh, felling the first tree, had launched construction work that had transformed the area into a humming complex of concrete and steel. This, therefore, was a proud moment. For him. For the men who had built it in record time. For the company that invested $30 million in it. For the State of Singapore.

As the gathering watched, Dr. Goh depressed a switch.

Floodlights lit up the night and the structure stood out in all its magnificence. Ship sirens went off in the distance as coloured lights festooning two tug boats came on.

Shell's oil refinery, the first in Singapore, was officially declared open.[2]

Connections

To be a "one-stop" agency, to solve all the problems that potential investors might have, required the ability to get things done in other parts of the government. The fact that Hon was a close and trusted friend of the prime minister and of the minister of finance provided him ready access to the centers of power and policy. Because of his civil service background he knew "everybody," which made it easy for him to pick up the phone and get instant action. The use of a network of personal acquaintanceships as a basis for problem solving across organizational units remains to this day one of the strengths of the EDB and one of the salient characteristics of Singapore as a whole.

Land Management

One of the priorities for the EDB was to make land available to potential investors and to provide them with rental or leasing arrangements that would be attractive to them without compromising Singapore's own long-range land strategy. Having been land commissioner for a number of years gave Hon deeper insights into how to make those arrangements optimally. For example, he was highly praised by the current group of ex-chairmen for what was considered at the time to be a very innovative leasing policy referred to as the "thirty plus thirty system."

First of all, Hon did not want to sell land outright because Singapore might find itself "stuck" with some companies that later proved to be "undesirable" for any of a number of reasons. Second, if the land was leased at too high or too low a rate initially or on a one-shot payment, Singapore would not only be unable to correct the rate later but also would have no steady income. The solution was to lease land for thirty years with an option to renew at the end of that time, giving Singapore the opportunity to refuse renewal or negotiate a more favorable rate. If the land was to be rented, a similar philosophy would operate in that the rental rate would be reviewed every five years with a guarantee that it could not be raised more than 50 percent—a condition that was important to companies to reassure them that they would not lose the land once their factory was built. This system of renting and leasing provided a continuing stream of income to what eventually became the independent Jurong Township Corporation.

Goh had designated the Jurong area, which at that time was basically a swamp, to be the future Jurong Industrial Estate. Developing it would require an infrastructure of roads and utilities. If the industrialization scheme did not work, it was quipped, this area would be known as "Goh's Folly," but both Goh and Hon had not only high hopes but complete faith that things would work. Hon had line authority to commit funds, and Goh let him know that he would back him completely. An example of the kinds of risks that they were willing to run was how they dealt with the public utilities officials who were not willing to lay pipe and build the technical infrastructure without prepayment, because they did not know if any industries would actually locate there. Hon made the decision simply to go ahead and pay them and risk all those funds against an uncertain future. This ability to take financial risks was one of Hon's major assets.

Hon's technical knowledge of land management also made him a highly persuasive negotiator, because he could marshal the facts necessary to make his argument. One story was told of a "planeload of lawyers from an overseas oil company" who arrived with all kinds of demands for a choice piece of land and very favorable leasing terms. Hon responded by simply laying out all of the facts, presenting the different options, and letting the facts speak for themselves. He was seen as a man of absolute integrity who was fair to all of the stakeholders—investors and the Singapore government alike.

Management Style—"None of Us Wanted Him to Look Sad"

Hon's prestige came from his personality, from his integrity, and from his gentle yet firm managerial style. In a 1993 group interview, many of his former subordinates emphasized his gentle but firm style by noting that if you did something wrong, he did not yell at you or rebuke you, even in private; "he just looked sad, and none of us wanted him to look sad." This style brought out very high levels of motivation in his people without close supervision. People were very loyal to him, to the point that it was said that "people would die for him."

Hon's style was a direct reflection of his Chinese socialization, his training in the British civil service, and his personality. As an administrator he introduced the concept of *total written documentation* so that everyone would always be fully informed, especially the boss. Hon demanded detailed monthly reports, went over them very carefully, and then reviewed them at a division directors' meeting where the directors and the heads of departments would go over all of the material. This system and the underlying assumption that the boss must be fully informed about everything at all times has continued as a core requirement of EDB management to this day. Hon delegated authority but kept himself well-enough informed to guide decisions and sometimes to overrule decisions that he felt were wrong. He also held weekly development meetings of what he called the "technical officers," during which time all relevant decisions were reviewed and hammered out.

Hon's gentleness with subordinates did not imply weakness. Indeed many examples were cited in which he made decisions with great strength. One story was told by a former subordinate of a textile company that had a consistent pattern of difficult labor relationships partly because communist agitators had infiltrated the factory and were periodically inciting strikes. Hon asked one of the senior officers to settle the strike, but the officer had no idea of how to accomplish that. He asked Hon, "How do you want me to do that?" to which Hon replied, "It's easy. Let me show you." He called up the bank that had the major outstanding loans to this particular company and had the bank pull the loans. This immediately shut down the company and put everybody out of work. It permitted the company to hire a brand new work force and start all over again. The lesson was not forgotten on the communists and, as Hon put it: "If you strike on ideological grounds instead of on economic grounds, you will be shut down and out."

Mentoring Subordinates

One of Hon's greatest contributions to the EDB and to Singapore was his mentoring of several generations of young EDBers. He was a strong and caring teacher, yet delegated sufficiently to allow his people to grow and develop on their own. Almost all of the former members of the EDB commented in one way or another on how important their time under Hon was to their career development. Not only did they learn administrative and management skills from observing him as a role model, but they learned a caring attitude toward subordinates from his gentle yet firm style. People who did not do well in the organization were "taken care of rather than punished" in that Hon would use his contacts to find them a job in another organization and engineer the move in such a way that they would not feel too much a failure.

Hon's skill in selecting people and mentoring them ensured that the talent needed for the future would be available. For example, he recruited Chan Chin Bock from the Ford Motor Company in Singapore and developed him into a highly successful manager of EDB's international operations, architect of some of its innovative training programs, and its third chairman. All of the later chairmen except Philip Yeo were originally hired by Hon Sui Sen and were allowed to develop their own philosophies under him.

Nurturing Future Strategies

The shift from import substitution to export orientation and internationalization began during Hon's later years as chairman. Also during this period major decisions had to be made to prepare to upgrade the labor force in order to be able to attract the more skill-intensive and high-tech companies. The international offices had to be opened and people found to staff them. To help with the growing drive toward internationalization in 1966–67, Chan Chin Bock was sent to open EDB's New York office and P. Y. Hwang was sent to open the Hong Kong office.

Hwang spoke Cantonese and his primary job was to bring in Hong Kong companies, but in addition he was to help recruit MNCs. He described how this worked at first.

One thing we had to do was to hang around the airport and intercept U.S. company representatives on their way to Japan, Korea, or Taiwan and talk them into making a "little side trip" to Singapore. Mr. Chan was to do the same thing in New York, intercepting people on their way to seeking low-cost manufacturing sites in Europe. Occasionally reps from the same U.S. company who had agreed to visit Singapore would run into each other there and be totally surprised to meet. "I thought you were supposed to be in Taiwan." "What about you, I thought you were supposed to be in Ireland." (1994 interview)

An early success resulting from this tactic was the recruitment of the Fairchild Semiconductor Company, which not only agreed to come to Singapore to build a plant there, but whose vice president subsequently went to the National Semiconductor Company and came back to Singapore later to open a plant for that company as well.

The Breaking Up of the EDB

Perhaps the most difficult decision that Hon had to help make and implement was to break up the EDB in 1967–68. Several reasons lie behind the decision. First, by 1967 or so the EDB had become too big, too diverse, too powerful and was in need of refocusing. Each of the departments had become professional in its own right and could now stand on its own feet.

Second, because the departments were involved in (1) promoting investments, (2) providing land, (3) making loans and providing other financial supports, and (4) deciding on incentives such as tax breaks, the potential for internal conflicts of interest became very great. To avoid such conflicts initially Hon had taught the organization to make rules as clear as possible, to not allow exceptional cases, and to give itself the flexibility to apply rules differently in different circumstances.

However, as I. F. Tang noted in reminiscing about this period, "With land and with loans one must bargain and one cannot have completely clear rules, so one often had to wear three hats when making deals. To avoid conflict of interest one had to keep promotion, land, and money separate" (1994 interview).

Third, the EDB had become a kind of economic czar, doing everything. It had successfully become the one-stop shop for investors providing land, facilities, services, and even additional funds when needed. One consequence was that the focus on bringing in new investors was being lost.

By 1968 Goh felt that Singapore had broken the back of its unemployment problem, and for the three reasons cited above he decided to divide the EDB into several parts. He kept the investment promotion division as the EDB's central focus, but broke off the land development function as the Jurong Township Corporation and merged all of the investment functions into the Singapore Development Bank (DBS). Hon Sui Sen was appointed to be the bank's chairman because "he knew how to set up new organizations."

Prior to this breakup, the EDB training unit had already been spun off in 1964, becoming the Singapore Institute of Management (SIM). The Ford Foundation had expressed an interest in providing a grant for training but could not give funds to a government agency, so SIM was created as a private organization and developed with Ford money. Other divisions were also spun off in 1968 with the creation of the International Trading Company (INTRACO) to handle the promotion of exports, the National Productivity Board to worry about wages and productivity, the Singapore Institute of Standards and Industrial Research (SISIR), and the Engineering Industries Development Agency to further technical training.

In December 1968, I. F. Tang was brought in as the new chairman of the EDB to permit Hon to take over the DBS. Hon Sui Sen's legacy is best captured in his own words as he looked back at the EDB on its twentieth anniversary in 1981.

The EDB is special to me in several ways. First, I spent some of the most challenging and satisfying years of my civil service career when I was its Chairman in the 1960s. The task then was to develop virtually from scratch an organization that would be the chief instrument and prime mover not only of Singapore's industrialization, but also because industry was to be a leading sector of Singapore's economy, of Singapore's rapid economic growth.

Then, in the 1970s, as the Minister responsible for economic development, I had to ensure that the EDB under successive, capable leaders would deliver the goods and maintain the pace of our industrial growth in the most difficult circumstances brought about by the oil crisis and by unsettling changes in the world economic order.

Last, but not least, it was during my years with the EDB that I developed close personal ties with many colleagues which have grown into lasting friendships. It is therefore not easy for me to express the emotions I feel on this special occasion. Perhaps I can describe it best as not unlike seeing a son attain his maturity. You are happy, secretly relieved, that he has developed so satisfactorily and made such a good start. But as the ever caring parent, you are anxious still for his future. In the same way, with the EDB, you are naturally pleased by its achievements in the last 20 years, but you try also to evaluate its strengths as you ponder the challenges it will face in its task of advancing Singapore into the world community of industrial nations." (Hon Sui Sen [1981], EDB, *Thirty Years of Economic Development,* 1991, p. 13)

Analytical Comments

The Legacy of the British Civil Service

Many people noted that much of Hon's style derived from his training as a civil servant. In particular, the following imperatives were cited by P. Y. Hwang as being characteristic of the British civil service tradition:

1. Train yourself to the highest possible level of competence;

2. Always be maximally rational, impartial, and unemotional in your dealings and decisions;

3. As a senior civil servant, your job is to be the "Chef." The glory goes to your political master—he will eat the food you prepare and he will make the speeches. You have to remain silent and invisible or be billed only as "a reliable source" or "a source that could not be quoted." Your job is to cook as well as possible, keeping in mind nutrition, what the taste preference of the consumer is, and sometimes even how to influence what he eats or should eat. If he chooses to eat unhealthy foods, you should point out the alternatives and their benefits.

4. Every position you take must be documented, filed away, and preserved so that it can be justified and tracked at a later time. (1994 interview)

Hwang also pointed out a weakness in the British system that the EDB managed to avoid. The British system would malfunction if and when the lower-level civil servants would not take responsibility but would constantly "ask for instructions" so that the boss would always be responsible and the civil servant could never be held accountable. In contrast, in the American system the subordinate was expected to take initiative and act, so long as the boss's interests were preserved and the boss was told what was done. In that system the subordinate is accountable and more visible. The EDB and most of the Singapore government ended up operating more like the American system, probably for two reasons: first, because so many of them were educated overseas and were exposed to many different role models; and second, because so many of them learned to deal with companies in which taking action and being responsible and accountable was highly valued.

These comments suggest that the system of honoring the hierarchy and, at the same time, expecting subordinates to take positions and be accountable was already in place in the way that Hon defined his own role and that of his first-line officers. What made it possible to stay within the hierarchy was the system of full information flow and the expectation that everyone had read all of the reports. There was therefore no necessity to go outside the hierarchy when exploring decisions or seeking information. As will be seen, the tradition of staying within the hierarchy eroded with subsequent chairmen, but the tradition of everyone being fully informed at all times became a strong and stable element of the EDB culture.

Many current and past members of the EDB noted that the system of writing reports had the effect of forcing people to think through exactly what they were saying and providing training in communication, as well as information for others to learn from. Almost everyone noted how much they learned from having to put things on paper and having bosses and colleagues critique ideas by putting notes in the margin or asking questions in meetings. Not only did this provide training in thinking and communicating, but it meant that written proposals and presentations would be perfected in the process of being developed. I once asked to see a draft of a presentation and was told that I could not see it until the boss had been over it, even though my informant and I knew perfectly well that it was only a draft and that I wanted to see it only to get a sense of its direction. But it was not a perfect product yet, so it could not be revealed to an outsider.

In summary, many of the basic stylistic characteristics of the EDB were launched during the tenure of its first chairman, and many of these were inherited from the British civil service. At the same time, many of the deeper values of integrity, openness, commitment to the mission, and learning to be responsible and autonomous were reported to be the product of Hon Sui Sen's personal example and his management style. This style preserved the strong hierarchy, but also created a climate in which information could flow freely within that hierarchy and in which lower-level officers felt empowered to act.

The Impact of Entry and Exit from the Malaysian Federation (1963–1965)

The work of the EDB initially consisted of analyzing fact sheets with lists of industries and products to develop the import substitution program—namely to manufacture the products that the local market needed which, prior to this time, had been imported. As this program matured it was assumed that a larger market would become available with Singapore joining the Malaysian Federation, which was being created as the British planned their withdrawal. Joining the Federation was also motivated by political necessity to reduce Singapore's vulnerability and, from the prior Malayan point of view, to ensure that Singapore would not become a communist-dominated state. Many Singaporeans had family ties to Chinese living in Malaya and most of Lee's ministers were Malayan in origin; so there were strong personal ties to what became the Malaysian Federation.

Nevertheless the EDB had to play a special role in selling this concept to the Singaporeans because of the fear that they would be losing too much autonomy in implementing their economic strategy. Once they were part of the Federation, all new proposals would have to be ruled on by the Malaysian government in Kuala Lumpur. To deal with this potential problem the EDB loaded as many projects into their pipeline as they could before they joined. This front loading, in fact, kept them going because none of the projects that they proposed after 1963 were approved. Difficulties in working together arose on both sides, resulting in Singapore leaving the Federation in 1965 and setting the stage for a major shift in attitude and self-perception.

Island Mentality: "We Have to Do It on Our Own"

The recognition that Singapore was now on its own and without the resources or the market that Malaysia represented was quite traumatic, and many remember vividly the emotional speech that Lee Kuan Yew gave when he made the announcement. As people now look back on that event, however, they regard it as a crucial stimulus to getting serious about their own economic development. It was also at about this time that the British were beginning to talk about closing down their military operations in Singapore, causing even more economic stress.

Singapore now knew in more vivid terms that "people were its only resource" providing a strong stimulus to the work ethic and to the sense of being an interdependent community that had to work collaboratively as a team. A sense of vulnerability based on being an island in a potentially hostile sea was also accentuated, accounting in part for the willingness of the population to accept a number of governmental controls that outsiders often regarded as excessive, yet which were viewed internally as necessary to make the economic plans of attracting foreign investments work.

Contemplating the psychological state of the leadership and the populace in the mid-1960s, one can see that the Singapore leadership would feel totally justified in continuing to impose various controls on the society, intervene heavily in economic affairs, and be confident that all of the elements of strong government intervention would continue to be supported by the populace. The important point to highlight once again is that the government's policies were ultimately very pragmatic in that they were built on the central assumption that foreign investors would only come to Singapore if they found it to be a clean, safe, incorruptible, and politically stable environment oriented to the needs of business. This pragmatism was revealed repeatedly in subsequent years as the government shifted its strategy to deal with new economic realities.

It should be noted that the validity of that assumption was confirmed in Singapore's own experience by their success in attracting foreign investors who confirmed that safety, cleanness, incorruptibility, and the various financial incentives were important in their decision making (see chapters 8 and 9). But even current members of the EDB acknowledge that the historic circumstances that made this strategy work are not necessarily generalizable to other countries in other times. The general lesson rather is that each country must think clearly about its particular situation and develop its own version of strategic pragmatism.

5

The Deal Makers: I. F. Tang and Chan Chin Bock

The long-range strategic thrust toward attracting foreign investments was well launched by the late 1960s, and the EDB now had to focus on making it happen on a larger scale. The spinning off of several parts of the EDB was intended to facilitate this focusing, and the talents and predilections of the next two chairmen clearly put the emphasis on the marketing and selling of Singapore.

I. F. Tang (1968–1972)

A clear sense of mission, a superb salesman, and an inspirational leader. (a former subordinate)

We are not selling coffee or tea, we are selling a country. (I. F. Tang, 1969)

Never run down anyone or another country because, in the long run, you may be partners and have to work together. (I. F. Tang, 1969)

In naming I. F. Tang as the second chairman of the EDB in December 1968, Goh described him as "a man who absolutely mesmerized you; he could convince you to build a battleship here."[1] Tang remembers the following comment from Goh as he was given his new "marching orders" for the EDB: "I am taking away your land, your money, and half of your people. Refocus yourself with the rest of the people and bring in more investments. And I expect you to do it because the people are all high quality" (1994 interview).

I. F. Tang's mandate was not only to refocus but to totally reorient the EDB's promotion program toward higher value-added industries such as petrochemicals, electronics, and pharmaceuticals that required a more skilled labor force. To do this Singapore had ultimately to become the "precision engineering shop" of Asia and prepare for the electronics revolution. In the short run, they had to train skilled technical personnel such as tool and die makers and precision machinists.

The EDB had already realized that to upgrade selectively the skills needed in the population, Singapore should develop joint ventures with companies from countries that had those particular skills, so they started a series of joint training programs with companies from Germany, France, and Japan. The UN had also provided some money for courses in light engineering services, and New Zealand had helped with setting up what eventually became the Singapore Institute of Standards and Industrial Research (SISIR).

The Singapore government itself was maturing, and the fact that many of its departments were now staffed by former EDB people ensured that continued coordination and cooperation could be counted on. So each of the separate government units could become highly specialized yet remain integrated with the long-range strategy because of the common philosophy learned in the EDB and the cross-representation on each other's boards. The basic premise that all parts of government had to work together cooperatively was thus strongly reaffirmed.

Background

I. F. Tang was an expatriate from China. He received his bachelor of science degree from the National Central University of China and a master's degree from the Harvard Business School. Most of his linkages were in the United States and he was working for the United Nations at the time the 1960 Mission to Singapore was formed. As the only Asian member of the mission, Tang decided to keep a very low profile, but did provide some advice on how to proceed. He did not want to be the leader, but he was willing to be assigned to the mission as its secretary, which meant that he had to pull most of the material together. He had no direct contact with the EDB until he was recruited by Hon Sui Sen in the early 1960s to be a liaison with the UN and pay periodic visits to the EDB while still fulfilling other commitments to the UN. When Tang's various UN duties were finished he agreed to come to the EDB in a technical role, and he took over the technical consulting division in 1963. Consequently, by the time he was made chairman he had had a variety of assignments in the EDB and was familiar with its basic method of operation.

Management Style

Tang was described as very business oriented, very sharp, very persevering, very shrewd, a good negotiator, and very personal. His subordinates learned a great deal from watching him deal with investors and also from listening to him when he explained the job. He was an inspirational leader who not only displayed his conceptual and sales skills by his own example, but he had a supervisory style that really motivated the senior officers in the field and at home to an extraordinary degree. He was able to make everyone feel important.

One senior officer recalled that when several of them were about to go on an overseas visit, Tang came to the airport to see his men off and, as he did so, he gave them the following message: "You guys are being sent overseas to promote Singapore; you just get them to come here, we in headquarters will take over once they are here; your job is 90 percent of the job, we'll do the rest." At the same time, another officer noted that Tang not only made the field officer believe that he was doing 90 percent of the work, but, at the very same time, was able to convince headquarters staff that getting the company to come and visit was only 10 percent of the job, and that the real ultimate effort was the 90 percent that the headquarters did to actually close the deal.

The view from a headquarters standpoint was that the effort in the field was, in fact, more difficult because you were out there on your own with very few things to go on. However, for the headquarters to put together the details of the deal, to negotiate with the various branches of government on land allocation, rental or leasing arrangements, tax incentives, level of training support, and so on was also very difficult. Senior officers and Tang would make only broad commitments to investors so the projects office often had to work very hard to "work out all the rest of the details."

For example, the international director in New York had made certain commitments to General Electric. When the company lawyer was in Singapore following up on the details with the projects office, the EDB staff realized that they had to renegotiate certain things because GE was getting some very unique concessions and a tax break that was actually too unfavorable to Singapore. The headquarters people put together an alternative plan that would be more favorable to Singapore without GE losing anything. They were able to "force this plan on GE" as the quid pro quo for the other special concessions that they were being given. Tang helped his people to see themselves as both salesmen and administrators, and showed them that the administrators really functioned as the integrators in the system between the field sales people and the government ministers, always working in the national interest.

New Hierarchical Style

Under I. F. Tang the formalism of preserving the hierarchy began to erode. Tang valued and preserved the hierarchy, but did not hesitate to go around it himself or encourage subordinates lower down to come to him directly. The norm was to get the job done; the niceties of seniority or formal rank mattered less. Information still had to be written down, but more informal communication channels began to be legitimated and used. As one senior officer recalled: "There were extensive corridor discussions where important information was exchanged, and these discussions reflected not only the openness of the EDB culture but the commitment to everyone being on top of everything with respect to all present and future clients. This also created a climate where everyone thought that they did the crucial thing and made the major contribution" (1993 interview).

Tang was a man of few words, but he knew the background of all his people and respected their opinion in relation to what he felt they knew specifically. Several examples of this kind of confidence were provided by M. Q. Wong, who was at that time the field representative in Japan, had a background in Japanese culture, and knew the language fluently, resulting in Tang periodically asking him informally and off line for a frank appraisal of the Japanese situation. When he did so he was always willing to listen and really pay attention, as illustrated in the initial negotiations with the Seiko Watch Company to get the company to manufacture in Singapore.

What was important here was the degree to which informal communications and "off-line" contacts were crucial in aiding the formal decision making. I was aware that Seiko was a family-controlled company, but under the Japanese consensus system the entire fifteen-person board had to be persuaded that building and making their product in Singapore was a feasible and worthwhile enterprise. All the various machinations and negotiations that had occurred in the board and that I either knew about and had engaged in had to be kept secret because if you put a lot of it in writing, local opposition in Singapore would mobilize and would jeopardize the project. So whenever I had "real data," I phoned Mr. Tang and gave it to him privately over the phone.

At one point two of the Seiko board members who were in favor of manufacturing in Singapore asked to have dinner with me and told me very emotionally that they really had some serious conflicts in the board, but they thought there was a good chance of success if I would come to one of the board meetings and personally answer the questions of some of the skeptics. I was willing to do this and was asked particularly whether Singapore would honor its various commitments. I replied that they definitely would and that I was not committing anything that I was not able to back up. Secondly, they wanted to know whether Singapore would really train the workers to a sufficient level of skill to manufacture this precision product. I replied that they should come and visit and see for themselves what the skill level was.

After this board meeting a couple of weeks went by and it was not clear what was going to happen, but I got a call one day in my Tokyo office saying that the chairman and the number two person were coming over to see me. They arrived in my office and told me that they were prepared to visit Singapore and make the commitment if I would agree to go with them and stay involved with the project.

Once they said this I knew that they would commit to the Singapore project even though nothing was on paper. I phoned Mr. Tang and told him, "The Seiko people will come," and urged him to ignore the various other negative inputs that he was getting from others at the office. I could hear on the phone that, even as I was talking, someone in the background was raising objections, and I heard Mr. Tang say, "Please be quiet. I'm listening to M. Q. and he has something important to tell me." This made me feel very proud and showed how much Mr. Tang had this ability to know when to listen. (1993 interview)

I. F. Tang's ability to motivate, inspire, and teach people under him was illustrated in the recollections of Ng Pock Too, an alumnus of the EDB and now president of a large company. Tang taught them that if you let a potential client leave Singapore without having gotten a commitment from him, you have not really done your job. To get that commitment, the idea was not just to argue for Singapore but to demonstrate Singapore's ability to be efficient by actually displaying those traits to the potential clients.

Mr. Tata of the Indian Conglomerate Tata Enterprises had been visiting Singapore and had formed a favorable impression but no deal had been closed and he was going to be leaving the next day early in the afternoon. Mr. Tang and I had had a long dinner with Mr. Tata the previous evening during which we tried very hard to close the deal, but it was still wide open at midnight when dinner was over, so Mr. Tang asked me to go home and prepare a letter of proposal that would lay out all the terms that Singapore would be willing to offer to Tata. It was to be ready to be signed by Mr. Tang at 9 A.M. the following morning. I went home and worked until 3 A.M., came into the office very early, collared a secretary, got her to type the proposal and had it ready on Tang's desk by the required time of 9 A.M.

I recall Mr. Tang saying, "Young man, this is fairly well done; now get it over to the minister in the form of a draft letter to Tata with a signed offer from Singapore, and when you have that, get it over to Mr. Tata before the time he leaves early this afternoon." That meant a whole morning of rushing around getting signatures, but I was able to deliver the letter before Mr. Tata left. Tata was so impressed by Singapore's ability to produce an offer on such short notice that it clinched the deal. (1993 interview)

Tang knew how to use each of his people and maximize their resources. He gave them lots of valuable principles such as doing their homework on a client very thoroughly because "if you can't really get him excited in the first fifteen minutes, you may never get him excited at all." This fifteen-minute rule derived from the experience they had when they were "cold calling" on CEOs of companies. A few would refuse to see them altogether, but some of them would say, "Okay I'll give you fifteen minutes; if you can get me interested in that time, I'll keep talking to you; otherwise we are done."

Tang also taught them all how to sell by being "credible"—remove any element of doubt in the investor's mind about any possible flaws that Singapore might have. Think out what concerns the investor might have and deal with all of them. Another key point in selling was to bring the prospective investor to talk to companies who were already manufacturing in Singapore and let them do the selling. Show prospective companies the training center so they could see the present and future skill levels of prospective employees and show them that Singapore itself wants to survive, hence will do a good job.

Analytical Comment

The early 1970s was a period of great success for the EDB with many companies such as GE, GM, Rockwell, Sunstrand, Beecham, Philips, and Sony investing in Singapore. The influx of companies was attributed jointly to the good promotional work of the EDB and the readiness at that time of many companies to seek out low-cost manufacturing operations "offshore." By late 1970 industrialization had taken off with 352 Singapore Pioneer certificates issued that year. Two hundred thousand people were employed in manufacturing, and per capita GDP had gone up to $5,107, compared to $2,780 in 1966.

Unemployment had dropped from 14% to 4% in spite of the completion of the British withdrawal from their naval bases. In fact, the specter of labor shortages and the prospect of having to import labor began to appear. I. F. Tang decided in 1972 to return to the private sector to pursue his own business interests and fulfill some residual obligations to the UN, and Chan Chin Bock was recalled from New York to become the EDB's third chairman.

Because of his background and his broad perspective from his UN work, I. F. Tang had brought to the EDB a genuine sense of professionalism in the areas of sales and project management. One of the critical elements that was noted by most executives that dealt with Singapore was how well prepared and knowledgeable the EDB officers were about their industry in general and the company they were dealing with in particular. As one executive put it, "It was frightening that they seemed to know more about my company than I did." This commitment to being fully informed and prepared clearly came out of Tang's teaching and coaching.

Not only did the young senior officers learn by observing him in action on projects, but he provided an important model of leadership that was to become one of the hallmarks of the EDB culture—how to preserve a tight hierarchy, yet be able to communicate fully and openly across all levels of that hierarchy. Tang clearly was able to be autocratic when that was necessary, but, even more important, he was able to get close to all of his people no matter what their level, and he was perceived as always listening to them. This attentiveness to what senior officers had to say gave them a tremendous sense of empowerment that is highly visible in the organization today.

Chan Chin Bock (1972–1975)

A brilliant marketer, teacher, and coach. (a former subordinate)

Total dedication to work—the ultimate organization man. (a former subordinate)

When Chan Chin Bock was made chairman, he was pulled back from his New York job as head of international operations, but he continued to run the international division from Singapore.[2] During his tenure as chairman he had the opportunity to implement a number of strategic initiatives that were to a large extent his own creations, as will be seen. Primarily he was to (1) expand and consolidate the international operation; (2) build up Singapore's skilled labor pool through the creation of innovative joint training centers; and (3) continue to bring in key MNCs to further the growth of the manufacturing sector. Whereas Hon Sui Sen was viewed primarily as a strategist and maker of broad policy, Chan saw himself and I. F. Tang as "project oriented" and "deal makers." This self-view is consistent with how former subordinates characterize him: "a superb salesman, someone from whom one could learn a lot by just watching and listening to how he handles potential investors."

Background

Chan Chin Bock's career started as a schoolteacher in an American Methodist Mission school in Singapore. As a sideline he began to write some of the editorial commentary for the *Straits Times,* though he did not have a byline there. He also developed a column with a byline that focused on new cars from various companies, and that brought him to the attention of the Ford Motor Company, which had a plant in Singapore. The plant union was led by a communist who took the workers out for a very serious 110-day strike in 1961–62. Because Ford's image was badly hurt by this strike, the company felt that it had to reestablish its credibility with the public. They noticed Chan because of his column on cars and because of his editorial writing skills and hired him in 1962 "to rehabilitate the public image of the company after the long strike." So when the EDB later recruited him in 1964, he was working in the Ford public affairs department.

Chan was not sure at the time that he really wanted to be the one to project the EDB's image and that the EDB job would be to his liking, so he took a three-year leave of absence from Ford instead of going totally with the EDB. If he found that he didn't like working for the civil service, or if in some other way the job turned out to be a mismatch, he had a guarantee that he could go back to Ford.

At this time Singapore was still one state among many in the Malaysian Federation, and most of the decisions were being made in Kuala Lumpur. But in the middle of Chan's three-year contract, Singapore left the Malaysian Federation and found that it had to go international and "do it on its own." As Chan saw the challenge and potential in the new Singapore, he decided to change his three-year contract and accepted a permanent appointment with the EDB. In 1966 Chan was made head of international operations and was asked to move to New York to work with J. P. Bourdrez, who had been suggested by Winsemius as a mentor, "to learn what was really involved in marketing a country."

In 1972 Chan became chairman and was pulled back to Singapore as a result of I. F. Tang's decision to leave. He and Tang had been working as a team all these years and they recognized that there was a wave of U.S. and European companies that were ready to invest in a place like Singapore because those companies needed help in fighting off the Japanese challenge and to maintain their cost competitiveness.

When I asked Chan why he decided to make the career move of joining the EDB permanently, he said, "The work couldn't stop." He felt a tremendous sense of challenge, he could begin to see that Singapore could survive on its own, and he could also see that he was one of the very few people in the organization who had the relevant experience to make it all happen. He had already been quite successful in promoting the early investments so, as he put it, he wanted to maintain the momentum and that required total commitment to his job.

Management Style

Chan is described as sharp and perceptive, someone who led by example, a workaholic, and one of the most dedicated people to an organization that subordinates had ever encountered. He was also perceived to be extremely skilled in his manner of presentation, perhaps because of his background as a teacher and his experience in public relations. Ng Pock Too, who had worked for him in several capacities, said:

His mind was forever on the job, day and night, and he would always weave work into conversation and discussion. He would explain points and persuade very patiently. He was like a missile when he latched on to a topic in that his focus would go very, very deep and he would leave no stone unturned and he would never stop until a project was locked up, tenaciously answering all the questions that might be asked.

  For example, the EDB had decided that one of the ideal companies to go after would be General Electric. GE had a lawyer by the name of Larry Ebb who was extremely good at asking questions and would just continue to ask questions forever. So GE spent all of three years checking Singapore out and Chan just patiently hung in there and encouraged his staff to hang in there. (1993 interview)

  Chan himself noted that he spent many a day in the GE headquarters offices building the relationship, though the projects eventually would come from all the different divisions scattered around the country. When GE finally did make the decision to go to Singapore, "they came in not with one project but with seven projects, which proved incontrovertibly that the ability to stay with the project and with individuals, answer all the questions, build strong relationships and patiently negotiate really pays off."

  Chan was personally dedicated to the EDB and Singapore, and he expected the same commitment from others. Ng recalls that if Chan had any instructions or ideas or needed any information, he would telephone from New York at whatever time the idea or question occurred to him, which often was in the middle of the night in Singapore. Ng would say, "Look, do you know what time it is? Couldn't you call in the morning?" and Chan would reply, "No, I want to discuss this with you right now." Chan often wanted to brief Ng on whatever had transpired, which forced Ng to get up and write elaborate notes in the middle of the night because if he just listened on the phone and then went back to sleep, he would often forget what he had been told. During those days family life and personal life were left behind. They were all "married to the EDB."

"Judgment Calls"

The early decisions to pursue particular companies like Hewlett-Packard and Texas Instruments were made primarily by Chan and Tang, and were viewed at the time as real "judgment calls" in that no one really knew whether the long-range strategy of pursuing companies that would ultimately add value to Singapore would pay off. They would often have to convince Goh that even though Singapore's resources and land were limited, they should allow a company like HP to become a small investor because, "If you bring in an important company with good managerial techniques and prestige, Singapore will learn a great deal even though the initial project might be very small." To find the right companies they had to stick their neck out, particularly since Goh always challenged them about being too generous with small investors.

Building Up Skilled Labor

One of Chan's major projects was to build up Singapore's skill base by creating viable apprenticeship and training programs both overseas and in Singapore. Companies were recruited in countries like Germany and Switzerland to accept small numbers of Singaporeans as apprentices, and larger programs were launched in Singapore with the creation of joint government training centers, in which a few companies were recruited to teach Singaporeans selected technical skills and thereby prepare them for the higher-tech industries that were to be attracted in the future. These centers were eventually established with the Rollei Company from Germany, Tata from India, and Philips from the Netherlands, and subsequently extended into training partnerships in country centers in Germany, France, and Japan. Each country partner was selected for its special areas of strength, that is, Germany for precision engineering training, France for electronics, and Japan for mechatronics.

Chan realized that Singapore needed to develop the skilled machinists that would eventually permit Singapore to obtain investments in computer disk drives, aircraft parts, electronic components, and a tool and die industry. The story of how he came to these insights, as Chan recalls it in 1994, is revealing.

While in New York, Chan became interested in the development of a costume jewelry industry in Singapore, so he frequently traveled to various parts of Rhode Island, where most of this industry is located. On one of the trips to Providence he met Henry Sharp, son of the founder of Brown and Sharp, the machine tool company in Providence. He got to know them very well and persuaded Sharp to visit Singapore "to look it over." As part of a family trip to the Far East that he had planned anyway, Sharp agreed to the visit. The EDB planned special events for Sharp's family and even recruited some younger people from Singapore to talk with the Sharp's teenage daughter.

Sometime later Sharp wanted to reciprocate the favor, and so he invited Chan and his wife to his Rhode Island home for the weekend. Knowing how dedicated Chan was to his work, Sharp said he would "invite a few people over for dinner from the neighborhood" because they would be good contacts. As Chan put it: "Sharp said, 'I'll bring them in for dinner and you can work them over.'"

This group included the chairman of the board of Textron and several CEOs from various industries. During the dinner it was revealed in various conversations, particularly by Sharp, that Americans were less and less interested in the kinds of jobs that required long apprenticeships, that students were more interested in taking jobs that might pay less but would be immediately available without their having to undergo long periods of training. The implication was that the machine tool industry, which required the development of skilled machinists through long apprenticeships, would be forever trouble in the United States.

As it turned out, Brown and Sharp itself never invested in Singapore, but the conversation gave Chan the idea that, if this lack of interest in apprenticeships was a general American phenomenon, Singapore might step into the breach by developing a high level of machining and machine tool skills. This idea took hold and led to the further realization that the training would have to be provided by investors who had those skills and were willing to develop joint industry-government training programs. Singapore would provide training facilities and financial support if the company would provide instructors and provide the basic training as well as apprenticeship opportunities for Singaporeans.

Willingness to provide training then became one of the important criteria for seeking out companies like Rollei. Even though the Singaporean subsidiary eventually failed because of Japanese competition in the camera field, it was viewed retrospectively as a valuable venture because of the skills that were passed on during the time that Rollei was active. Through ventures like these, Singapore was able to build up its precision engineering skills plus electronics (what the Japanese called mechatronics), which became ultimately one of Singapore's great comparative advantages. Chan speculated that the whole disk-drive industry, which became very mature in Singapore, would not have happened if they had not built up their precision engineering skills.

To carry out the manpower training strategies and shape the program, Chan deployed Lee Yock Suan, one of the EDB's and Singapore's best brains, and at that time the EDB's first director of manpower development. Lee subsequently left the EDB to go into politics and became the minister for education.

During Chan's tenure as chairman, the manpower development program was strengthened and the international division enlarged with the opening of offices in London, Stockholm, Frankfurt, Zurich, Chicago, and Tokyo. Chan and Tang both realized that in the early 1970s a great many companies under threat from Japanese competition were seeking low-labor-cost manufacturing sites, which led to the successful promotion of companies like HP, National Semiconductor, TI, Air Reduction, and GE. The strategy to upgrade Singaporean labor was launched with an overseas apprenticeship program and a number of joint training ventures with MNCs, thereby laying the foundation for a new set of high-tech, capital-intensive industries to come into Singapore.

With the oil crisis of the mid-1970s Singapore, like many other countries, found itself floundering and in need of a more fundamental reassessment. The EDB was seen at this time to need more of a strategist than a deal maker, so they brought in Ngiam Tong Dow as chairman in 1975. Chan returned to New York to refocus international operations, and P. Y. Hwang, who had been Chan's managing director, was sent to London to convince the European companies that they would soon be facing the need to find lower-cost manufacturing sites also.

Analytical Comment

Chan's story highlights several important themes in the evolving EDB culture. First, each of the first three chairmen set the example of thinking things through very carefully and created mechanisms to ensure thorough preparation. The commitment to write things down and the process whereby proposals for action had to go through the chain of command forced clear thinking and provided feedback opportunities at any point in the chain. Tang's dictum that one must be totally prepared for any question a potential investor might have about Singapore highlighted the importance of doing one's homework before leaping into action.

Chan characterizes himself as the first one to bring in "professional management from a local perspective" in that he was coming in from the outside with no ties to government and no particular external industrial expertise, but with a good sense of what Singapore was all about. From Chan the EDB learned how important it was to build relationships and patiently cultivate them, even if they did not pay off immediately, or ever. In those relationships EDB officers learned a great deal even if the targeted investor decided not to pursue a venture in Singapore, and implicit in those relationships was the notion of "partnering" with their potential and actual investors to pursue future projects that might not be visible to anyone yet. The concept of investors as partners was to become an important theme.

Both Chan and Tang viewed themselves not a strategists but as deal makers, yet in the kind of criteria they used to target companies as investors to be wooed, they furthered several critical strategic priorities, especially the thrust to go for capital-intensive high-skill industries that would, in the end, educate Singapore's population. As Chan points out in his own "retrospective": "I believe that the most significant achievement of the EDB is our role in establishing the skills infrastructure. We started preparing for a 1992 industry in 1972" (Chan Chin Bock, 1992).[3]

In implementing this strategy, Chan provided a good example of how to stay open and take a broad view of the environment and its potentialities. For example, as the EDB worked with various countries such as France, Germany, and Japan on the possibilities for joint training ventures, they first observed what those countries were particularly good at, and then promoted at government level the development of the joint training programs, with training curricula provided by country experts. Once the companies had been selected, the EDB worked very hard to solve any problems that those companies might have in investing in Singapore. This combination of strategy and detailed implementation is striking and leads one again to the concept of "strategic pragmatism."

In a sense, the first three chairmen represented additive components of the culture. Each chairman continued the core elements learned from the previous one, but added some new dimensions as well. And, though most of the comments about the chairmen emphasized their sales, marketing, and administrative skills, it was actually their ability to combine those skills with entrepreneurial instincts and skills that led ultimately to successful partnerships with companies.

6

Building and Consolidating: Ngiam Tong Dow and P. Y. Hwang

The period 1975 to 1985 started with a world recession triggered by the oil crisis of the early 1970s and ended with another world recession. In the interim, the EDB restructured itself and moved forward on its internationalization, manpower development, and local industry development initiatives. The EDB had two chairmen during this period, both of whom had grown up within the EDB and had performed a variety of other jobs before returning as chairmen.

Ngiam Tong Dow (1975–1981)

> The years spent in EDB (1961 to 1963) (1964 to 1965) and as Chairman (1975 to 1981) were for me some of the most rewarding years in my public service career. In EDB work, there was always an exciting sense of tangible accomplishment, of doing something worthwhile for family and country, over the long haul and for the long term. (Ngiam Tong Dow, 1992)[1]

Ngiam Tong Dow was brought in as chairman in 1975.[2] Chan Chin Bock was needed in New York to intensify work on investment promotion while the EDB took stock of itself under someone who was more of an administrator and strategist. The EDB was now about fifteen years old and was clearly succeeding in its industrialization program. Each annual report emphasized the continued growth and reaffirmed the basic strategy of obtaining foreign investment while at the same time encouraging local industry. A clear bias toward the large multinationals had, however, been established, which meant that Singapore's economic fortunes would be tied more closely to global economic forces as these played themselves out through the MNCs.

In terms of the structure of the EDB itself, what is noticeable is the growth of an experienced cadre of leaders. Ngiam, for example, had spent four years learning the ropes in the EDB before going to the finance ministry, where he became permanent secretary, before being reassigned to the EDB, but this time as chairman. His alternate chairman operating out of New York was Chan Chin Bock (the previous chairman), his deputy chairman was I. F. Tang (who had rejoined the EDB on a part-time basis), and his executive deputy chairman operating out of London was P. Y. Hwang, who had been with the EDB since 1964. All four were members of the Board, where they were joined by S. Dhanabalan, a former EDB chief of projects, and four outside members.

The EDB itself was reorganized and streamlined to permit fuller support of the international investment program. The new divisions were Investment Services, Projects, Manpower, Administration, and International Operations. Shirley Chen, who later played a major role in the development of this culture study, came on board during this time as secretary and legal officer.

Background

Ngiam was an economist by training, having received his education in Singapore and at the University of Malaya. He joined the EDB in 1961 and was therefore one of the original officers involved in getting the investment promotion program off the ground. He left for a year in 1963 to go to Harvard University's Kennedy School of Government and rejoined the EDB in 1964. He became the permanent secretary of the ministry of trade and industry and held this job at the time he was appointed chairman of the EDB concurrent with his appointment as permanent secretary. Today he is permanent secretary in the prime minister's office, permanent secretary in the ministry of finance, and the chairman of the Development Bank of Singapore and a director of Singapore Airlines Ltd.

Management Style

Ngiam was described by Ng Pock Too, a former subordinate, as follows: "He was more of an administrator and bureaucrat, a strong organization man, much less accessible to the people, a solid thinker with a good strategic mind, who was also a salesman but worked much more on facts and statistics and solid arguments" (1993 interview).

Ngiam was perceived to be "very authoritative." He ran an extremely tight ship and was viewed as the kind of person who clears his desk every day. One day when a subordinate wondered aloud where all the work was, Ngiam said, "I don't work; I make decisions; I make others work; I'm responsible." On another occasion when a phone call came in, the subordinate heard Ngiam say, "Yes, yes, that's right," and then he hung up the phone. A little while later another phone call came in from overseas from one of the field officers who was complaining about a negative decision that had been made and was now trying to get it reversed. Apparently as Ngiam was listening, the field officer was making his case because at a certain point Ngiam said, "Yes, I know what the decision was, I backed the decision." After a few more minutes Ngiam said decisively, "Put down the phone; you've heard the decision; you're costing the government money, end of discussion."

The sense of his own strength can be illustrated by an incident when Ngiam chuckled over how negotiations with the Japanese were conducted. The Japanese, because of their consensus system, would always bring a whole team of negotiators to the table, sometimes ten or fifteen people. Ngiam would arrive by himself, which always surprised the Japanese and made them think that he was not very strong or serious. Yet he clearly was not put off by their numbers or unanimity and could hold his own in negotiations.

Because Ngiam had been in a high senior government position as the permanent secretary of the ministry of trade and industry and had an excellent track record, when he came back to the EDB he provided a whole new set of connections to various government departments and thus reinforced the tradition of the EDB as the one-stop agency that could solve all of its investors' problems. He believed strongly in this principle and used his connections as much as possible.

Ngiam developed his people and backed them when necessary. For example, on the recommendation of Chan Chin Bock, Ngiam sent Ng Pock Too to the Harvard Business School's Program for Management Development, which according to Ng was "a profound experience which taught him to think strategically." Another alumnus related that Ngiam had asked him to set up a local industries section and to prepare a board paper to create a light industries department. This project challenged some of the work of the Development Bank and caused a lot of opposition there, but Ngiam defended the proposal vigorously and pushed it through.

The Petrochemical Complex

One of Ngiam's special interests was the evolution of a petrochemical complex in Singapore. Several studies had been done showing that, with the availability of naphtha as a feedstock from the refineries, a variety of petrochemicals and plastics could be made in Singapore. In the early 1970s Sumitomo expressed an interest in establishing a joint venture on such projects, but the proposal created a good deal of controversy because of the softness of the market and the high initial capital investment that would be needed. Hon Sui Sen, who was then finance minister, decided to back it. The project was initiated in 1972 but the complex was not really finished until 1982, illustrating the single-minded, go-get-it mentality, patience, and total commitment of the EDB.

The Singapore Air Show

Ngiam introduced strategic planning workshops in the EDB, and the output of one of the conversations in the first of these workshops was the idea of having a Singapore air show. If Paris could have an air show, why couldn't Singapore? Such a show would bring many CEOs to Singapore and would help build the aerospace business, which had been moving very slowly. Ng Pock Too was working on the concept and met an executive from the *Financial Times* who was willing to put up money to sponsor a conference of aerospace executives, so the first hurdle of how to finance it was overcome. The head of the civil aviation department, however, firmly rejected the idea because of his concern about the use of the airspace, the tight quarters, and the danger of an accident. No amount of arguing could convince him. Ng tells what happened next:

I kept thinking about it and one day ran into Philip Yeo, who was then in the ministry of defense. Yeo said that I was looking "down" and asked me what was the matter, so I told him I had this great idea for an air show but couldn't get it off the ground because there was no airport runway that they could use. Philip Yeo listened and a month or two later called me up and said that he had an idea—they were about to move the Singapore Air Force from one airport to another and there was an old terminal that was in perfectly good shape and a set of runways that would be available for two weeks during the moves. If I wanted it I could have that two-week block for the show. So I got back to the *Financial Times* people and they put the whole package together and we had a very successful air show in 1981, which has since become a regular event.

What impressed me was the willingness of Philip Yeo to take the risk to provide the space and the facilities, because if there had been any accident or anything had gone wrong it would have definitely been the end of Philip Yeo's career. (1993 interview)

In a subsequent interview Philip Yeo pointed out that to avoid accidents they had asked the pilots to fly over water, but this led in turn to complaints from the pilots because of the difficulty of defining the horizon. To solve that problem and enhance pilot safety, they decided to strategically place a large number of boats around the area and in so doing define the horizon accurately.

This willingness to take major risks is characteristic of the leaders of the EDB and is reminiscent of the story about Hon's willingness to expend much of the EDB's budget on building the infrastructure of the Jurong Industrial Park long before they had any clients to occupy it or pay for it. As Ng put it: "Whoever leads the EDB must be an entrepreneur, must have a strategic mind, must have guts, must be a strong tough person and must be a risk taker" (1994 interview).

Building Up the Technical Curriculum

As Singapore moved toward more high-tech, knowledge-based industries, it became evident that there would be a shortage not only of skilled technicians but also of graduate engineers at all levels. One of Ngiam's projects became the upgrading and expansion of Singapore's technical education, which led to the creation of the Nanyang Technological University and the expansion of the polytechnics. Ngiam noted that he ran into officials with very traditional attitudes in the ministry of education, who felt that if the applicant pool increased they simply should raise the standard so that they would get ever higher quality and better engineers. Thus another of Ngiam's accomplishments was to gradually influence the education establishment to enlarge their enrollment pool at the university level while maintaining their standards and, at the same time, create a number of alternate programs for getting more engineers.

Analytical Comment

What is most striking in talking to Ngiam Tong Dow and in analyzing what his colleagues and subordinates say about him is how different his managerial style is and yet how similar his strategic vision is to that of EDB's other chairmen. He clearly was perceived to be more autocratic and decisive, yet he gained the allegiance of his subordinates because of the clarity of his vision, his ability to communicate, and his support of their projects. Part of that communication skill lies in creating concise but powerful images. For example, in commenting in 1994 on how the role of the EDB was changing, he noted: "The task of the EDB is like climbing a mountain; the higher you get, the harder it gets" (1994 interview).

In commenting on the need for Singaporean business to become more bold in venturing overseas he stated: "Our companies should go overseas, but the *directing mind* should always remain in Singapore. One should create the conditions to keep the *directing mind* here by having law and order, creating a good education system for children, having more lively minds around, and reducing regulations on business as much as possible. . . . Our local businessmen expect too much of a tax break which is a legacy of the paternalism we have had. . . . We have to be in every industrial pyramid and in every growth triangle; wherever we can play a useful role, we should be there."

And in referring to what it takes to be successful as an EDB officer, he said: "They must have *animal energy,* be real activists. And the chairman of the EDB should be the *directing mind* for economic development."

Ngiam felt that other departments in Singapore's government were becoming too strong, and he wished that the EDB could again be as strong as it was when Lee Kuan Yew, Goh Keng Swee, and Hon Sui Sen comprised the basic team. As an example, he cited how difficult it was to get the petrochemical complex approved over the demands of a consultant hired by the environmental ministry. Not only did the consultant insist on having both a very high chimney and under-ground pollution control (which Ngiam and Sumitomo thought excessive), but he required detailed information about so many of the chemical processes that Sumitomo felt this was tantamount to industrial espionage. In the end, Simitomo and the EDB had to accede to the environmental ministry's requirements on pollution, but they drew a clear line against sharing information on the chemical processes themselves.

Viewing himself as a prime example, Ngiam noted that the EDB was in effect Singapore's first business school, given that many of the most senior executives in Singapore today, especially in the banks, are ex-EDB officers. He reinforced strongly the self-image of the EDB as a basic training ground for future leaders both in government and in business.

In summary, Ngiam Tong Dow highlights the degree to which the EDB had to shift course in response to global economic forces, yet its spirit and culture seemed to remain intact, and its ability to continue to attract the big investments remained as strong as ever. Ngiam had continued to hold the job of permanent secretary during his EDB years and, because of his various other commitments, asked to be relieved as chairman in 1982.

P. Y. Hwang (1982–1985)

When I first returned from Europe in 1982, Singapore was riding high. Business was booming. The challenge was how we could keep up the growth rate. EDB joined in the intensive national programme to upgrade Singapore's efficiency. The transition for EDB was to prepare ourselves to sell on quality, not only on price or quantity. It is something like selling Rolls Royces. You don't have to sell very many, unlike popular models. But it is not always easy to persuade people that quality is good value for money, and you have to seek out the right customers." (P. Y. Hwang, 1992)[3]

We have to have humility about how to do things and we have to learn from others. We have a very small island mentality and can only survive if we are a little Holland, Belgium, Sweden, or Denmark, or a significant part of a larger whole like Switzerland or Austria. We cannot afford xenophobia and we are very multiracial. We notice what problems others are facing, we seek examples of who is fixing these kinds of problems, and we apply the solutions to our own area. (P. Y. Hwang, 1994 interview)

Background

P. Y. Hwang was one of many Singaporeans who was educated overseas.[4] He describes himself as a "medical school dropout at the U.
of London" who went on to graduate with a degree in biology from
Cambridge University, where he knew Joe Pillay in the 1950s and
was something of a student activist. Goh Keng Swee at that time was
still working on his doctorate in London. After graduation, Hwang
went to work for a Singaporean company selling chemicals. He met
Pillay again and was introduced to I. F. Tang at a lunch in 1964 and
was promptly hired into the EDB. Because his English was good, his
first job was to digest a mass of "stuff" that no one had been able to
do anything with, and use it to write the overdue 1964 Annual
Report for Parliament. He interviewed everyone he could to find out
what they were doing and, in that process, not only obtained good
material for his report but learned what the EDB was all about. His
next and primary job was to set up the Technical Services Division
to help in EDB's investment efforts; so he set up a library to provide
such services and later started up the design center to develop Singapore's skills in product design.

In 1965 Hwang wanted more variety, so he left for awhile to build
a factory for his friend whose chemicals he had been selling. The
factory was to make plastic moldings, and he found himself on the
other side asking the EDB for a loan. After Singapore left the Malaysian Federation, the EDB in 1966 asked Hwang to come back. The
EDB had realized that it had to go international to attract companies,
so P. Y. Hwang and Chan Chin Bock were asked to set up the international wing—with Chan stationed in New York, and Hwang in
London. Previously, they had used only local businessmen as "hon-
orary reps" in various countries, but these people did not go out and
promote aggressively enough.

In 1969 Hwang was promoted to deputy managing director and in
1975 he was moved again to London so he could travel around
Europe to try to convince companies that what had happened to U.S.
industry by way of encountering stiff competition on manufacturing
costs, thus forcing companies to seek lower-cost labor offshore,
would happen to them as well, so they should come to invest in
Singapore. In 1978 he was asked to be Singapore's ambassador to the
European Community, based in Brussels. By observing how Holland,

Sweden, and Switzerland were managing their economic growth, he noted that they all had gravitated toward English as the dominant language, had excellent infrastructures, and had gone for higher value-added businesses. He also noticed how Brussels was developing the concept of becoming a center for regional headquarters organizations and started to sell this idea for Singapore.

In late 1985, from his position as chairman of the EDB, Hwang went to Temasek Holdings, one of Singapore's investment arms, as its deputy chairman. Among his other involvements he is also chairman of Intraco Limited and a director of five other Singaporean companies.

Management Style

P. Y. Hwang was described as having yet another managerial style from the other chairmen, a style best characterized as "the international civil servant." His approach to problems was often more intellectual, analytical, and evaluative, which resulted in less hands-on management, less risk taking, and more detachment from his subordinates. Whereas some of the other chairmen were described as being closer to their people, "one of the boys," Hwang was seen as more scholarly and "so well informed about everything" that there might not be much to talk about with his people on an informal level. He was highly respected, however, and very effective as a chairman because he was skilled across the board. It was noted that his breadth of knowledge and cosmopolitanism led to his being selected ambassador to the European Economic Community prior to his EDB chairmanship. Although he often had to perform in a selling/marketing role, it was not as natural to him. In his analytical/evaluative role, however, he showed his strengths. This was reflected in his eventual appointment to Temasek Holdings where investment opportunities have to be carefully analyzed and evaluated.

Maturing and Redirection

Many of EDB's earlier strategic thrusts reached their maturity under Hwang. For example, during his tenure the Brown-Boveri Government Training Center was founded and eventually evolved into the Precision Engineering Institute in 1988. The German-Singapore

Institute was launched to offer courses in advanced manufacturing and automation technology. The Japan-Singapore Institute for Software Technology was founded and the French-Singapore Institute was launched to train technical professionals in electrotechnical engineering disciplines. Four years after its conception, the Science Park was opened to stimulate R & D activities; and through the Robot Leasing Scheme, low-cost financing and technical consulting were offered to companies to encourage them to automate.

When Hwang came in as chairman in 1982, however, the transition to high tech had already reached its peak. The 1980s oil crisis and global recession had a negative impact on Singapore and forced a major reexamination of its economic strategy. The EDB had to broaden its mission to stimulate the service sector, to develop a higher profile, and to help local industry more. Teamwork among the various government agencies was also beginning to break down, leading to a sense that the EDB had to be revitalized. All of these circumstances led to Philip Yeo's appointment as chairman in 1986.

Analytic Summary

By 1985 the EDB had had twenty-five years of success and growth. There had been some mistakes, some bad investments, and some false starts; but overall the picture was very positive. Most striking is that during this period Singapore had faced several economic crises that had to be overcome—the separation from the Malaysian Federation, the confrontation with Indonesia, the withdrawal of the British naval bases that had contributed 20 percent to Singapore's economy, the 1970s global oil crisis, the growing competition from other developing countries, and the 1980s oil crisis and world recession. Listening to the various chairmen reminisce about these times, several themes come through that clearly have become cultural bedrock:

- Dedication to Singapore and its growth
- Optimism and self-confidence
- Commitment to learning, adapting, innovating
- Strategic pragmatism—a commitment to partnering
- A marketing and sales philosophy built on technical competence

• A global outlook based on a sense of vulnerability as a small city-state

The five chairmen differed a good deal in terms of their management styles and their strategic priorities. These differences created some of the paradoxes and anomalies of how the EDB operates. For example, the organization learned that it could function under an extremely autocratic or a very delegating kind of leadership, or under a strategist or a project-oriented deal maker. It could also be a government agency, yet make investments and operate with a market philosophy. Many of the management systems acquired early in the EDB's history offered sound ways to run the organization; so they evolved but did not change fundamentally. For example, the system of writing everything down, which had been acquired from the British civil service, continues to be a mainstay of today's management, yet it has evolved to adapt to today's realities. In the next chapter we will examine how Philip Yeo's leadership both enhanced and further evolved the EDB culture under his mandate of "revitalization."

Redefinition and Renewal: The EDB under Philip Yeo

The Next Lap in economic development, which has already begun, will test EDB's mettle even more. Because economic development is dynamic, we have to continually maintain and improve Singapore's competitive advantage. To achieve this objective, we must endeavor to encourage and promote high value-added international and local manufacturing and services investments whilst encouraging and supporting our local companies to go international. . . . My task now is to maintain the cutting edge of the organization to meet its external challenges whilst internally making EDB a great place to work. I recognize that our achievements will be highest when an officer says, "We respect the people we work for, are proud of what we do and enjoy the people we work with" (Philip Yeo, 1992).[1]

I don't believe in charters, hierarchies, or layers of seniority. I believe the best and brightest can do the job. So my fundamental concern is how to create enough young talent, and I spend most of my time looking for good people (Philip Yeo, 1994).[2]

Philip Yeo, the current chairman of the EDB, has clearly had a major impact on the organization and is playing a key role in Singapore's continuing economic development.[3] He presides over the EDB at a particularly complex period in Singapore's economic history. This chapter will therefore provide somewhat greater detail about his vision and style. When he was first appointed in 1986, he personally provided the force for reexamination and revitalization because he was a very energetic, quick-thinking, quick-acting, and hands-on kind of leader. He also brought into the organization some "new blood" at the highest level in appointing as the managing director, Tan Chin Nam, then chairman of the National Computer Board, a position he maintained until August 1994, along with his EDB responsibilities.

According to most EDB informants, Tan provided not only new marketing and strategic tools, but also the administrative skills to launch the EDB into a whole new series of programs and activities. Yeo and Tan had worked together in the ministry of defense and the National Computer Board and were obviously an effective team with very different but complementary managerial styles. Their entrepreneurial styles had been tested in that they had been instrumental in the rapid introduction of information technology into Singapore's government and had created the vision of Singapore as "the intelligent island" with a plan to fully connect all of its sectors by the year 2000.

Background

Philip Yeo was born in Singapore in 1946 and received his primary and secondary education in local schools but then he, like so many others, took advantage of the scholarship programs available to go overseas. He received an applied science degree in industrial engineering from the University of Toronto in 1970, a master's degree in systems engineering from the National University of Singapore in 1974, and a master's in business administration from the Harvard University Business School in 1976, under the auspices of a Fulbright scholarship.

He joined the civil service in 1970 and became permanent secretary (defense) for logistics, research, and technology in 1979. He then became the first chairman of the newly formed National Computer Board in 1981, joined the EDB as a board member in 1982, and became its chairman in 1986. As Philip Yeo himself put it: "I was conscripted to engineer a kind of a turnaround of the EDB because, in order to bring Singapore out of its recession, the EDB really had to shift its emphasis from just promoting investments in manufacturing companies (which continued) to promoting *services,* particularly those related to manufacturing, and to develop a program to stimulate and *help local enterprises*" (1993 interview, my emphasis).

In the history of the EDB, their strategic pragmatism had always led to innovations of all sorts as problem areas were identified, but the economic changes in the 1980s created an entirely new set of challenges. The recession not only forced a reexamination of Singapore's overall economic policies, but it provided the necessity and the opportunity for the EDB itself to take a major growth step in terms of its basic assumptions and strategic priorities. It was one of those transition times that organizations experience where change is not incremental but discontinuous.

For the first time in its history, according to many interviewees, the EDB was perceived in the mid-1980s to be "complacent and bureaucratic" and even, according to some, to have acquired some "dead wood" that Philip Yeo "had to clear out." What was perceived as dead wood by the younger EDB'ers was of course perceived by those with a longer perspective as a group of people who were competent, but whose style and areas of expertise were more adapted to the "hosting role" of the EDB. As a new entrepreneurial thrust was needed, some of these people had to be moved to other career roles where their skills were more congruent with the jobs to be done.

The EDB's strong technical emphasis was also perceived to be in need of enhancement by bringing in more marketing, finance, and strategy as a regular part of its thinking. Although the EDB had always been international in its outlook, the evolution of MNCs into global organizations now provided the opportunity, indeed necessity, for the EDB to work with these companies on a truly global basis and develop brand new concepts of what "partnership" with a company really could mean. The EDB as "business architect" was evolved in this context. "To carry out this mission in the global environment of intense competition, the EDB needs to be a 'business architect' in helping our corporate clients, multinational corporations and local companies configure their global business from a Singapore home base or OHQ (operational headquarters)" (Philip Yeo, 1991).[4]

Management Style

Philip Yeo is undoubtedly one of the fastest thinking and fastest moving managers I have ever met. His style is therefore not easy to characterize. In his person he represents many of the paradoxes that one experiences in Singapore as a whole. Much of his philosophy and style comes through in his own words.

I'm a man of few words; I give a few instructions and then I expect you to take care of the rest. If I have to go into detail on how to do something, I might as well do it myself. (a subordinate quoting Philip Yeo's answer when asked for some guidance on a task, 1993 interview)

I must move fast . . . it's the rules of the game. When a thing is new, move like crazy—expand fast. It's the two-year magic. That's why I did ten projects [the computerization of the first ten ministries] all at one go. (Philip Yeo, 1991)[5]

The fundamental difference between an engineer and someone attracted to the arts is an interest in how a thing works. As a kid I liked to take things apart—though putting it back together again was another matter. Curiosity plays a part—and looking for tangible results. But I would not consider myself an arts person. I may enjoy music. I may listen but there is nothing productive in it—I hope you understand; I'd rather sit down and crack a problem. (Philip Yeo, 1994)[6]

Philip Yeo was the most open and articulate of the chairmen I interviewed when discussing his own management style. Although he described himself to his subordinate as a man of few words when giving instructions, he is in reality highly verbal when expounding on his philosophy and goals, and very persuasive when articulating his vision for Singapore and the EDB.

As he related it, his first activity after taking over the EDB was to assess the people it had on board. He discovered two problems. First, a lot of people had simply accumulated length-of-service raises without really changing or enlarging their job; so there were some older, more senior officers who were not really doing anything very innovative or broad. Most informants noted that these people were dealt with by giving them essentially three-months notice and help in finding better jobs in other companies or departments. Everyone emphasized that the policy of "taking care of people" was strongly sustained. Although people had to be moved out of the EDB in the process of "right sizing," they were "not just thrown out onto the street, but relocated in other jobs."

Second, Yeo had also noticed that the EDB had many good people but the organization was very compartmentalized, a phenomenon he attributed not to the people but to the natural aging process of an organization. Evidently over the years, the pattern of free flow of information throughout the organization had eroded somewhat and functional groups had arisen that did not fully share relevant information.

To reduce this compartmentalization and to get access to all of the EDB's activities, Yeo created what he called the "float system." This involved making "float files" that consisted of all the written reports on each project, scanning those files, identifying important issues in the various projects they referred to, and writing comments or questions directly on the files. The reports and the comments were then transmitted to all of the people who might have any relationship to that project, so that they would all be made aware of everything about it, including all of Yeo's comments. He said he had learned this system in the National Computer Board where it was his way of keeping himself informed and making sure that everyone else was informed.[7]

Those float files were supplemented with other processes that enhanced frequent communication. For example, Yeo had overseas officers return to the home office once every year instead of once every three years. He visited every office at least once a year himself, during which time he asked questions and made himself available to the office in relation to the various promotional activities of that office. Many companies expected such visits from the chairman and expected to be briefed about Singapore and the Southeast Asian situation as part of their partnership with Singapore. Others wanted reassurance that the commitments and promises made by the EDB were agreed to by its senior management.

To highlight his emphasis on quick and open communications, Philip Yeo also said that he expects each international office to have a mobile phone so that when he is traveling he could always be reached, even if he "might be between appointments someplace." In other words, he wants to inform and be informed as soon as anything relevant happens—a view strikingly comparable to what Chan Chin Bock had put forward as his reason for calling from New York to Singapore at any hour of the day or night. As Yeo put it:

> *If you are in the business of competing for investments, if you know things sooner than your competitor, you are going to be more successful.* For example if other countries are also competing for a particular company to come there, it is absolutely crucial to be informed of every event pertaining to that, so that one can react to it and make things happen while the others are sitting and waiting.
>
> *If you have no natural resources except your people and your skill, you have to compete in those terms.* Even though Singapore has no oil resources of its own, we are able to attract companies in the chemical and oil-related processes by virtue of being able to offer better services to those kinds of companies. (1993 interview, my emphasis)

A further point about creating a total open communication system is Philip Yeo's willingness to pay for it by authorizing travel and anything else that it takes to make the system work. In that regard, he talked at length about the *daily report system,* which is electronic and provides every overseas officer or every project officer the opportunity to submit a daily report listing which companies have been visited, what activities have been carried out, what the prospects are for a deal with those companies, and any other pertinent information. This system is still in the process of evolution and is not yet fully utilized, but the intention is to collect and channel information electronically and automatically so that it becomes available wherever needed.

In the meantime, every officer continues to use the computerized *weekly reporting system* that had been instituted earlier. These reports are required and are assessed not only by the immediate supervisor, but are circulated throughout the office and reviewed once a week at the "operations committee" meeting chaired by Tan Chin Nam. At this meeting each department reviews its major prospects, and information is provided to everyone on all of the activities.

As has previously been pointed out, the written reports also provide a system for supervising and appraising. Several people referred to Yeo as a "very operational, hands-on kind of manager," which is reflected in his saying with great pride that he not only scans all the float files and makes corrections or redirects about 10 percent of each file based on his intimate knowledge of industries, but he also reads all the daily reports and evaluates the information, writes questions on them, and ultimately makes judgments about the quality of the various officers based on the reading of those reports.

This kind of a system of course depends very much on people telling the truth. Yeo felt that there were so many cross-checks on what the various senior officers were reporting that there was strong pressure for people to be extremely honest and truthful. Some of this cross-checking occurs through the personal network that Yeo has established with various executives in the companies, with whom he has often become personal friends. So if one of the officers writes a report on a given company, Yeo can often check it directly with executives from those companies.

Interestingly enough, even though there is this strong emphasis on information transmission and open communications, Yeo has pointed out that *building up a personal network and treating clients as friends and members of the family is much more important to business success than having accurate analyses about those companies or giving them good written analyses of Singapore.* He cited the example of a company that was dealing simultaneously with Singapore and another nearby country. The company was getting only formal information from the other country while the EDB had a lot of personal contacts in the company. Needless to say, the company chose Singapore. The assumption appears to be that no matter how essential and how accurate written information is, one also needs personal contacts and a relationship of trust before one can really get at the truth and make an accurate assessment.

New Blood

Philip Yeo's overall impression was that the EDB had good people but not enough of them because they had stopped recruiting some years before. The kinds of people that he now wanted, particularly for the expansion of the overseas operations, were what he labeled "scholars who were coming back from their education or subsequent work looking for new posts within Singapore." By scholars he meant people who had performed very well on the high-school-level exams and who had won government scholarships to continue their education overseas. When such people were recruited by the EDB, they were further assessed in terms of personal qualities. Philip Yeo said they needed: "People who were flexible, who had high levels of initiative, who displayed a lot of autonomy and ability to work on their own in the overseas environment, who had the persistence to chase projects because some of these projects took years to develop, who had traveled a lot and who generally displayed overall brightness irrespective of their particular area in which they had taken their majors" (1993 interview). There was still a bias toward technical people, largely because the scholarship program had that bias, but there was also the recognition that broader and more diverse kinds of education were increasingly relevant to the tasks the EDB had to perform.

To ensure that Singapore had the necessary people, the EDB launched the International Manpower Program, a major effort to identify and recruit Singaporeans and others currently overseas in schools or in jobs. As companies identified their future needs for technical and other kinds of talent in Singapore, the program would attempt to locate specific people and get commitments from them to work in those jobs as they became available. The EDB was thereby able to promise a company that if they located their R & D department in Singapore, there would be sufficient talent available to staff it.

Corporate Meetings and Shared Visions

Soon after taking over, Philip Yeo asked Tan Chin Nam to organize a major corporate planning exercise to help reposition the EDB's strategy and to encourage the development of a shared vision for the future. Such internal planning seminars had started under Ngiam Tong Dow's chairmanship, but Tan took the meetings to a different level of complexity and involved a much wider group. Both Tan and Yeo brought with them a much more contemporary and "professional" approach to strategy, communication, and marketing, and both intended to use knowledge that had been developed worldwide in these fields. For example, Tan Chin Nam had become familiar with the research on the factors leading a country to be competitive carried out by Michael Porter of the Harvard Business School, and he arranged for Porter to come to Singapore. Porter was to run a seminar and a planning exercise for Singapore in exchange for being given sufficient data to include Singapore as one of the countries in his research project.

Tan's logic was that when you transform an organization, you have to create a new vision, so the seminar that was eventually conducted by Porter and Jagdish Sheth, another well-known authority in this area, was designed to help the EDB and other sectors of Singapore to achieve that new vision. The impact of the seminar was considerable in that it brought about a new strategic perspective. It provided a way to look at the organization from a total systems point of view and showed participants a new concept of what strategic marketing is all about. The new management believed that the EDB ought to become more systematic in identifying world-class marketers' and strategists' sources of success, and not only train EDB officers in some of those models and methods, but also use these valuable international perspectives to educate other Singaporean agencies and the business community in general.

Tan launched a number of annual activities that linked various organizations within Singapore and provided a more visible merchandising image to the rest of the world. CEOs from Singapore companies and the MNCs were often involved in these meetings, also providing opportunities to educate them and to tap their knowledge and opinions. By working with the Singapore Institute of Management, Tan could bring in major marketing "gurus" like Philip Kotler from Northwestern University and Ted Levitt from the Harvard Business School to give seminars to large numbers of people. Over the next several years, often working with other government ministries and boards, he created a national marketing workshop, two global strategy conferences, a national business forum, and most recently, a regionalization forum.

The annual corporate planning meetings of the EDB itself provided an opportunity to review the year's achievements and set the direction for the next year. The process and its impact was described by Lee Suan Hiang, deputy managing director of the EDB:

I was made head of a task force on marketing improvement, which drew on not only my prior design skills and interest but also on my experience with what different companies were doing in the marketing area; so, in a sense, I was an ideal candidate internally to implement some of the plans that Mr. Tan had to upgrade the whole marketing function.

They created among other things a set of standard operating procedures regarding how to handle marketing, how to handle ministerial visits, large conferences, and other kinds of formal events, drawing on the collective experience of the various EDB officers. This got to be quite specific in terms of how to dress, how to behave properly in various kinds of functions, and how to project a more professional identity in general. (1993 interview)

Most of the interviewees who had worked in the EDB since 1986 commented on the degree to which the EDB became conscious of itself as an agency with an image, and the importance of professional marketing and public relations in the communication of that image to the world. Many brochures were produced to communicate the EDB's various programs, and these brochures reflected sophisticated public relations skills. With Philip Yeo and Tan Chin Nam as highly visible and dynamic leaders, the EDB was able to stimulate and launch the initiatives that started Singapore on a new cycle of economic growth, which was symbolized by a 1991 government publication called *The Next Lap.* This book lays out in text and pictures the challenges that Singapore faces in all aspects of its political, economic, and sociocultural evolution and enjoins the population to continue its efforts to achieve economic maturity and the quality of life that goes with it.

Regionalization as a Major Initiative

Many of the strategic initiatives fostered by Philip Yeo were outlined in chapter 3. Probably the most important of these was the concept of regionalization and the "growth triangle" initiated by Senior Minister Lee Kuan Yew. This initiative dealt with Singapore's security vis-à-vis its neighbors, its need to expand its land resources, its future economic development through becoming business architects for the MNCs, and its need to leverage its own local businesses into MNCs through direct overseas investments or various kinds of joint ventures.

In May 1993, the EDB cosponsored a major conference to facilitate the exploration and further development of the regionalization concept. Representatives from the government, private industry, and academia were invited both to provide ideas through a set of working groups and to stimulate a more shared vision of regionalization in all of Singapore's sectors because they would all be needed to make the vision a reality. The introduction to the conference proceedings stated the goal well.

The Forum . . . will be a platform for the exchange of ideas on adopting a sharper regional focus for the next phase of Singapore's economic development. The regionalisation programme is a major initiative and a national imperative. It requires the cooperation and support of all parties—government agencies, statutory boards, the private sector and academia. The Forum aims to reach out to these parties, to invite feedback and discuss issues relating to the regionalisation programme, and to promote ownership, involvement and commitment to the programme. (EDB, *Proceedings of Regionalization Forum*, p. 3)

Several months before, working groups had been formed involving over 300 representatives of each sector to address questions of how best to position the public sector for the regionalization thrust and how to enhance public-private sector partnership. Through breakfast and dinner meetings, focus group discussions, and questionnaire surveys, they had reached tentative conclusions and recommendations. At the forum itself each working group reported its recommendations, which were then discussed and finalized. It is important to note that in the *design* of the meeting, the EDB sent the "teamwork" message in that every working group had to be co-chaired by one government and one private sector official.

Various speakers and working groups then made observations and proposals to the plenary session for final consideration. These can best be summarized by paraphrasing the following points from the conference proceedings.

1. Because of a growing distrust between the government and the private sector, new partnerships and teamwork attitudes have to be developed. It is not clear precisely what the growing distrust was about, but a few clues are listed below.

    a. The civil service had become too bureaucratic and conservative; and this led to conservative loan policies by Singapore banks, a monetary policy that made it hard to use local currency, limits on lending overseas or borrowing by nonresidents, excessive requirements for collateral, and in general a perception that the environment was overregulated;

    b. Favoritism toward the government-linked corporations (GLCs) on the part of other government departments in the use of information and incentives;

    c. Local companies' dependency on the government, based on a history of support and subtle disincentives to the pure entrepreneur. Several government speakers stressed the desire to have businessmen take a long-range perspective rather than looking for a quick return, which favors the technical entrepreneur more than the purely financially driven one.

2. The key role for the government should be to provide information and help, but the initiative for how regionalization should work must remain in the private sector. To this end, several concrete proposals were made along the lines of having the government share its information on overseas markets, working conditions, and opportunities so that the entire business community, not just the GLCs, would have access to this valuable information.

Local boards such as the Jurong Town Corporation should be prepared to help local businessmen, but it was acknowledged that the scale of local business may not be sufficient to bring rents down to an affordable level, and the corporation may not be prepared to offer subsidies because of its own need to be self-supporting.

3. More teamwork is needed within the private sector. This should include: sharing information, networking, and supporting industry associations at home and "Singapore houses" abroad, where in each major locale all the relevant information for doing business in that area is collected and made available to future investors.

4. Prime Minister Goh Chok Tong provided several key guidelines based on Singapore's experience with MNCs.

    a. maintain a diverse portfolio, do not put all your eggs in one basket;

    b. maintain traditional ties with neighbors where good relations already exist;

    c. go into new markets with a long-term view;

    d. make sure that the investments benefit not only Singapore but also the host countries (help them by training and developing their people);

    e. be a good corporate citizen in the host countries;

    f. let the private sector take the initiative with the public sector playing a supportive role.

5. Develop a new generation of Singaporeans who will be able to speak foreign languages, feel comfortable living overseas, have knowledge of other cultures and business environments, and yet create a quality of life at home that will make people want to return to Singapore. It was noted that with regionalization there may also be a loss of loyalty to the home base, resulting in more people staying overseas.

6. Additional proposals were presented for further study:

    a. exchange members on boards;

    b. the public sector should share more of its expertise;

    c. privatize some of the public sector activities;

    d. break large public projects into smaller units so that more local business can get involved;

    e. create "country investors clubs" so that new investors can learn from previous ones;

    f. create a global business program to train managers and their families for overseas service;

    g. market Singapore's name more;

    h. create a new position in government to liaise private firms with the statutory boards.

What is notable in this exercise is the degree to which the process of organizing the forum reflects the goals to be achieved. Not only were the working groups formed with all the sectors represented, but they were given enough time to come up with concrete ideas and proposals; and the forum itself provided an opportunity for these proposals to be analyzed and, if they made sense, to be "ratified" as mandates for new action programs. This total process illustrates well how ideas "bubble up" from below, then are processed through the hierarchy, leading eventually to consensus and commitment across the levels and sectors represented. Teamwork is not just advocated, but becomes part of the process of the meeting itself.

What is also clear is that these groups felt free to be quite specific in offering their critiques and practical remedies. The problem-solving process does not stop with vague diagnoses or broad visions, but is pushed through to very specific "initiatives" and "schemes" that are refined, tried out, and evolved into longer-range workable solutions.

Accomplishments

The EDB has successfully launched a number of new initiatives reflecting these various strategic thrusts.

1. Joint ventures with Indonesia to build industrial parks, estates, oil storage facilities, and resorts on the Indonesian islands of Batam, Bintan, and Karimun—all close to Singapore.[8]

2. Joint ventures with Malaysia, to build an industrial park in the province of Johor, adjacent to Singapore.

3. Joint planning and ventures with the city of Suzhou, China, to build an integrated industrial township.

4. Joint ventures to build industrial parks in Wuxi, China, and Bangalore, India.

5. Plans to use tourism as a way to get into a region if there is insufficient infrastructure or skilled labor to develop the manufacturing sector. Joint ventures to build resorts, hotels, and the infrastructure needed for tourism, which then provide a base for developing manufacturing later.[9]

6. Aggressive expansion of the service concept with promotion of information technology, telecommunications, financial services, the arts, publishing, advertising, public relations, fashions, design services, film, music, and broadcasting.

7. An aggressive international manpower development program to recruit people with skills that are not available in Singapore.

8. Various kinds of support programs to stimulate and help local industry, especially in relation to regionalization.

9. More complex joint ventures with the current MNCs and local companies to create industry clusters and to develop Singapore as a business and information hub.

Moving ahead on all of these fronts has created a much more complex multifaceted organization that relies on teamwork, especially across divisions and on projects where individual EDB officers will be "multitasked" and will have to work across many areas.

Analytical Summary

The "turnaround" that the EDB has achieved since 1986 is clearly the product of a team effort. Philip Yeo, as the highly visible chairman, is an extremely dynamic, proactive individual who produces concepts, information, and proposals for action quite rapidly and gets involved in projects at a very detailed level. Tan Chin Nam is much more of a careful conceptualizer, theoretician, articulator, organizer, and team builder. Tan is described as being very good at setting up administrative systems that really work, and he is clearly the type of leader who builds strong teamwork by patiently encouraging and stimulating others while being relatively modest about his own contribution. Tan described most of the activities that the EDB launched in terms of a vague "we," whereas, in fact, he is apparently the architect of most of them. Because Tan is a strong believer in teamwork, he will create a concept, carefully sell it to people in the ministry and within the EDB, and then put together a team to work on it with himself acting as a kind of stimulator, animator, and low-key chairman. He often refers to "twinning conferences" where other organizations share sponsorship of the project with the EDB. He is a strong believer in strategic alliances as the model of the future.

Both leaders espouse and act in accordance with what I have previously called a "nonhierarchic hierarchy," in the sense that the EDB has at least seven or more formal levels supported by strong patterns of deference to authority. Yet there is egalitarianism, openness of communication, "boundarylessness," and norms that supported going around the hierarchy whenever the task called for that. The only constraint is the norm to keep the intermediate levels of supervision fully informed when levels are bypassed, and to accept authority when it is exercised, for example, when a superior would critique a proposal that had been submitted or when Philip Yeo would write comments on his float reports. The hierarchy was built on mutual respect, competence, and prior experience, but subordinates felt empowered to assert themselves when the task called for it. In fact, Philip Yeo recruited people who were self-starters and assertive. He did not want what he labeled in one of his interviews "passengers" who were just along for the ride. He wanted leaders at every level who were willing to accept and meet challenges, who were willing to help "drive" the train.

It is noteworthy that all the previous chairmen had spent some of their working career within the EDB. Although Philip Yeo had spent four years as a board member, he came into the role of chairman as an outsider. He brought with him new energy, new ideas, several key new people, and new activities. He did have to "right-size" the organization, launch new initiatives and hire new people to fit the new requirements of the late 1980's and early 1990's. But with all of these new initiatives and people, one still sees most of the basic cultural themes in operation. The EDB's strategic priorities and some of its methods of operation certainly evolved dramatically under Philip Yeo, and many new elements were brought in; but the basic elements of the culture as such did not change. In fact, it is the stability of many of the EDB's basic beliefs and values that is striking, even as the challenges the EDB faced escalated dramatically.

Much of the explanation for this stability lies in the fact that the new leaders coming into the EDB grew up in the Singapore culture, knew many of the players already, and believed in and personally valued the kind of culture that the EDB had evolved. Not only had this culture produced great economic success, but to a considerable degree *it was a culture similar to what other dynamic government ministries, boards, and agencies had also evolved. This meant that outsiders coming in from other agencies often had, at the outset, the same beliefs and values as those of the EDB.* And of course this parallel evolution was partly driven by the fact that the EDB had seeded some of those other agencies with its own alumni over the previous two decades.

What is striking then in looking at the thirty-five-year history is that many of the critical cultural themes that were launched in the early 1960s proved to be relevant and still viable in the 1990s. The marketing of Singapore had become a competitive enterprise that required the most sophisticated tools available, but the EDB culture readily adopted those tools and implemented them successfully. Philip Yeo summarizes the EDB philosophy well as he articulated it in the 1992–93 Annual Report:

The charter of the EDB is broad, yet clear—to create good jobs. Economic development means job creation. Jobs create prosperity and the rest, quality of life, etc., follow. If you have no jobs, there is no quality of life to speak of. No higher standard of living to aspire to.

Our primary goal is clear. It doesn't change. But the means to it may change. We are a very flexible organization. If we want to excel, we must be creative. In the EDB, we must always try new approaches, new solutions. If it doesn't work, try again, start something else.

We concentrate on creating. The EDB does not hang on to projects. We come up with new solutions, we kick off projects, we prototype them for a while. We then transfer these projects to more appropriate agencies to mother and expand them. You have to know when to give up, when to pass it on. Otherwise you cannot take on something new. If the EDB is saddled with all our creations, we will become a dinosaur. We should remain slim and fast. (EDB, 1992–1993 Annual Report, pp. 5–6).

We have now completed the description of the EDB as seen primarily by its own members. The EDB presents a fairly articulate view of itself as was reflected in table 1.2. The components of its self-image fit together. It now remains to be seen how well this self-image jibes with how others saw the EDB.

II

The EDB from a Client/Investor Perspective

The culture of the EDB derived primarily from the management style of the early leaders as they grappled with the economic realities that Singapore had to face and learned from their own experience what worked and what did not. In the previous six chapters I described some elements of the historical context in which those leaders operated and highlighted the diverse mix of causal political, social, and economic elements. These various historical, cultural, and personal strands produced a particular managerial and operational style that clearly had a powerful impact on potential investors. What was that impact? How did non-Singaporean managers view the EDB and Singapore? Why did companies choose to invest in Singapore?

Some of the answers to those questions are the focus of the next two chapters. Even though the EDB's efforts were worldwide, a great deal of that effort was directed at U.S. companies, in part because these companies were beginning to look "offshore" for manufacturing just at the time that Singapore was launching its strategy. The next chapter will therefore focus exclusively on U.S. companies, and chapter 9 will look at companies from Europe and Asia.

In reviewing the data the reader will notice that they are basically slanted toward explaining why companies decided to invest in Singapore. Ideally I would have searched out an equivalent number of companies that did not invest in Singapore to try to find out whether it was aspects of the EDB culture that turned them off. It not only proved to be very difficult to find such companies, but it was also the case that the successful investors made enough critical comments to make it possible to infer where the problems lay. Those comments are pulled together in chapters 12 and 13.

8

The EDB as Perceived by U.S. Investors

In this chapter I will examine how a number of U. S. businessmen and entrepreneurs who decided that investing in Singapore was a good idea justify their decision retrospectively. How did the EDB present itself to its potential clients, and what impact did that have on them? How did the investors reach the initial decision to invest in Singapore and then the further decision to expand and to continue to invest, leading in many cases to a complex partnership with the EDB and various local companies?

The primary data come from personal interviews and lengthy phone interviews. The EDB has also analyzed the case histories of twenty of their key "partners" and segregated out both why the EDB wanted these companies and why, according to the EDB, these companies decided to invest in Singapore. In addition, the reactions of companies are often reported in various monthly and weekly publications such as the EDB's own *Singapore Investment News,* the *Straits Times,* and various promotional publications.

The data from these several sources are quite consistent with each other, and certain themes repeat themselves in company after company. I have deliberately kept most of the stories in spite of the repetition to show that, though these themes come from different companies in different industries and at different stages in the EDB's history, they tend to reflect the same kinds of EDB characteristics. The stories are organized roughly in chronological order to reflect both early and more recent decisions about investment.

The Mobil Corporation

The Mobil Corporation is of interest because it already had a presence in Singapore prior to 1961. It not only made early investments but found the environment conducive to continued investment up to the present time. Mobil thus represents the ideal kind of "partnership" that the EDB says it is seeking with a MNC. The EDB's own case files show that Mobil first entered Singapore in 1893 as the Vacuum Oil Company. According to the case material, contact with the EDB first occurred in 1962 to explore the possibility of investing in petroleum facilities, but Goh was not optimistic about how much productive capacity this would add to Singapore. However, Hon Sui Sen and E. J. Mayer persuaded Mobil executives to look into investing in a refinery that would serve as a supplier for the region. The construction would provide many jobs for a number of years, the refinery would stimulate related industries and provide much needed fuel. The size of the investment would also give impetus to the whole industrialization program. Mobil would, at a later time, also implement an intensive training program for local personnel to prepare them for supervisory and managerial jobs.

After a year of exploration Mobil decided to invest $39 million in such a refinery because (1) it needed a regional center, (2) there were fears of a possible nationalization of its operations in Indonesia, (3) they were offered a good site in Jurong, and (4) the EDB offered very good economic incentives in terms of tax relief through the Pioneer program, low-interest loans, exemption from import duty on materials needed for construction, and foreign exchange for services and payment of royalties and dividends.

The refinery opened in 1966 and was producing 30,000 barrels a day by 1970. In 1973 Mobil invested an additional $150 million to increase its capacity to 180,000 barrels per day, making it the largest of Mobil's wholly owned facilities east of Suez. Further investments were made in 1977, 1978, 1981, 1982, 1990, 1991, and again in 1992 with a S$150 million contract for construction of a catalytic hydrodesulphurization plant for the production of premium quality diesel fuel with very low levels of sulphur. Mobil's total investment in Singapore will have reached S$2.4 billion, making it Singapore's second largest investor after Shell.

A. V. Liventals, the vice president for Middle East and marine transportation and the local manager in Singapore through much of the 1980s, was interviewed by me in 1993. His first contact with the EDB was in the early 1980s when he was in Saudi Arabia helping to build a large petrochemical project for the Saudis. One of Mobil's goals at that time was to have the Saudis themselves take over the running of the complex as soon as possible, so they had to rapidly train large numbers of people in the requisite skills. They would pick young Saudi candidates for training and send them to various other places where they could learn. Since they had refineries in Singapore, Liventals made an arrangement to send twenty-four people per year for several years to be trained in the Singapore refinery. He got good cooperation from the Singapore government in loosening up immigration requirements for foreign workers, providing housing for them in exchange for guarantees that they would leave and that they would be "well behaved" while in Singapore.

This high degree of cooperation from the government foreshadowed how things would work later when in 1988 Liventals was assigned to Singapore to open a large aromatics plant. Mobil had acquired land in the 1960s when they were building and expanding refineries and had sufficient land to expand into various downstream chemical activities. The employee who first made the deal to acquire land in the Jurong township (which at that time, was mostly swamp and chicken farms) told Liventals that the land Mobil initially wanted was not given to them by the government, but that they were offered an alternative space that was in fact much larger. It was lucky that that initial request did not work out because only by getting the much larger piece of land could they afford to do the later expansion.

Liventals pointed out that the government policy on foreign labor was very critical because on any construction job it is likely that there will not be enough local labor available to complete the job, given the fact that the government imposed a cap based on the ratio of local to foreign labor. In the middle of a project with time deadlines Mobil often needed much more labor and would have to exceed the cap. They would then have to go through the EDB to various government agencies and deal with the sensitivities of the National Trades Union Congress (NTUC) arrange for extra housing, again guarantee the behavior of the immigrants and ensure that they would leave when appropriate. He said that they have always gotten what they needed from Singapore even when that meant exceeding the ratios and going beyond the guidelines that the government had set.

In response to the general question of what impressions he had of working with the EDB, he stated the following points:

The government was not only very aggressive but very professional in its recruitment of foreign capital. At the beginning they needed the foreign money and what was attractive to the investor was the sense that these people really wanted us, they had a hard-working labor group, a government that was pro-business, and this strong attitude of "we want you."

Access to them was always very easy—you could simply pick up the phone to your EDB contact and within twenty-four hours you would always get feedback of some sort. Their efficiency was impressive—they always worked in real time on a business clock, not on bureaucratic time or a government clock. Their power centers were well coordinated so that you got more rapid action in solving problems—they didn't function like a bureaucracy, they were on top of things. (1993 interview)

When I asked how this came to be, how they avoided becoming more bureaucratic as so many other government agencies had become, he mentioned the following factors:

1. They have a strong tradition of accountability for results.

2. They have to make things happen, leading to a "let's do it," performance-oriented attitude.

3. They talk to each other; they have open channels inside and with the outside so that the whole organization responds. If the person you talk to on the phone one day isn't available on another day, someone else will know all the relevant facts and be able to deal with it.

4. There is a tight hierarchy but communications are open—the senior man's vote is "it," but they communicate with each other.

5. They are very smart to take little steps and learn from them rather than overreaching themselves. For example, on the regionalization initiative they are working in small steps with the geographically close islands and learning what it's like to work with other governments before they get too deeply into overseas activities.

6. Another reason for their success is that even though they have lots of pride, they have very little chauvinism. Very little is done without careful disciplined research and, in that process, they use outside resources and are willing to learn from whoever has relevant knowledge.

7. They always picked the best people and, through creating a fairly strong elitism, managed to get very good people to the top.

8. They have great respect for their leaders and that, in combination with a high sense of discipline and a very strong work ethic derived

somewhat from Confucianism, makes them very effective. (1993 interview)

Alan Murray, Mobil's CEO in 1993, made the following kinds of comments about his perception of Singapore and the EDB:

They have an overall favorable business climate, are well motivated and have well-trained human resources available; they have favorable incentives and tax treatments, and Singapore puts an emphasis on productivity.

For example, when Mobil was involved in labor negotiations, the typical short-run philosophy in other parts of the world would be to just give each side a little of what they wanted. In contrast, Singapore always took a long-range point of view and asked the question, "How can we resolve the issue in such a way that not only will everyone get what they want, but that productivity will go up?" They did not display the typical short-run, knee-jerk reaction to labor problems, but had a long-range plan that emphasized consistent growth and productivity.

The strength of the EDB is that they were very clear about their long-range goals and knew what they were trying to accomplish. At the same time, they were able to make shifts in emphasis from labor-intensive to capital-intensive to high-tech to now more broad business architecture.

They were good people to do business with, good partners, partly because they have high motivation, high skills, good education and, most important, the ability to constantly upgrade their mode of thinking and their goals.

Singapore was willing to recognize the fundamentals—to create a long-range plan emphasizing education and training, to develop their talent and also to recognize that this would require a great deal of discipline. People were willing to accept this discipline because they could see progress in their standard of living and recognize that the more disciplined approach actually did produce a fairly high rate of success. They could see their way of life changing in front of their eyes, and this success of course bred more motivation. (1993 phone interview)

Murray noted that such accomplishments always require some leaders like Lee Kuan Yew who really see what's needed, but that the philosophy referred to above permeated various other leaders in Singapore, which made things work so well: "These were leaders who thought broadly, who were worldly, who were productivity conscious, who were long-range thinkers, and who were very open and frank in conversation and negotiation."

How the EDB works with its partners on an ongoing basis was revealed in some detail by Liventals.

On a number of occasions, perhaps five or six times during my five-year stint in Singapore, I was asked to attend, by invitation, a "think tank breakfast."

These were organized by the EDB, usually at one of the nice hotels, for anywhere from twelve or so industry guests and four to six EDB people. The industry guests were always a carefully picked group to be representative of industries dealing with the particular topic that was to be discussed that day, and that usually meant that no companies that were directly competing with each other would be involved. The four to six EDB people were usually directors or deputy directors from the industry sector that was involved with the particular topic. Sometimes Mr. Tan Chin Nam would show up at the beginning and say some things by way of welcome, but the directors and industry officers then took over the meeting.

Depending on the topic, there would usually be a short slide show indicating "here is where we are now" in terms of a certain set of issues. This would lead to a definition of a problem or a plan or a set of questions followed by a set of proposals or ideas of what the Singaporeans felt they needed to do. Then they threw it open to the industry executives with the question, "What do you think?"

There would then follow a very polite but open discussion, relatively low on advocacy, but the industry executives would express their concerns or disagreements which would usually be listened to, sometimes argued with in the form of the EDB people presenting all the logic on their side as to why they had come up with a particular proposal.

In this way the EDB would not only learn a great deal about what local executives thought, but it was also a very good way of co-opting those executives and getting them to think more about Singapore in a helpful way, leading ultimately toward regular dialogues. (1993 interview)

The attitude from the beginning was to "consult the people you have available for whatever information or help you need." For example, when the government issued new regulations, they didn't just one day drop them in but rather floated them and let them be discussed widely before actually implementing them.

Analytical Comment

Both Murray and Liventals were very impressed with the ability of the EDB to be helpful and solve problems. They had many reasons for investing in Singapore and most of these focused on Singapore's "understanding of business, creating a good climate for business, and doing things in a businesslike fashion." Although the use of the English language did not come up as a special factor, one can conjecture that this kind of climate plus the use of English made Western managers feel very comfortable that they would be welcomed, understood, and helped.

The DuPont Corporation

According to the EDB's case files, DuPont's relationship with Singapore goes back to 1973 with the establishment of a sales office for the distribution of explosives. In 1974 the company explored the possibility of manufacturing a new explosive in Singapore, but this idea was rejected by Singapore because of problems pertaining to safety and security. However, in 1978 Berg Electronics, a division of DuPont, started to explore manufacturing possibilities and the EDB labeled this a high-priority project to be "intensively promoted" because this kind of electronics plant fitted well into the strategy of emphasizing more sophisticated, capital-intensive industries that would lead to more training for Singaporeans. The EDB also felt that DuPont's entry would eventually lead to other projects and it was important to have a company of DuPont's stature represented in Singapore.

According to the EDB, DuPont was impressed from the outset with the government's open attitudes and policies toward business, Singapore's sense of organization and discipline, the ability of workers and executives to comply with DuPont's stringent safety and housekeeping policies, the proximity of customers and suppliers, and the general momentum of Singapore's electronics industry. In spite of these favorable conditions, the EDB had to work hard to convince DuPont that Singapore had the tool and die making skills needed, that the unit costs of production were competitive, that the appropriate economic incentives and tax breaks could be put into place, and that a suitable site could be provided (the latter required some "intense" coordination with the Jurong Town Corporation).

As had been hoped, not only did this subsidiary grow over the next five years, but a number of additional projects developed. In 1991 DuPont opened a Delrin compounding plant to manufacture its engineering plastic, a regional distribution center and a Corporate Data Center at the Singapore Science Park. In 1992 it opened a Lycra polymerization plant, and is currently constructing an Adipure plant to produce the acid necessary for the production of nylon. In addition, the company is planning a world-class, vertically integrated nylon complex.

Edgar Woolard, chairman of DuPont, was interviewed in 1993 and provided some perspective on DuPont's evolution. DuPont decided to invest in Singapore in the late 1980s. They had been a presence in Japan for a long time and were also operating in Taiwan and in Australia, but they were beginning to try to look more broadly at where the customers of the future would be and how DuPont could become more important to the Asian automobile, electronics, and fiber (textile) customers.

They realized that they needed plants that were big enough to provide economies of scale but not so big that they would be geographically locked in forever. They also realized that, given the nature of the Asian situation, their customers (other companies) would be moving around a lot between Malaysia, Indonesia, China, Korea, Thailand, and other countries in search of the best tax breaks and lowest labor costs.

DuPont decided it did not want to chase customers by having to redo their plants all of the time, so they saw Singapore as potentially the best central locale, even though that involved overruling some inside protagonists who wanted to be based in Taiwan, South Korea, or Japan. The Japanese were perceived to be very capable but not very adventurous in that arena, and there was no particular petrochemical base in Japan to supply all the potential customers in that region. So the strategic question they put to themselves was, "How could DuPont become a leading chemical company in Asia for that whole region?"

DuPont needed to put in local facilities that would be perceived as highly efficient, low cost, and high quality and as having a short supply chain. They needed not only a strong ingredients base to supply the polymer and fiber plants for their various customers, but also land, people, reasonable costs, and a stable customer base. When they examined all the trade-offs, they discovered that Singapore offered the best mix. So in the late 1980s they began to explore Singapore actively and found the following positive factors:

They (the EDB) were the most knowledgeable government people we had met, who knew exactly what it took to make a business successful, who knew business trends around the world, who had a truly international focus and, most important of all, had a "can-do" attitude.

Singapore was politically stable, gave reasonable tax breaks, had a very strong infrastructure, a skilled labor pool, and a very fast decision-making cycle so that as problems arose, we could count on them being settled fairly quickly. The EDB is one of the best in the world in what they are trying to accomplish. (1993 phone interview)

As the plant has now been under construction for over two years, there is of course a whole group of people from DuPont working there; the consistent feedback is that as problems arise, the Singaporeans show spirit, determination, speed, and timeliness in solving them. They are driven by a spirit of "let's figure out how to get a win-win situation for both Singapore and DuPont." Detailed questions that require negotiation come up constantly, but what impressed Woolard was that they are always resolved, and resolved in a way that makes you feel that it was fair. He viewed the EDB as very efficient, very determined, very quick to identify barriers and then solve the problems.

In addition Woolard explained why they felt they could trust the EDB and Singapore with as big a capital investment as they were making: "*What they said, they stuck to.* We had a lot of experience in other countries where something would be discussed and agreed upon one day, and then the next day or in a week we would get a call back saying, 'Well, we didn't quite understand,' and/or, 'We can't do that now.' In other countries things would constantly come unglued, whereas in Singapore, once they said something, they stuck to it. Or, if they did have to renegotiate, the logic was always very clear and very plausible" (1993 phone interview, my emphasis).

Compared to other countries, Singapore was easier to work with because there was no graft, no under-the-table payoffs. DuPont also knew they could trust Singapore because other MNCs always said that Singapore lived up to its commitments. Woolard remembered visiting the prime minister on one occasion and being told, "All we have here in Singapore is our integrity, and therefore we cannot compromise it."

Woolard emphasized repeatedly that the EDB has an attitude of understanding what is important for their country *and* for business. This did not mean that they just gave in to everything that business wanted. They bargained on many issues, and on many of them DuPont either compromised or Singapore got its own way. For example, DuPont wanted to build their plant onshore but Singapore, for various reasons, wanted the petrochemical complex offshore on one of the islands where they had already started some work. Singapore prevailed, which meant that DuPont had more of a problem with transporting labor and materials over to the island. But as in every case, if it ended up costing DuPont more to build on the island, they would get more help with taxes or with the infrastructure.

Woolard pointed out that DuPont takes a very long-range view of things and that has led them to explore further the possibilities for research in Singapore, using scholars from India and China. DuPont would do this to form good relationships with the universities in the area and to build a major presence for themselves in Asia.

DuPont also found that the EDB was very interested in the tremendous safety record that DuPont has amassed over the decades, particularly a very low accident rate in the plant construction phase. The EDB was very interested in learning those safety techniques, leading to a sharing of the technology of safety for other EDB projects. So the relationship is one that is leading them to be able to begin to learn from each other, and for both to benefit.

In the petrochemical complex, several plants have already started. They started on time and are successful, so the bottom line for Woolard is that Singapore has been an excellent place in which to invest and build relationships. Although Woolard did not mention it as a factor, in the EDB's own case analysis the fact that Singapore was an English-speaking country was listed as an additional factor making it more attractive than other Asian locations. The EDB analysis also points out that there were at least two other projects with DuPont that the EDB failed to get for various economic, marketing, and environmental reasons.

Analytical Comment

DuPont, like Mobil, was an ideal partner in that the nature of their investments changed in line with Singapore's own strategy of going to higher value-added, capital-intensive kinds of industries. It should be noted that among the various factors listed for liking Singapore, a very salient one is again the EDB's responsiveness to the needs of a business and its willingness to deal in a timely fashion with whatever problems cropped up.

The Lubrizol Corporation

Lubrizol is a $1.5 billion U. S. company roughly in the Fortune 300, primarily manufacturing specialty chemicals that are used as additives in a variety of products (particularly crankcase oils). It is the world's largest supplier of such additives, with 35 percent of the world market; 70 percent of their revenues come from outside the United States. The company employs roughly 4,000 people and has made it a point to treat people very well, so that they have experienced only a 1 percent turnover domestically and in their overseas operations. The company was formed in 1928 by six people, one of whom was a professor of chemistry at Case-Western Reserve University. They are a highly technology-driven company and manufacture in twenty different countries. Singapore is today the largest manufacturing site they have in the Pacific basin, but they also have plants in Australia, Japan, and India.

Roger Hsu, my informant, came to Lubrizol in 1952 with a doctorate in organic chemistry from Case-Western Reserve University. He came to the United States from Shanghai in 1949 at age twenty-one. In the 1960s he went to Case-Western Law School, obtained a law degree, and became the chief legal officer of Lubrizol for roughly twenty years until his retirement. In addition to that he had responsibility for international business development, where his job was to find opportunities, create companies and then, once they were up and running, turn them over to local management. He retired at age sixty-five, but has remained an employee in the role of counselor to the chairman.

Lubrizol's entry into Singapore had multiple causes. First, Hsu had to be well informed on all the various international possibilities, so he already knew a good deal about all the countries in the Pacific rim and had an impression that Singapore was more interested in long-range planning than, for example, Hong Kong. When they first began to think about the Pacific rim, they did not have a big enough market there to warrant building a regional headquarters. But as the market grew, the need for such a regional organization also grew and, at that point, Hsu became more interested in Singapore precisely because they had a better location, a longer time horizon, and a more stable, business-oriented government. He noted that Japan was a little bit too provincial and that Korea and Taiwan were not sufficiently stable or predictable to do business there.

Hsu also mentioned that through a mutual friend he had met Chan Chin Bock some twenty years earlier, long before their actual Singapore project got going. Chan was at that time the EDB's Director of International Operations based in New York, and he became a good source of information and insight. Because Chan was very objective, they formed a good relationship and Hsu developed a high degree of respect for him partly because he felt he was not getting a "sales pitch," but objective data. The conversations with Chan confirmed and modified some of his views of Singapore, but he did not think that he learned anything that fundamentally changed his own conclusions about the pros and cons of Singapore. He had also met I. F. Tang in connection with some help that he was providing to the UN on a program to help developing countries.

When I asked him how, in the end, he came to choose Singapore, he said:

Singapore was unique. Hong Kong was status driven and corrupt; Singapore had more of a philosophical approach, a general direction that was *long term* and not the quick dollar here and there. They had their eyes set on developing their resources, thinking about the education of their people. They had a real spirit of cooperation with business and a free-market philosophy within boundaries. They were democratic but they viewed it as a managed democracy, which was appropriate since it is not clear that people could have handled too much freedom. They were strategically very well located. Japan was too provincial and Taiwan and Korea were not safe enough. (1993 phone interview, my emphasis)

When they began to think seriously about moving into Singapore in the early 1970s, Hsu did most of his "negotiating" with I. F. Tang who was then the chairman. When I asked how this negotiation worked, he pointed out that it really wasn't negotiation so much as *joint problem solving.* Hsu felt he needed more information on the government's long-range plans, especially regarding land for a $20–30 million plant they were planning. They needed to know that they could expand and think in terms of a twenty- to thirty-year plan. Since they were planning to use local labor, he also needed to know whether Singapore was in a position to provide that labor and also offer the kind of help they needed with taxes, financial incentives, and recruiting.

Hsu recalled that he and the EDB people would get together and each articulate their objectives and then identify problems and solve them, which did not feel like negotiation. In fact, he described it as a set of very pleasant experiences—open discussions with very high-quality people. Lubrizol also felt a real compatibility with Singapore's goals to have "clean industries," because the company had always had high standards for running nonpolluting kinds of plants.

Analytical Comment

The Lubrizol case highlights the degree to which the EDB had its own strategic agenda that, in this case, according to its own retrospective analysis, was not entirely met. Although Hsu painted an entirely positive picture of the Singapore relationship, it appears that the EDB was somewhat disappointed that, in the end, the investments that Lubrizol made fell short of the EDB's expectations and, though Hsu did not perceive the process to be a "negotiation," apparently the EDB did. In particular the EDB did not want to release a large, choice piece of land with waterfront access unless the company invested on a scale sufficient to warrant such land. When such investment was not forthcoming, the whole land deal had to be renegotiated. Though the projects that eventually were built were satisfactory to both parties, the total investments made by the company fell short of what the EDB had originally hoped for.

Polysar Corporation

Bud Green, a vice president of the Polysar Corporation, was assigned to be the director of their mainland China business, to be conducted from the regional headquarters that were to be set up in Singapore in 1986. The EDB was very anxious to develop the regional HQ concept and therefore very willing to help Polysar establish one. Polysar was viewed as one of the kinds of companies Singapore really needed because of their potential in Southeast Asia. When they agreed, a lot of publicity and fanfare was given to the decision, which really made Polysar feel wanted.

Why did they decide to locate in Singapore? Green listed a whole series of reasons:

• It is a great place to do business; you never face any impediments.
• The EDB really wanted us to come there.
• The EDB had a very flat organization that communicated well internally so we could always get what we needed.
• Singapore is very efficient; things get done.
• Once they decide to do something, they do it so fast.
• They are a monetary powerhouse in the way they extract money from the population and recycle it through the Provident Fund.

- They are very pragmatic, especially in overlooking communism in dealing with China.
- They have a moderate tax rate.
- They have a very central location; it is easy to get everywhere.
- It is a good place to set up a technical facility regarding rubber because of its location.
- It is a nice place to live.
- They use English as their business language.
- They are a very hard-working people. (1993 phone interview)

Analytical Comment

Chemical and petroleum-related industries played an important role in Singapore's economic development, and it is clear from the comments made by various executives from these industries that the EDB recognized their importance and went after them. One of the interesting findings thus far is that each company made its decision on the basis of a set of criteria. It was not any one factor that led to the Singapore decision, but a complex mix.

Let us next turn to another set of industries that played a central role as well: the electronics and computer industry.

Texas Instruments

This case is of particular interest because of the recent four-way joint venture (TECH) with HP, Canon, and the EDB to manufacture semiconductors, and the fact that TI's so-called fifty-day miracle was such a prominent story in the late 1960s and early 1970s. Elements of the story were supplied during a 1994 phone interview by Robert England, TI's worldwide product line manager for memories.

TI has been in Singapore since 1969, starting with their integrated circuit assembly and test factory that was put up and made operational in fifty days (the fifty-day miracle). TI was one of the first high-tech semiconductor companies operating in Singapore and helped to build the infrastructure for that industry. In connection with the fifty-day miracle, England remembered that the first bit of manufacturing was done in a school gymnasium because there was no manufacturing space available, and that the basic drawings for the layout of the manufacturing operation were done by the EDB officer who was TI's liaison officer.

In connection with TECH he remembered that when the wafer fabrication facility was being built, it was imperative that they get started very quickly. The MRT (the local transportation authority) was building a station nearby and the pile driving would disturb the fabrication unit because of the vibrations. The EDB talked to the MRT and succeeded in getting the MRT to speed up its construction schedule so that all the pile driving would be finished before the wafer fabrication facility had to become operational. The EDB had the clout to do this because of its track record in helping Singapore become economically successful.

In thinking more generally, England noted that the EDB is unique in the depth of their understanding of particular industries and the key companies within it. They go out of their way to find out what you need. Where other countries would send out visiting delegations to potential investors, the EDB had its own representatives based all over the world learning first hand what was going on in various industries that might be of strategic importance to Singapore. Such depth of understanding was necessary to be able to help to put together as complicated a project as the TECH joint venture. He noted that the way the EDB educates, trains, and rotates their people to ensure that they have a global outlook is impressive—"They target their industries and really study them."

He also emphasized that the EDB could coordinate and facilitate the procurement of land and smooth the way with other government agencies who would have to cooperate to make the new venture work. One of the main problems was that the new factory would need twenty acres of land, which, in that land-poor city-state, was outrageously out of proportion to what was available. Had TI gone directly to the JTC, "they would have been laughed out of the office, because even one acre is beginning to be hard to find." So the EDB had to work with all the other government agencies to locate a parcel of land, to convince them of the importance of this project so that the land would be made available, clear the way for a complex leasing arrangement (because land could not be owned), provide the infrastructure such as utilities, make arrangements with suppliers of the superpure chemicals that would be needed, make sure that the needs of the chemical companies who would be involved as suppliers were met, clear the way for certain special imports by providing customs clearances, and so on. If TI had had to do all of this on its own or through a local lawyer, it would have taken them four to five years. Instead, "the EDB became the roadblock buster." TI would call up the EDB with a question or problem, the EDB would say, "Give us a couple of days," and the problem would be solved. England noted that he knows of no other country where the internal agency is so effective in getting all the problems solved so quickly.

Analytical Comment

Apart from illustrating very vividly the "one-stop" concept and providing an example of the helpfulness of the EDB, this account highlights the importance of the EDB's studying their industries, getting to know the individual companies, and fitting this knowledge together into a strategy.

Hewlett-Packard

Hewlett-Packard (HP) was an early investor that found many areas of compatibility and is today one of the main partners in Singapore's growth strategy. The EDB's own case analysis shows that the initial relationship was complicated because the ministry of trade and industry turned down HP's 1970 application for tax relief under the Pioneer certificate program, disappointing the EDB. In spite of this failure to get the tax relief, the manufacture of memory cores proceeded from the factory that had been opened and, in 1972, HP came back with a new proposal to manufacture their new electronic mini-calculators for the world market.[1] This proposal was accepted and Pioneer status was granted because it fitted better into Singapore's strategy and because HP was the kind of world leader in precision electrical/electronic products that would contribute to the upgrading of the electronic assembly industry in Singapore.

Over the next fifteen years HP continued to invest in Singapore in various manufacturing projects, in an integrated circuit design center, an information Network R & D Center, and ultimately in the joint venture with TI, Canon, and the EDB to manufacture advanced semiconductors. HP found Singapore to be a very congenial environment and developed a very symbiotic "win-win" relationship with Singapore because the HP long-range growth philosophy fitted so well Singapore's own need to grow technologically.

From the EDB's point of view, HP's twenty-five-year history in Singapore is also a prototypical success story in that both HP and Singapore have benefitted from HP's presence there. HP has evolved into a major player in the computer industry, and its Singapore operations have contributed heavily to that evolution, including some successful product designs executed by local engineering and R & D staffs. In 1995 HP was given the "Distinguished Partner in Progress Award" by the Singapore government, listing among its accomplishments the following:

The company was one of the pioneers in TQC in Singapore, the first to set up a networking products operation and the first to have a gallium arsenide wafer fabrication facility. Operations began modestly with the assembly of core memories, and 62 employees, 47 of whom are still with the company. R & D work also started modestly in 1984, with a laboratory for HP keyboards. Today, the product line comprises automation and advanced products such as calculators, palmtop computers, inkjet printers, IC's, LED components, personal computers and network products. The staff now exceeds 6,700 people.

HP Singapore also holds the worldwide product charters for portable inkjet printers and handheld personal computing devices such as calculators, palmtop computers, electronic organizers and personal digital assistants. The charter gives HP Singapore responsibilities in marketing, research, design and manufacture of the products. Among the notable achievements are the award winning HP Deskjet 300 series of printers and the HP38G graphic calculator, all created in Singapore.[2]

At the award ceremonies HP's CEO Lew Platt reinforced the concept that Singapore could take over many of the functions previously performed in the U.S. organization, a goal that has been implicit in Singapore's overall strategy going back to the chairmanship of Chan Chin Bock in the 1970s.

HP Singapore has made important contributions to HP's expertise in low-cost, high-volume manufacturing. It has earned expanded responsibilities in R & D, marketing, sales and administration. And its commitment to quality is widely recognized—both within HP and outside.

In the years ahead, the convergence of the telecommunications, computing, publishing and broadcasting industries will create the rich information structure envisioned in Singapore: The Intelligent Island. HP people and technology will make this information revolution possible.[3]

Cheah Kean Huat, managing director of HP Singapore, is facilitating this expansion with a new $238 million factory to be completed in 1996, making the HP Singapore site one of the most complex in the world.

Digital Equipment Corporation

Digital Equipment Corporation (DEC) started their Singapore operations in 1980 from a base that they already had in Taiwan and Hong Kong. In 1980 there was a change in technology from core memories to semiconductor-based operations. This technology not only displaced core memory but required much less direct labor. Asia had been a good place for the labor-intensive work but, as DEC got into this new technology, they looked again at where else they might go to manufacture something that was much less labor intensive. They did not want to expand in Taiwan (where they already had 1,500 people) or in Hong Kong (where they already had 2,400 people), so they looked at Singapore, the Philippines, Korea, and Malaysia and evaluated them all. Singapore at this time did not have the lowest labor cost, but it won out over the other countries because of several factors as assessed by Ed McDonough, the international manufacturing manager in 1993.

1. The extremely well-organized government. When DEC first got involved with Singapore, they did so through the EDB office in New York and found that the EDB people had done their homework. As he put it: "The EDB knew more about us than we did. It was the most organized government that we had ever dealt with. Other governments mostly did not know much about DEC, partly because it was not a well-known player at the time" (1993 interview).

McDonough had also been looking at Singapore in 1974, when he was with the Control Data Corporation. At that time they already had operations in Korea and Hong Kong, and he was looking at the Philippines, Indonesia, and Singapore. He was working through their local plant management and was impressed with the efficiency of government, how well organized they were when you met them, and how competent and professional they were, rather than political. "In all the other countries you encountered politicians and bureaucracy."

2. Singapore had tremendous tax saving advantages.

3. Singapore was a duty-free port with minimal customs involvement, which was both a factor in saving money and in terms of efficiency. If you had to pay customs duties and if things could be held up, that opened things up wide to bureaucratic delays and

corruption because your materials could be held up unless you paid off bribes. "Singapore has no corruption, which made it much easier to work there."

4. The ready availability of suppliers and raw materials.

5. The quality of the technical talent that was available.

6. The good infrastructure. Singapore was very ready to rent out temporary facilities and to help provide an indirect labor force trained to do what DEC needed. This was all handled through the EDB. DEC had only one or two expatriates in Singapore. They took a Chinese manager from Hong Kong as the plant manager, hired a local personnel manager from GE, and then hired their manufacturing staff locally. They found that there were very strong people available locally with very good technical talent, but they needed training. The EDB was willing to share in the cost of sending people to the United States for this training and generally getting things operational.

McDonough noted that the EDB's doggedness and determination persist today. He gets two to three visits a year from the EDB, especially now that DEC is considering an expansion of their operation in Batam through a joint venture between Indonesia and Singapore. This expansion is motivated again by the excellent base of raw materials available in Singapore, good local sourcing, and an excellent infrastructure for getting the job done.

He noted that Singapore organized itself very well for industrial expansion. For example, the Batam expansion is very sensible because it is just a half-hour ferry ride from the city to that area. It is a good illustration of how the government operates with temporary housing for employees who are building the plant.

McDonough often repeated that he found Singapore to be a very sophisticated environment, and if he had to choose a place to live in the region, he would certainly pick Singapore over other places like Taiwan or even Hong Kong. He noted that in Korea and Hong Kong things were much more political, and in Japan (where they also have operations), things were much more "closed." He found Singapore a very open environment.

When we talked about the controls and the autocracy, he smiled and said, "It's just like Switzerland—they have a lot of controls too," but he never at any time felt that the controls in Singapore interfered with anything that DEC wanted to do or with the personal lives of DEC employees. He noted that the Singapore plant is one of the highest-quality plants they have in Asia, which again reflects their technical skills and infrastructure. All in all, his impression of working in Singapore is that it is an entirely positive experience. He sees no problems in the future.

In a subsequent interview with a former DEC manufacturing manager, it was noted that the manager of DEC's Far East operation was himself Chinese and had a definite preference for Chinese employees because he felt they had a better work ethic. From this point of view, his first choice was Taiwan or Hong Kong, but he also favored Singapore because "it was 80 percent Chinese." He thought of Hong Kong as more cosmopolitan than Taiwan, and Singapore as more cosmopolitan than even Hong Kong, to the point that their Hong Kong–raised plant manager had a tough time adjusting to Singapore and had to be recalled after a year or so. These comments highlight the perception that though Singapore is stereotypically considered "Chinese," not only is it ethnically more diverse—that is, there are many Malaysian and Indian employees at all levels—but the Chinese population itself is diverse and to a considerable degree different from the Chinese population in Taiwan and Hong Kong.

A final comment made by this DEC manager concerned the fact that whenever you went into Singapore with a proposition, they always wanted to know immediately what technology you would transfer and what training you would provide to local Singaporeans. The government had all the financial support necessary for the training, but the company had to be willing to provide it and to transfer technology. DEC more than some of the other companies was acutely aware of Singapore's own strategy and that the EDB had its own agenda. The fit between that agenda and DEC's was clearly good in that DEC opened up their regional headquarters in Singapore in 1994.

Analytical Comment

I was able to observe the process of "knowing about the companies" because of my own involvement with DEC as a consultant and my interviews in 1993 and 1994 of the Boston EDB director under whose auspices companies like DEC fell. DEC at that time was in considerable turmoil because of major downsizing and massive management changes. To my surprise, the EDB director knew in great detail what was going on in DEC, and at a level of detail that would have required considerable research and personal contact.

The Apple Corporation

Apple's entry into Singapore was related in 1993 by John Sanders, the retired vice president of manufacturing. He had been hired by Apple as materials manager in late 1980 and had successfully revitalized and modernized one of Apple's major service support centers. One day after he had been at Apple for about nine months he was taken out to lunch and told that Apple had been looking offshore for some time and had decided to open a factory in Singapore. They offered him the top job. He had just moved into a house and finished redecorating it, but was talked into saying "yes" because it would only be a two-year assignment. So he closed up his house and took the job.

In March 1981, he and a finance manager went to Singapore to look over the operation. Other managers had already made the deal, gotten all the relevant tax breaks, and negotiated a site on which a partially finished factory was already located. He said that when he and his finance man arrived at the old airport at 3 A.M., they were immediately regretful because it was "old, tacky, and dirty." But they were met by K. C. Teo from the EDB and were taken straight to their hotel, briefed immediately, and told about the meetings that were set up for the next day. Sanders was impressed by how well organized this was.

The EDB had already decided where the plant should be located and took him out on the next day to show him this "five-story flatted factory." The area was completely surrounded by mud, some of the floors were not even in yet, so it was quite a challenge for Sanders to try to ship product by his July target date. The main help from the EDB at this point was that Teo recommended the various contractors and service people to whom Sanders should talk to get the factory fixed up.

Sanders stayed about a week, during which he hired an architectural firm who supplied the project manager. He had no more direct dealings with the EDB, but he got the feeling that the EDB was extremely powerful—"they could move mountains and would help in whatever way they could." He went back in April and at that point brought with him the finance and human resource managers so that in May they could hire their entire staff. They had put ads in the paper for the various technical staff they needed (with Ernst and Young being their local agents) and were absolutely astonished to discover that they had several hundred applications from very competent people, many of them from various other companies such as National Semiconductor and GE. They stayed for two weeks sorting resumes and applications, hired their entire complement of people, and arranged to have them come to the United States for a week or two of job orientation and training.

Initially Apple wanted to make only peripheral cards in Singapore, but eventually they decided to make motherboards and ultimately a final product. He was able to start in July (as planned) with 2,000 units and was able to double this every month until they were working at the 32,000-unit level. He noted with great pride that in the United States the Dallas factory, which was doing a comparable job, had yields of 50 percent or less on their basic boards while the Singapore plant had a quality level yield of 80 percent or more. He said they were so successful that Apple's CEO wanted to shift all manufacturing operations to Singapore. Sanders's own people developed better testing methods, automated a great many things, and eventually reached yields of 99.3 percent. It was a model operation, which received a steady stream of visitors from all over the world. He had such an excellent staff that he could receive all the visitors within the confines of his factory, and today this factory and the subsequent one he built are state-of-the-art factories in the world.

Sanders said that Singaporeans are delightful to work with. Whereas in most other parts of the world you have absenteeism problems, most Singaporeans wanted to come to work and the infrastructure supported it. Banks were open on Saturdays, and other services were made easier so that people really could put in full work time, resulting in a zero absentee allowance. He felt that Singaporeans put out at least 30 percent to 40 percent more effort than their U.S. counterparts; this observation would be supported by a quote he remembered from Lee Kuan Yew, who told his people to "do what your boss tells you and do it better."

He himself used management by objectives and noted that, once objectives were negotiated, he could basically leave people alone and they would accomplish what they had promised, or more. His overall judgment was that Apple would be a totally different company today without Singapore. They were so productive and got costs down so low that the Singapore operation really helped Apple to be successful. To illustrate, he told one story about choosing a location to manufacture finished products. He had been told that the Koreans could do it for $185 per unit and, unless somebody could do it for less than that, other locations would not even be considered. At a meeting of manufacturing managers Sanders said he promised that the Singaporeans could do it for $150 per unit, delivered in the United States, and committed himself to that figure. Several people were skeptical but he won the vote seven to three, set up an automated line, got all his people working together, and developed good suppliers and a just-in-time delivery system. He was able to land products in the United States for $149 per unit as promised because of lower costs, faster production runs, and better use of shipping and containerization, as well as very clever designs for testing. He said this worked because "they are sharp, sharp people." I asked him why the Singaporeans were so sharp, so technically competent, and so hard working, to which he replied, "It's their educational system, the discipline that's drilled into them, their desire to be the best."

John Scully, Apple's CEO, visited in 1985 and, when he saw the factory and how well it was working, accepted a proposal from Sanders to invest $15 million more to build a new factory. They needed a new factory because it was difficult to work across several floors, and they wanted to design a state-of-the-art factory on just one or two levels. Scully was so impressed that he immediately approved it, so in 1986 they built the factory and, in fact, came in $2 million under budget. At the same time they were building a factory in Ireland, which came in at $2 million over budget, a fact he used as another example of how effectively things worked in Singapore.

The EDB was very supportive all along and, as one example, he recalled that at one point they discovered some union organizers in the Apple plant and Sanders knew that, even though Singapore unions were at this time fairly benign, it would not sit well in the United States to have a union come into the factory there. So he called Teo, his EDB contact, and explained the situation and the U.S. attitudes. Teo listened and said he would see what he could do. Sanders said there was never another recruiter in the factory.

In summary, the factors that were mentioned in favor of Singapore were:

1. Singapore had such a great infrastructure.
2. Their small size.
3. Their good fortune in having a leader like Lee Kuan Yew.
4. Their financial strategy in that they have no debt and lots of cash.
5. They know "how to do things right." For example, he pointed out that Singapore Airlines will buy an airplane, run it for six years, depreciate the cost, and then resell it at a premium, thus enabling them to buy new planes.
6. As a final point he reiterated that if you give a Singaporean an assignment, you do not have to follow up; you know that it will get done.

In March 1994 I visited the Apple factory and was hosted by managing director Peter Tan and Bernard Lim, his financial controller. We spent an hour reviewing their impressions of the EDB and then toured the plant where they were making Powerbooks. Most of the factors mentioned by other executives were reiterated by Tan and Lim, and the tour revealed a spotless, highly automated factory built with a particular eye to efficient use of space by having various of the lines *above* each other instead of next to each other. It is notable that Peter Tan was a Singaporean hired from another electronics company and was replacing a U.S. manager.

An Entrepreneurial Point of View

Gary Weitz, who has been involved in three different high-tech start-ups in Singapore, was interviewed in 1993. He first met the EDB in connection with the Adaptec Company through his contacts with the SCI Systems Corporation who were slated to be his major prospective customer for the computer controller boards he was proposing to manufacture and sell both to SCI and to Seagate, the major manufacturer of disks. The SCI people put him in touch with the EDB's K. K. Chung, who became the project officer. The Adaptec idea fitted well into Singapore's strategy of going for higher-tech firms that would provide stimulus and training for their engineers, so Chung helped Weitz put together the business plan "to sell to the higher-ups." At the time, to help a small start-up was "going against the grain," but the plan was approved and Pioneer status was granted.

Subsequently Chung provided advice on how to get started and recruit people, but he did not really provide much direct help because Adaptec was a small start-up, and much more attention was going to the big companies like Seagate. Adaptec started with a small number of people but became highly successful, first building their finishing factory, then going into the new surface-mount technology to build their own boards, until today it has a $10–20 million investment and employs 600 or so people. The company went public, so Weitz moved on.

The next venture in 1990 was Metracom, which made radios for the public utility market. In this case he needed introductions from the EDB to the venture capital people and noted that the EDB seemed very closely tied to that community, leading eventually to his being able to raise the money needed for this venture. This company was also successful and eventually went public, but the EDB had no direct role beyond providing the necessary contacts.

In mid-1992 Weitz was involved in founding Co-Active. He needed a low-cost manufacturing operation and went first to his friends in SCI, from whom he was able to get the initial investment. He then went to the EDB with an expansion of the concept to get support for founding a local engineering and marketing center. He tried to reach his original contact K. K. Chung, but was told by return voicemail that Chung was unavailable (he had been promoted and may have been in another country at the time), but that Bernard Tan had been assigned as senior officer and would meet with Weitz at 2 P.M. the next day. He described that as being "forced *down* via phone or voicemail, but it worked very well because Tan really knew the technology and the business issues and helped put a viable plan together." Chung kept in touch via sending regards, but he was off doing "other things," so he could not function as the regular contact.

As Gary Weitz reflected on why Singapore is a good place to conduct business, he came up with the following factors:

• It is a small country that can control and coordinate everything.
• It has the support of its people.
• They are smart, pick the best and brightest for government service, and pay them well.
• They make a master plan and stick to it.
• They do their homework on the companies.
• They are technically astute.
• They know how to bet on companies and on individual people.

Analytical Comment and Summary

The personal comments of a number of U.S. executives from several types of industry illustrate both the range and similarity of reasons why they chose to invest in Singapore initially and why they continued to expand there, even as the costs of doing business there were rising. Several things are striking about these accounts:

1. There were always *several reasons* why Singapore was chosen over other Asian countries;

2. The kinds of *reasons given were very similar* across quite different types of companies;

3. The reasons *reflect very well Singapore's own concept* of how to become attractive to the foreign investors; and

4. The reasons reflect both Singapore's *pragmatism* ("they solved all our problems efficiently, they were a 'one-stop' shop") and their own *strategic priorities* ("they always wanted to know what technology we would transfer and how much training we would do").

A consistent theme that also surfaces in all of the cases is the willingness of the EDB to get directly involved to whatever degree was necessary. The project officers for a given client company not only were well versed in the problems of that company, but they were prepared to get their hands dirty if that was needed. This high level of knowledge and the willingness to help clearly differentiated the EDB in the eyes of their clients from similar organizations in other countries.

Overall the most salient theme is that businessmen felt comfortable in Singapore because they encountered in the EDB a group of helpers who thought like businessmen, who understood the needs of business, and who were really organized to help business. This contrasted sharply with what investors encountered in other countries and in other parts of governments that they dealt with. As the historical chapters tried to show, this positive orientation toward business and industry was very much shared by the early political leaders and was, in fact, the cornerstone of their development policy.

9

European and Asian Client Perspectives

Information from European, Asian, and local Singaporean companies was based on face-to-face interviews, telephone interviews, and a three-item questionnaire that asked selected executives to answer the following questions:

1. In what way has the EDB helped you in developing your business?
2. What are the special characteristics of the EDB that are helpful?
3. How could the EDB be even more helpful to you? What should they do in the future to improve their performance?

Responses were received from Sony, Hitachi, three different divisions of the French multinational Thomson, and from two local companies, International Video Products and Seksun Precision Engineering. In addition, interviews were conducted with Shell Singapore and EPAN Cable and Wire Company, a local supplier for several of the computer companies working under the LIUP scheme (Local Industries Upgrading Program). The responses to questions 1 and 2 are reviewed in this chapter, and the responses to question 3 are reviewed in chapter 12.

Shell Singapore

Shell's history in Singapore goes back one hundred years, and its commitment to Singapore was reaffirmed in 1961 with the opening of their refinery and subsequently with many other projects such as becoming a major investor in the petrochemical complex. In a conversation in 1994 with Peter Chen, the current CEO of Shell Singapore, and his manager of human resources the following points were expressed:

Shell considers the EDB to be a partner and trusted friend. Not only was
Shell the recipient of the first Pioneer certificate, but recently it was given
the first Distinguished Partnership certificate. The characteristics that made
the EDB valuable were as follows:

• Nothing was too difficult for them, they always were able to solve whatever problems came up. They cut the red tape. We don't even think of red
tape anymore.
• They were highly professional in that they really knew the industry inti-
mately and could therefore help in joint planning, become partners with
Shell in dealing with other parts of the government. They have a clear, open,
speedy, well-thought-out, integrated approach.
• The EDB always played a very important coordination role (the one-stop
concept).
• The EDB works with Shell in their manpower recruitment effort by having
Shell and other companies go along to campuses when recruiting is done.
• The EDB is very future oriented in creating a recruitment program for
Chinese workers (i.e., the EDB has an employment agency in China).
• The EDB has a good program for short-term foreign workers that are often
needed in the construction phases of products. Instead of minimum wages,
they use a levy on the companies for the number of foreign workers used,
encourage training, and create situation where trained foreign workers can
stay on if their skills are needed.
• When they do things, they explain the logic so that everyone has a deeper
understanding of why things are done the way they are.
• They are always very innovative in thinking of ways around constraints.
(1994 interview)

The Shell view reflects closely the view of U.S. companies reviewed in the previous chapter. The question then arises of whether
non-English-speaking organizations have a different view. We look
first at some data from French companies.

Thomson

Three different divisions of this French organization provided responses, again emphasizing a broad range of reasons why they considered the EDB helpful. A senior manager from the Consumer
Electronics Division Asia put the reasons as follows:

• The EDB provided the impetus for the setting up of an Asian Operational
Headquarters in Singapore;
• Their initiative in establishing the growth triangle (Singapore, Riau Island,
Johore) has led to the setting up of a major TCE facility in Batam, currently
with a workforce of 1,900;

• Various financial incentives and tax holidays that have helped to alleviate the cost of doing business in Singapore;
• Collaboration in manpower training, specifically the launching of a Post Diploma in Consumer Electronics at French-Singapore Institute, with 108 employees trained under the scheme;
• Assistance in problems relating to employee passes for expatriates to augment the technical/management expertise required to develop our operations. (1994 questionnaire response)

This manager also took the trouble to specify the special characteristics and abilities of the EDB that made them particularly helpful:

• Visionary outlook that helped to lay the foundation today for tomorrow's business, social, and technological scenarios;
• Close support with industry to effectively respond to investor's needs;
• Ability to scan the environment for new opportunities to help existing investors enhance their business—the Board is run more like an enterprise than a statutory body;
• Close government links in the region;
• Strong international outlook and an understanding of the global business game;
• More generally EDB has always behaved as a partner:
   • With a style for a personalized working relationship
   • With great availability and responsiveness;
   • With good knowledge of the company and not only of the business or activity;
• Dedication, competence, efficiency of the team.

The vice president of the Thomson Consumer Electronics Video Group first gave some general reasons, but then listed the many specific ways in which the EDB helped his organization.

During various stages of our development in Singapore, EDB has been a key factor of our success by providing invaluable information and support to our operations and implementation of business in the region. It provides us with the necessary link with major players of the Singapore economy and assists us in communicating with them.

By regular contact with us, EDB has been very supportive in the adaptation to the business environment changes.

Their action is not only focusing on the needs of today, but also on the evolution. They help us on the preparation of business evolution.

I can name some of the key areas where we appreciate EDB's support:

• Financial support to the implementation of product development in Singapore.

- Efficient support during implementation of our video company, IVP in Singapore.
- Link with educational system and universities to train and prepare future executives and staff.
- Staff recruitment and overseas talents.
- Liaison with TDB (Trade Development Board) and MAS (Monetary Authority of Singapore).
- Provide visibility of Singapore strategy for the future.
- Preparation and implementation of business extension in Batam and now China.
- Development of the local supply capability (LIUP program).
- Constant information on the support schemes and support (National Science and Technology Board, National Productivity Board)
- Support on trade regulation and evolution: GSP (Generalized System of Preferences)

In summary, EDB is an exceptional support to the business in Singapore by being a central point of the relation between all organizations and national bodies in Singapore.

The main characteristics that make them helpful are:

- Easy access and involvement of key department heads.
- Very business oriented (1994 Questionnaire).

Finally, the vice president for Asia Pacific from SGS Thomson Microelectronics also noted in some detail the many different ways in which the EDB had been helpful and the characteristics that made them so.

Since the beginning of our presence in Singapore in the late 1960s, EDB has been very supportive of our business development needs as a foreign investor. The support extended is wide-ranging across many varied areas:

a. Helped to secure suitable land to build our two factories; assist in the formalities for the amalgamation of the adjoining land for expansion and liaison with other government departments to get the necessary approvals/permits,

b. Supported our applications to the Labour Ministry for issuance of work permits to bring in professionals as well as workers to meet our manpower needs,

c. Endorsed our applications to the minister for grants or various fiscal incentives,

d. Approved the issue of special low-interest loans to support our expansion plans into new technologies,

e. Supported our training needs either directly through Intech grants or indirectly through other government-regulated schemes like SDF (Skills Development Fund),

f. Helped to expedite approvals required with relevant government bodies and statutory boards, e.g., building construction, temporary occupation permits, changes in plans, etc.

EDB personnel also keep in close touch with our organization both locally and at the corporate level to understand our future plans, needs, or potential problems encountered by our company, with the aim to support our growing operations here and ease bottlenecks where possible.

Furthermore, they constantly bring to our attention changes in legislation so that we, the investors, are aware of its impact on our operations.

SGS-THOMSON would definitely not have developed as fast or grown to its present size in Singapore without the active support of EDB.

One pronounced characteristic of the EDB is the proactive business approach taken when dealing with investor/business community compared to the sometime bureaucratic style prevalent in other government departments/bodies.

Likewise, there is also a distinct difference as to the quality and calibre of its staff. EDB's staff tend to be more dynamic and commercially minded rather than bureaucratic in dealing with matters desirous of their attention.

It is this "proactive business" and open approach adopted by the EDB that the business community finds extremely helpful as it now has a government body that understands and empathizes with their aspirations and needs and could therefore be relied upon to channel their views to the government policy-makers/regulators.

Another special characteristic of EDB that is helpful is its integrity and persuasive influence with other government bodies and statutory boards. In view of their considerable knowledge of both sides of the coin, EDB officers are frequently requested by the business community to help resolve disputes/problems with the government bodies.

The reasons for working with the EDB given by these French companies are not fundamentally different from the ones previously reported. And, as will be seen, the Asian responses that are reviewed below once again emphasize the same range of issues.

Sony

Sony's response from their managing director was brief and to the point:

EDB has a one-stop package business service to SPEC's (Sony's) operations. In Singapore, SPEC has been working closely with EDB and taking them as a partner. In view of EDB's efforts, SPEC looks forward to working with EDB through our strong business partnership.

EDB management is flexible, efficient, and effective. SPEC is also satisfied with their open-style management.

Hitachi

Hitachi, by contrast, emphasizes a range of issues that makes the EDB a desirable partner. The managing director put it as follows:

Our company is a joint venture between the EDB Investment Pte Ltd (15 percent) and Hitachi Ltd of Japan (85 percent). With the managing director of EDB as a vice-chairman in our board, we have the privilege to gain invaluable advice and comments during our discussions on the company's business development plans.

The opportunity for direct exchange and feedback with the top level of the EDB had enabled us to set our business plans and direction with due consideration to the country's economic development strategy. Also, with regular information through circulars and the EDB newsletter, such as the "Singapore Investment News," we are kept informed of the latest happenings in this sense.

On many occasions, the prompt and efficient service of EDB officers has helped us expedite our development projects in areas that require governmental procedures and/or support.

The EDB has the *foresight* (this is supported by their prompt and strong actions) to ensure the survival of the country's economy. This is evident in their commitment to realize their vision (e.g., M-2000, IT-2000, Regionalization 2000, high-tech industrial projects, etc.) such as identifying and attracting the kind of investment that is desired, and with their competent staff keeping in touch with advanced technology trends in the world.

In this respect, the EDB is also able to offer us valuable advice on what projects to undertake in order to complement their economic strategy as well as to ensure our continued survival in a very tight and competitive business environment.

In this response the simultaneous emphasis on short-run problem solving and longer-range strategic help comes through very clearly. We shift now to the point of view of local companies. What is immediately apparent is that the EDB's many specific schemes to solve specific problems, their intensely pragmatic approach, finds a ready audience.

International Video Products

The manager of training and systems development for this organization highlights the close relationship that exists between the EDB and the direct business issues of his company, especially during start-up operations. He also emphasizes the great importance of the joint training and development schemes for upgrading technical talent.

EDB has a team of professionals that provided information on various schemes available for investment and contacted us for the opportunity to develop our business. They further facilitated the process for business development such as manpower needs, sites for factory construction, and reservations for expansion based on our business needs.

Arrangements were made to meet restrictive ministries or statutory boards to expedite our application for permits for building, grants, and tax incentives.

The strong linkages and working relationships with the government ministries and statutory boards enable the speedy set-up of business and operations. Thereafter they provide linkages and identify business opportunities in Singapore as well as overseas such as Batam Industrial Park, Indonesia, Vietnam, and China. These had strengthened our relationship with materials suppliers and service supports for our business needs, thus enabling us to sustain competitive advantages, especially in materials cost for consumer electronics products like ours. Next, their International Manpower Division assisted in promoting our organization for recruiting specialists for our R & D and engineering function. Also they facilitated the obtaining of permits for semiskilled and skilled staff.

Training and transfer of technology plays a key role during our initial set-up of operation in 1988. Under the INTECH scheme, we managed to have more staff trained overseas as well as engage specialists to transfer the technology in design and manufacturing. Also under the same grant, the French-Singapore Institute has developed jointly with Thomson Consumer Electronics (TCE) the Post Diploma in Consumer Electronics Course.

The reader will recall that one of the major strategic shifts that occurred in the mid-1980s was the creation of more incentives for *local* industry, based on the recognition that local industry had been neglected in the rush to woo the large MNCs. This manager's comments suggest that these incentives were perceived and utilized by local companies.

Seksun Precision Engineering

The managing director of this local organization gave a detailed response to the question of how EDB had been helpful and what its characteristics were. Note that many of the items are "small" in monetary value, but were obviously important to this organization.

1. Tax incentive–investment allowance.
2. Extended Local Enterprise Finance (LEF) scheme–special interest rate for mechanization.
3. Grant of S$15,680 under the Small Industries Technical Assistance Scheme to assist the company in quality control system ISO 9002, under the Local Industry Upgrading Program (LIUP).
4. Grant of S$11,200 under the Small Industries Technical Assistance Scheme (SITAS) to assist the company to engage a consultant for carrying out feasibility study under the Small Enterprise Computerisation Program (SECP).
5. SITAS grant of S$21,420 to assist the company to retain the consultant for implementation consultancy under the Enterprise Computerisation Program (SECP).
6. The Local Industry Upgrading Program (LIUP) initiated by EDB is designed to foster closer linkages between local companies and their customers (multinational corporations and larger local companies) for mutual benefit. The company benefited from this program in upgrading operational and technical efficiency. The Production Planning & Control (PP&C) project under LIUP has been successfully completed.
7. The Enterprise Development Division (EDD) of the EDB has launched the Business Collaboration Programme to encourage local enterprise to go into collaborations to generate synergy or economies of scale. One of the initiatives is to form an Enterprise Collaboration Forum (ECF). The objective of the ECF is to encourage selected local enterprise to meet once a month to explore and consider business collaboration opportunities. Business collaboration can be in the form of product and/or process development, manufacturing partnership, shared resources, new project joint ventures, economic groupings for joint marketing or bulk purchasing.
8. EDB has been very helpful in granting the company in-principle support to recruit and obtain two-year work permits for skilled PRC workers. EDB also assisted the company in granting in-principle support in our application for the Housing and Development Board for an industrial site at Yishun Industrial Park A and in liaising with the various government departments and statutory boards to obtain approval for the construction of the factory building on this site. To finance this expansion program, EDB also approved our application for a factory and machinery loan under the Local Enterprise Finance (LEF) Extension Scheme.

What makes the EDB helpful is:

1. Liaison with various government departments to explain our needs so that quick action can be taken by the respective departments.
2. Since 1987 we have seen and felt that EDB's policies of handling SME in all industries have changed. Although they are still looking after MNCs, inviting them to set up plants in Singapore by providing favorable conditions, they are also concurrently looking after the Singapore SME (e.g., upgrading their skill and competitiveness through full financial support in the various schemes introduced by them and faster response in handling local SMEs' problems).

EPAN Cable and Wire Pte Ltd

Lim Chiang Peng, managing director of Epan, was interviewed in Singapore in 1994. Lim was working for the National Productivity Board when, in 1978, EPAN went to the NPB for financial help. At that point he resigned and agreed to take over the company as managing director. His first contact with the EDB was when he went to them for money to buy machinery under a loan program for small and medium-size industries. The EDB approved the idea, and the bank then provided the capital investment with the EDB underwriting one-half of the loan.

Over the years he has worked with many different people in the EDB, but he always felt that the EDB knew his company and its needs. They were more commercialized, more business oriented, and less bureaucratic than other agencies. Over the years they have helped in various ways, getting space for a factory, organizing trade missions to other countries that allowed him to become familiar with new markets and technologies, and providing linkages to foreign companies that led to EPAN's membership in the LIUP program.

He explained how the LIUP program works for him. It was started in 1985 as a scheme to stimulate local companies to expand and upgrade by becoming the prime suppliers to the MNCs. The EDB would bring several companies such as Apple and HP together to define their need, in this case, for computer cables. By having several companies as customers, a sufficiently large market was created to enable the local supplier to expand. By dealing with sophisticated MNCs, the local supplier had to upgrade and ensure that he reached the quality necessary to be the chosen supplier. The EDB played the role of broker, bringing the managers from the MNCs together to develop the concept. From the point of view of the MNCs, the advantage was less trouble and better prices. EPAN is happy with this program because it is one of the more innovative ways that the EDB has invented to stimulate local companies to grow, while providing favorable economic circumstances for the MNCs.

Analytical Comment and Conclusion

I have deliberately presented as much of the original data as possible and allowed these stories to be repetitive so that the reader can get an appreciation of the uniformity of attitudes and perceptions I encountered as I started to investigate company experiences with the EDB. Note that the points brought out by the Asian and European companies are essentially the same as those revealed in interviews with American companies. There seems to be a great deal of agreement on why the EDB has succeeded in attracting these companies.

The overwhelmingly positive tone is, of course, a product of working primarily with a sample of companies that are happy with their experiences in Singapore. However, the third question in the questionnaire elicited a number of caveats, criticisms, and suggestions that will be reviewed in detail in the chapter on problems and issues. There are also other companies that did not find the Singapore strategy congenial and who either chose to go elsewhere or were actively discouraged by the EDB. But it is interesting to note that the EDB leaders are convinced that when a potential investor chose not to invest in Singapore, it was invariably because the strategy did not fit. It was never thought to be because of poor service or dissatisfaction with the EDB's efforts. These perceptions are hard to check because it is not easy to locate the decision makers who chose *not* to invest in Singapore; in any case, such optimistic self-perceptions illustrate the extraordinary self-confidence that the EDB developed.

For our present purpose it is important to see how the EDB's basic assumptions created an approach to potential investors that meshed with what many companies were looking for. From a Western perspective, one is struck by the fact that the EDB appeared to do everything "right" vis-à-vis its customers and was therefore able to attract a large number of foreign investors as called for by their strategy. If "delighted customers" is one characteristic of an effective organization, the EDB would rate high on this dimension. What is less clear, however, is whether the local companies are as delighted as the MNCs. As we will see later, in spite of all the schemes developed to help the locals, problems remain in this arena.

By way of summary, table 9.1 presents a list of the factors cited by the companies, organized into major categories. As was emphasized by the informants, there were generally many reasons why an investor chose Singapore. We should be cautious in looking for the one or two "key" causal factors. Most of the managers involved in these decisions considered most of the factors on the list shown in table 9.1 and made complex mental calculations to decide on Singapore rather than some other Southeast Asian country. It should also be noted that different ones of these factors had primary importance at different stages in Singapore's evolution. For example, low wages ceased to be an attracting factor as Singapore's success brought wages up to much higher levels in the 1980s.

Table 9.1
Master list of pro-Singapore factors

Geographic location
  Access to markets
  Access to suppliers
  Access to raw materials
  Access to Asian customers

Cultural factors
  English language
  English laws
  English systems (i.e., accounting system)
  Chinese heritage—a window to and contact with China

Government strategy and attitudes
  Political stability
  Absence of any form of corruption
  Congruence with Singapore's long-range strategy
  Degree of business orientation of government
  Degree to which government seeks and wants industry
  Logic of Singapore's strategy, rules, and constraints
  Clarity of rules
  Consistency in applying rules and keeping promises
  Cooperation in solving problems
  Internal coordination to speed problem solution
  Willingness to become real partners with companies
  Quality of social services and planning
  Sophistication of financial community
  Ability of government to change strategy and laws in response to new
  economic conditions or other circumstances

General economic factors
  Low labor costs
  Size of local market and market potential in surrounding area
  High labor productivity
  Tax holidays (Pioneer certificates)
  Export enterprise certificates
  Investment allowances
  Financial support of all sorts (low-interest loans for cost of buildings
  and machines, installation expenses, housing, utilities)
  Equity participation by Singapore government
  Fixed-rate loans from DBS
  Opportunities for joint ventures, acquisitions, takeovers
  Training grants for training of Singaporeans

Favorable rental or leasing arrangements

Access to potential customers

EDB characteristics

One-stop service

Accessibility

Efficiency and speed in solving problems

Willingness to be involved in day-to-day problems

"Can-do" attitude

Deep knowledge of relevant industry and companies

Business orientation

Persuasive with facts

Willingness to make special concessions when needed

Help in locating suppliers, contractors, construction companies

Various incentive schemes

Capital assistance scheme, which allows EDB equity participation in selected industries

Small industry finance scheme and other tax incentive and loan schemes

Land and facilities

Willingness to provide enough land

Willingness to let company hold on to land

Development of land in neighboring islands

Buildings and spaces to fit what is needed

Infrastructure

Modern airport

Modern port facilities, ease and efficiency of moving things in and out

Good roads

Water and other resources

Good transportation system

Good communication and information technology

Mature commercial and banking system

Adequate housing

A clean and safe urban environment

Labor

Talented, committed, and highly productive workforce

Strong work ethic, sense of discipline

Absence of strikes and stoppages

Technical skills available—high-quality machining and tooling

favorable immigration rules and costs of importing labor

III

The EDB Culture from an Analytic Perspective

The next two chapters try to bring together the two perspectives discussed thus far into a coherent picture of the EDB organizational culture and the cultural context in which it operates. The concept of culture is first described briefly. The reader is reminded that the concept of culture is an abstraction. It is not directly visible. But its manifestations, the overt behavior of the organization, is visible. To fully understand an organization, one must not only be able to make sense of the overt manifestations, but also be able to see the underlying pattern of shared assumptions by which the organization operates. If one is looking for the strong causal factors that explain how any social system works, it is those underlying tacit shared assumptions that are the strongest causal forces and that can be thought of as the "essence" of the culture.

10

The Core Assumptions of the EDB's Cultural Context

The Concept of Culture

Culture is an intrinsically abstract concept that integrates and explains the shared overt and visible behavioral rituals, beliefs, and values of a group. So far I have attempted to describe the EDB in these overt terms but, in terms of culture, what I have been describing is like the surface of a lily pond—these are only the visible, palpable aspects of the EDB culture. Just as one cannot understand the dynamics of the lily pond without examining the stalks, the roots, and the composition of the water and mud under the surface of the pond (the elements that create what is on the surface), so one cannot understand culture without looking for the roots, the nutrients, and the principles of growth that explain the surface phenomena one sees in the organization.

This way of thinking about culture is shown diagrammatically in figure 10.1. The most surface level of the culture, exemplified by some of the descriptive material covered in the previous chapters, can be thought of as the observable *artifacts* of the organization. The artifacts are very palpable and vivid, but they are hard to decipher because of the likelihood that the observer will project his or her own cultural assumptions onto them. Observing the patterns of color and distribution of blossoms on the lily pond does not reveal the nature of the root system, the depth of the pond, or the nutrients or pollutants that may be in the water or the mud underneath.

To begin to understand a culture, one must then move to the next level of inquiry by asking members of the organization *why* they do certain things, which usually elicits what one could call the *espoused values* of the organization. At this level one has the official

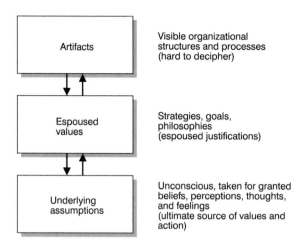

Figure 10.1
The levels of organizational culture

philosophy, the mission statement, and the various justifications that members use to explain their behavior. The observer will often note, however, inconsistencies between the espoused values and what the overt behavior or artifacts suggest.

To resolve such inconsistencies it is necessary to go to a further level of inquiry, the level of *shared tacit assumptions.*[1] Shared tacit assumptions are the real drivers of the observed behavior and are therefore what one can think of as the underlying *essence* of the culture, the hidden part of the lily pond. Such tacit assumptions often complement each other in complex and subtle ways and, if the organization has a reasonably long history, become patterned into a system or paradigm.

In other words, to fully understand the meaning of different observed behaviors and the espoused values, one must understand the underlying paradigm that the members of the organization use to structure their reality. One can think of such paradigms as "shared mental models" that structure how the members of an organization perceive, think about, and feel about themselves and the environment around them. Once one has identified the components of the paradigm, one can then also track the possible origins of those components in historical and broader cultural terms.

Such shared mental models do not reveal themselves easily, precisely because they are tacit and taken for granted. To decipher a cultural paradigm at this deeper level generally requires the joint efforts of an outside participant observer working with one or more insiders who are willing to try to explain observed anomalies or inconsistencies by exploring their own assumptions. Neither one alone can do it, but their joint inquiry efforts can bring the tacit assumptions to the surface. Once a tacit assumption has been surfaced, it can then be validated by (1) external testing of how much of the explicit behavior of the organization it explains, and (2) internal testing of how much it makes sense to the members of the organization itself once it is made conscious and visible.[2]

In the case of the EDB, this kind of inquiry made it apparent that two different paradigms were operating. One paradigm consists primarily of a set of assumptions that Singapore's leaders held about economic development. These assumptions are shared by the EDB, but they also provide a broader context within which the EDB operates. The other paradigm consists of a set of assumptions about how the EDB structures and manages itself. In this chapter I will present the contextual paradigm and in the next chapter the paradigm that underlies more specifically how the EDB operates. The two paradigms together must be viewed as a total system rather than as individual elements. What makes the EDB work is the simultaneous and coordinated effect of all of the different shared tacit assumptions.[3]

The Contextual Paradigm—Assumptions about the Role of Government in Economic Development

The contextual paradigm is shown in figure 10.2. It consists of six interlocking and interrelated shared tacit assumptions that reflect the mental models of the early leaders of Singapore and are largely taken for granted today. I call this a contextual paradigm because these assumptions are shared by the Singapore government in general and thus provide a cultural context within which the EDB operates. At the same time they are assumptions held by leaders and members of the EDB itself and thus influence more directly how the EDB operates.

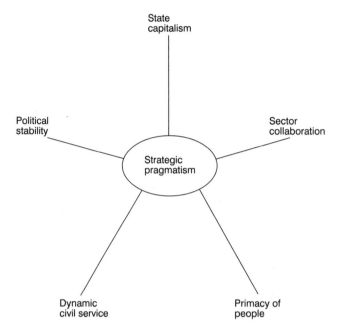

Figure 10.2
The shared tacit assumptions of the cultural context

"State Capitalism"—Government Involvement in Private Enterprise

Our government has always been a development capitalist. Jurong Industrial Estate was developed by our government and the EDB in the early 1960's to spearhead our industrialization. Singapore Airlines was a major and successful development project; so were NatSteel and the Jurong, Keppel and Sembawang shipyards. Likewise the Singapore Technologies Group of companies were nurtured and developed over two decades. When they succeeded, we put them in the marketplace where they deserved to be. We have never played around with venture capital in the U.S. way. We are not out to make short-term capital gains. The EDB investment company intends to use our funds in a deliberate and developmental way. For example, recently we took a 26 per-cent share in the Texas Instruments-Hewlett Packard-Canon-EDB joint investment in a US$300 million plant for DRAM 4M wafer fabrication. Our aim is to help create a new business in the semi-conductor industry. When the project is running smoothly after its gestation period, TI has the option to take up our stake. We can then move our development capital to another worthy project. (Philip Yeo, interview in *Singapore Business,* August 1991, p. 26)

Government is the great worrier. No individual has the resources to do what a government can do. When government abdicates, individuals suffer. (Philip Yeo, quoted in the *Financial Times*, 18 April 1994)

One of the original motivators for government involvement in economic development was the shortage of entrepreneurs willing to bear some of the risks of development. As the above quote suggests, ideologically the leadership always had a strong market orientation and would have preferred for the private sector to manage the entire development effort, but all of the chairmen emphasized that there was not enough money available to create a defense industry and an infrastructure if the government itself did not invest. Such investments were always made with the intention of privatizing as soon as possible, as in the case of Singapore Telecom and Singapore Airlines. It appeared that the EDB and many of Singapore's ministers operated as government functionaries, but ideologically they *thought like capitalists.* If one had to spell out the tacit assumption that lay behind their behavior, one could state it as follows:

Singapore's leaders and the EDB assumed and took it for granted that government could and should play an active entrepreneurial role in economic development, and should therefore exercise leadership through a quasi-government statutory board like the EDB.

In chapter 2, I attempted to show historically why this assumption came to be so strongly held and how it evolved, but there is little doubt that Singapore started with a concept of what some analysts have called "state-run capitalism"[4] and that the EDB started with the assumption that being part of the government and employing some civil servants was the "normal and correct" way to do things. The fact that the first chairman of the EDB was a senior civil servant clearly reflected and reinforced this assumption.

A comparison between Singapore and Hong Kong highlights this assumption in that Hong Kong was a city-state where "true" private entrepreneurship was highly encouraged and rampant. In contrast, Singapore has had a much more "controlled" but development-oriented entrepreneurship. The government has controlling interests in some companies and/or created companies with government subsidies and financial support during the early, risky periods. Such companies were typically managed either by civil servants (if they had the talent) or by professional managers brought in from the outside. Some of these civil servants eventually became independent entrepreneurs or general managers themselves.

From the point of view of understanding the success of the EDB, we should note how important it was to investors that the EDB and the rest of the Singapore government "thought like businessmen" and seemed to "care about business." Officially and by job titles, EDB members could be thought of as bureaucrats, but their mental model was clearly that of entrepreneurs, marketers, salesmen, and long-range strategy planners.

Absolute Long-Range Political Stability

A closely connected second core assumption that came to dominate Singaporean thinking is really a cluster of three interconnected assumptions that can be stated as follows:

Singapore's political leaders assumed (1) that economic development must precede political development, (2) that long-range successful economic development could only occur if there was political stability, and (3) that political stability could be achieved and maintained only by firm but benign government controls that steer all segments of the society.

The complicated historical roots of these assumptions were reviewed in chapter 2 reflecting (1) the events of the 1950s as Singapore in the postwar and post–Japanese occupation period began to fight for its own liberation from colonial rule, (2) the island mentality and accompanying sense of vulnerability that was felt particularly by Singapore's leaders, and (3) the strong sense of mission that the leadership developed that Singapore could and should become an economically developed nation. In other words, economic development became the primary mission to which all else was to be subordinated. As one of the ministers put it during my interview: "The key to Singapore was to put economics over politics. If politics leads while people are still hungry, they will simply look for new leaders; but if you figure out how to feed the people, the leaders who succeed in doing that will gain credibility and will succeed in building the society" (1993 interview).

If Singapore's leaders felt that certain kinds of social controls were needed to ensure economic development, these were imposed, but always with the accompanying rationale of how this would help economic development. If the controls or incentives did not work, they were abandoned and other policies or controls were put in their place. But the basic assumption that economic development justifies social control was never challenged as long as Singapore was succeeding in its development efforts. And what drove this process was always the concern to make Singapore an attractive place for foreign investment and thereby to improve the economic lot of Singaporeans. As Lee Kuan Yew had argued, the best way to avoid communism is to give people jobs and housing. And as the leadership saw it, to create jobs and housing requires a highly disciplined, politically stable society.

It is especially important to understand the depth of feeling around this assumption because without such understanding the observer or visitor to Singapore cannot appreciate why the society seems to be so controlled, even on seemingly trivial issues such as prohibiting the importing of chewing gum or imposing severe penalties for urinating in public places or failing to flush after urinating in public toilets. Political stability was seen to be necessary to create an environment that would be clean, safe, and attractive. Singapore's leaders knew that stereotypes of Asian cities were filled with perceptions of dirtiness, crime, instability, and corruption. Singapore, under the British, had itself developed something of a reputation as a ribald, dirty city, which may in part explain Lee Kuan Yew's almost obsessive efforts to present the new Singapore in a new light. If foreign investors were to be attracted, Singapore had to be attractive to them, and that meant creating an environment that would immediately be perceived not only as stable but as attractive, clean, safe, and efficient as well. From the point of view of the leadership, the population had to learn fast how to create such an environment, and that meant going down to detailed behavioral incentives and controls.

Collaboration among Sectors

A third assumption that undoubtedly grew out of the joint experience of the early leaders of Singapore reflected their sense of how the basic sectors of the society should relate to each other:

Singapore's political leaders assumed that economic development could only succeed if business, labor, and government actively collaborated with each other in fulfilling the common goal of building the nation ("Singapore, Inc.").

Interorganizational collaboration was considered vital in order to provide the *incentives* and *infrastructure* needed to develop the manufacturing and service sectors, that is, roads, communication facilities, land, financial support for investment and training, a well-trained and motivated labor pool, housing, etc. One of the most notable aspects of this way of thinking was the decision to give the trade unions some responsibilities as owners and managers by having them own and operate one of the taxi companies and one of the insurance companies in Singapore. Some industrial relations analysts might regard this as co-optation and undermining the labor movement but, from Singapore's point of view, getting labor on their side was paramount, especially in view of the proximity of a communist China to the north. The Winsemius report had stressed that the only way Singapore could pull itself out of its economic doldrums in the 1950s was to get *everyone* in the society to pull together to make it happen.

"Everyone" meant not only the major for-profit sectors of society, but also the various departments of the government and civil service. According to one senior minister, all the members of the Singapore government felt collectively responsible for Singapore's future. The cabinet functioned as a collectively responsible body and therefore shared information among members. There was no "turf" that the different ministers had to worry about. He also noted that "this culture is proliferated through newcomers learning right away that if they try to be too individualistic or to develop their own turf they immediately learn from their elders that this is inappropriate."

The communication system of having everything done through reports and papers circulated to everybody appeared to be an important structural element in making this kind of openness and transparency occur, and thereby stimulating collective responsibility. Teamwork was thus built into Singapore's basic governance model, a point that is especially important to grasp in light of the stereotype that Singapore's fortunes were primarily or even solely the product of Lee Kuan Yew's authoritarian style of leadership. He certainly provided the energy and strength, but he was always surrounded by a set of colleagues whose team effort was then, and continues to be now, crucial to Singapore's success.

The concept of the EDB as a one-stop agency hinged on these collaborative relationships. The EDB had to have the persuasive power to get the Jurong Town Corporation to provide the right kind of land deal, the immigration service to issue the permits for importing needed labor, the ministry of labor to allow necessary wage concessions, the ministry of trade and industry to authorize Pioneer status and other financial incentives, and so on. In the previous chapters we saw how important it was for the foreign investors to be able to count on the EDB to solve all these intergovernment agency problems. We also saw in Ng Pock Too's account of the creation of the first Singapore air show the importance of Philip Yeo in the ministry of defense making airport time available for a civilian event.

What made much of this kind of collaboration possible was not only the common mission of building Singapore, but the high level of acquaintanceship and trust that existed within the leadership group. Many of them knew each other from school days, many had worked in the EDB early in their career and then gone on to other government posts but retained much of the EDB spirit, and many of them saw each other regularly because of Singapore's small size. The EDB cultivated these relationships and made sure that if problems needed to be solved, the EDB would have available the necessary connections and trusted relationships to solve the problem, a characteristic that reflects, of course, elements of the Chinese culture in general.

One former chairman of the EDB articulated it as follows:

The EDB must have influence over other government agencies, i.e., be perceived and function as the most senior coordination mechanism for economic development.

The chairman (CEO) of the EDB must be a trusted friend, leader, and effective administrator (not necessarily an economist).

Intersector and interorganizational collaboration can only be achieved by building a network of human relationships characterized by high degrees of mutual acquaintance and trust. (1994 interview)

The strength of this assumption in the *contemporary* context was made clear to me in my first briefing at the EDB headquarters during the 1993 visit when I was shown figure 10.3 to illustrate how the EDB relates to the rest of Singapore's government. The figure shows nine different government agencies, all of whom have to coordinate to help "Singapore, Inc." become strategically what it wants to be.

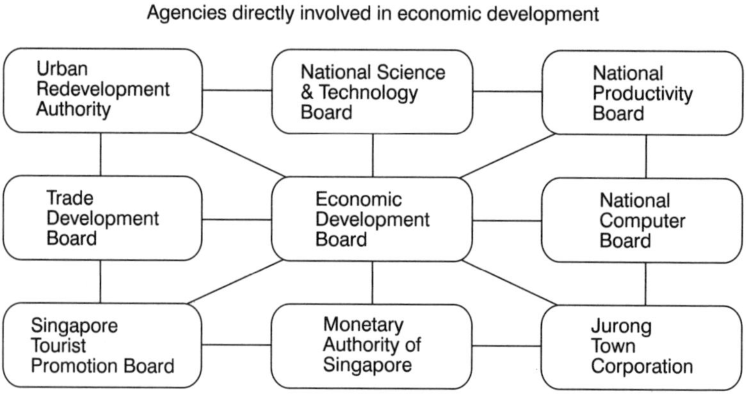

Agencies directly involved in economic development

Figure 10.3
The EDB's direct linkages to other government units

In this process, the EDB is trying to be very open in sharing information and is trying to encourage the other organizations to be
equally collaborative and sharing. In many instances this means
trying to get those other agencies to overcome their "civil service
mentality." The EDB is defined to investors as the "lead agency, the
coordinator and facilitator across the various other government agencies, working with the philosophy of minimizing internal and external boundaries."

To build relationships with all these other agencies, three different
mechanisms are used: (1) *infiltration,* by which I mean either that
EDB alumni become key members of the management of various
other agencies as their career progresses, or current EDB managers
hold joint appointments in both the EDB and other agencies; (2)
creating EDB babies, that is, new government boards have actually
been the result of concepts and needs identified by the EDB itself or
were spinoffs from the EDB; (3) *stimulation or animation,* in that the
EDB views itself as a pioneer who gets things started, not as an
organization that actually runs things. But clearly, the key underlying
assumption continues to be that things work best if you work in a
partnership collegial relationship with others in the service of
higher-order goals such as Singapore, Inc.[5]

Minister for Health Yeo Chow Tong, who is now minister for trade
and industry, the ministry to which the EDB reports, reinforced this
point in his 1993 interview by noting that the success of the EDB

was largely due to the fact that it was given the authority to cut across all the various turfs that exist in the government and, by virtue of the relationships they had built with the other government agencies, they were in the position not just to make promises but to actually deliver on what they had promised.

Similarly, in his May 1993 visit to China, Senior Minister Lee Kuan Yew made a point of saying that "Singapore has something which is valuable to any Chinese city which is not easily obtained (and) that is *the experience of how to integrate development*" (*Business Times,* 13 May 1993, italics mine).

An overt manifestation of this "skill" is that Philip Yeo, on selected visits to companies, will bring along the CEOs of the Jurong Town Corporation, the National Computer Board, Singapore Telecom, and the National Science and Technology Board. The purpose of having this delegation come along is to have available the key people who could answer any technical questions that might arise around a given project, and make commitments as needed. Second, the presence of these other CEOs make the teamwork within Singapore highly visible. Not only is it obvious that the different boards get along well with each other by virtue of their joint presence but, even more important, any promises of future services that would be delivered by Singapore could be checked on the spot with the relevant executives from the other organizations. Clearly the assumption of sector collaboration has survived over the decades and become one of the differentiating features of Singapore's strength.

An Incorruptible, Competent Civil Service: Clear Rules and Kept Promises

A fourth assumption that makes up the paradigm was based on (1) the Chinese cultural legacy that rulers must be exemplars of virtue,[6] (2) the British traditions of a "clean civil service," and (3) the early recognition on the part of Singapore's leaders that overseas investors would only be attracted to a developing nation in which there was not only political stability but also a competent government, a clear set of rules, and an absence of corruption. In assumption form, this point can be stated as follows:

Singapore's political leaders assumed that favorable economic conditions for investors would be guaranteed only if the government and civil service were competent, incorruptible, and operated with an open and consistent set of rules that were vigorously enforced.

The idea of a competent civil service system goes back in history. Bellows in his 1989 study of the Singapore bureaucracy quotes a 1970 speech that makes the point well:

The Singaporean civil service is a British creation (although its elitist, meritocratic character and policy making functions are consistent with Confucian tradition). . . . The PAP leaders, who formed a government in June 1959, learned first-hand that a bureaucratic apparatus was essential for political survival.

. . . prior to independence, the civil service performed a number of political tasks: to protect and strengthen its own position, to defeat the pro-Communist attempt to control the government, and to make it probable that PAP leaders would remain in power after independence. In the post-independence period, the civil service remained in the center of the political process, with the following two key roles to play: 1) to initiate and nurture social well-being and economic development and 2) to develop national identity, to facilitate political integration, and to cultivate civic/ethical behavior among its citizenry.[7]

One of the most consistent points made by managers who had decided to invest in Singapore was "they had clear rules and they kept their promises." What often impressed managers was the determination of the government to meet the needs of the investors, without, however, compromising their own values and rules. In other words, the investors did not always get what they wanted or demanded, but they always knew where they stood and they came to respect Singapore for being efficient without being either expedient or corrupt.

As one executive put it: "The government has high credibility, there is little corruption. One must be completely open about what one owns, and the pay for politicians and for bureaucrats is comparable to what private sector managers get. Consequently they get good people, and the civil service and government have high prestige" (1993 interview).

The sense of mission, the importance of what was being done, and the high standards set by Hon Sui Sen lent a high moral tone to the whole enterprise. This sometimes showed up in paradoxical overcontrol of some things, while other things were allowed to slip because they were not considered so relevant. One executive noted that during his stay in Singapore in 1970 he became aware that the

Singaporeans were very sympathetic to the fact that Westerners were often not used to working in a different culture. For example, because in Singapore they drove on the "wrong" side of the street, Westerners might occasionally get into trouble with parking and other traffic violations. He was told that people from his company could always count on help from the locals in taking care of tickets, etc., but he said with emphasis, "If you are ever caught in a blue movie, you've got to leave the country."

When asked what this moralistic attitude might be all about, he related it to Singapore's effort to overcome its prior reputation as a very "loose" place after the British left. He perceived Singapore as wanting to crack down on "loose morals" and to show the world that they could get things under control. So they were very hard on drug use, smoking, gum chewing in public, littering, long hair on men, and most important, any form of pornography. They felt themselves to be a kind of pioneer society that required very "straight" living.

This executive felt that if rules dealing with industrial matters were violated, punitive action was decisive and swift. For example, one clear rule was that a company was allowed to use foreign labor only up to a certain percentage of its workforce. One company kept too many of its own nonlocal people on the local payroll. The company was warned but did nothing, leading the government to order the manager of that organization out of the country, even though it was a large and prestigious multinational. The implication is that many of Singapore's rules are felt very strongly. Clients will be helped in any way that is needed so long as those basic rules are not violated.

Competence and a high degree of energy and motivation were also assumed, but these traits were not to be used for personal advancement. The strong sense of dedication to the mission of developing Singapore was supposed to override personal ambitions, and if it did not, if officials were discovered to have taken bribes or in other ways personally broken the rules, punishment was swift and very public. An example occurred recently where one of my informants, the then-chief executive officer of the Trade and Development Board, was discovered to have personally profited from some of his connections. He was swiftly tried, convicted, and imprisoned, and the press made an example of his case to reaffirm the incorruptibility of the government.

To maintain such standards requires not only a personal ethic but an institutional structure to monitor, control, and punish. Bellows in his analysis of Singapore's civil service summarizes some of these mechanisms of recruitment, coordination, and control by identifying several key institutions: (1) the Establishment Unit of the prime minister's office, which handles the assignment to the most senior posts; (2) the Public Service Commission, responsible for the training and development of the top civil servants; (3) The Pyramid Club, created in the mid-1960s of 150 or so top leaders from government, business, and academia, which facilitates contact and discussion among the various sectors; and (4) the Corrupt Practices Investigation Bureau located in the prime minister's office and empowered through the Corrupt Practices Act to investigate any and all corrupt practices in the public or private sector. No one is immune from investigation under this act.

If any civil servant is identified—with evidence—as corrupt, the CPIB will sue him in court. The Prevention of Corrupt Practices Act broadly defines offenses as corruptly soliciting or receiving gratification as an inducement for doing or forbearing to do any act pertaining to any official transaction. It provides punishment both for carrying out corrupt acts as well as conspiracy. The result is practically no corruption.[8]

The obsession with cleanliness and rules was highlighted in the recent controversy over the caning of American teenager Michael Fay for allegedly vandalizing cars by spray-painting them. The punishment of caning seemed harsh to many Western observers, but it must be understood in the context of how serious vandalism is to the Singaporean government. One can speculate that from Singapore's point of view, if vandalism and destruction of property (Fay had also "acquired" some twenty-five street signs) are not harshly dealt with, it would undermine the whole image of Singapore as a safe, clean, and incorruptible state.

I was in Singapore when Fay's sentence was announced but not yet carried out, so took the opportunity to ask Singaporeans what they thought of the whole affair. They gave the predictable response that laws are laws and Americans should not be immune from them, but also provided a less predictable response that caning, as a punishment method inherited from the British, was used primarily *because it works.* They pointed out that immigrants sometimes attempted to remain illegally in Singapore after their legitimate stay as guest workers. They would be deported, but often would be found later to have reentered Singapore. Jail was said not to be an answer because for most of them the conditions in jail were believed to be better than the conditions from which they had escaped. However, when caning was introduced for second offenders, illegal immigration dropped dramatically.

The facts pertaining to such matters are hard to come by, especially where different cultural interpretations and values color the facts themselves. For our purposes, the most important point is the strength of the beliefs that Singaporeans hold about their system, and the degree to which they justify those beliefs and assumptions ultimately on economic and pragmatic grounds.

Primacy of People and Meritocracy

The fifth and perhaps most important shared tacit assumption was revealed in the discussion with Senior Minister Lee Kuan Yew himself as he reminisced about the origins of the EDB:

We realized that the only resource Singapore had was its people and their potential; it must therefore pick the best of them and develop them to the maximum of their potential. (1993 interview)

This theme was strongly reiterated in 1991 as Singapore looked to its future:

People are, and will always be, our most precious resource. . . . The future will be no different. In the next lap the size of our population and the quality of our people will determine how successfully we fare. . . . Singaporeans will have to work hard, work smart, and work together. . . . As Asians, we believe that education is the key to a better life. . . . Our schools will not only push for higher levels of academic achievement. They will also keep alive our Asian values and traditions. . . . produce morally upright, diligent, compassionate citizens. . . . Our young people will eventually graduate and enter the workforce. It is crucial that they have good work ethics. The school in tandem with the home will instill and reinforce good personal habits which will lead to good work attitudes.[9]

It would not have been possible to build an effective economic development board, a collaborative set of relationships between government, business, and labor, and a competent, noncorrupt civil service without a deep belief in the value of people and faith in their abilities. This belief showed up in the commitment to English as a common language, the development of a common primary educational system, and the heavy investment that Singapore has made in the education and training of its population. Commitment to people was also reflected in the government's decision to solve the unemployment and housing problem, premised on the assumption that the best guarantee of political stability was an improving standard of living for the population. When Singaporeans are quizzed about their reaction to the social controls imposed on them by the government, one of the most common answers is that they accept them because they can see the positive economic results that derive from those controls.

A commitment to people is combined with a commitment to competence and merit. To create sector collaboration it is necessary to have a good network of trusted relationships, but even more important, the members of the network have to be competent—the best and the brightest. In a 1971 speech Lee Kuan Yew put it starkly:

Outstanding men in civil service, the police, the armed forces, chairmen of statutory boards and their top administrators have worked out the details of policies set by the government and seen to their implementation. These people come from different language schools. Singapore is a meritocracy. And these men have risen to the top by their own merit, hard work, and high performance. Together they are a closely knit and coordinated hard core. If all 300 were to crash in one jumbo jet, then Singapore will disintegrate. That shows how small the base is for our leadership in politics, economics, and security. We have to, and we will, enlarge this base.[10]

It is this emphasis on merit combined with economic development as a priority that creates in organizations like the EDB and in other government agencies the impression that one is dealing not with bureaucracies, but with private sector organizations. Whenever one reads about the EDB or meets members of the EDB, one tends to forget that one is dealing with a government organization made up of civil servants and employees of a statutory board. The EDB runs as if it were a private company with all the concerns for efficiency, productivity, and service that one associates with a well-run organization.

Merit is defined primarily by academic performance in an educational system taken over from the British. Cambridge O- and A-level examinations are a crucial measure for advancement to higher education, and getting a degree at a prestigious university is a further measure of merit. A bias toward science, engineering, and technology is also implicit in "merit," and, as I will indicate in later chapters, raises some questions about the future.

Strategic Pragmatism

I have put strategic pragmatism at the center of the culture diagram to symbolize that this assumption is, in a sense, the critical glue that ties the paradigm together. In assumption form it can be stated as follows:

It is possible and essential to have a vision and master strategy for the development of Singapore, and at the same time one must use all of one's practical intelligence to pragmatically and innovatively make it happen without at any point compromising the vision.

What I am trying to convey here is that all members of the EDB and most other government officials, ministers, and members of the business community have been able to combine and integrate their long-range vision with their day-to-day commitment to doing things intelligently to solve the problems of the moment. The common comment that "things work in Singapore" can be seen as one result of that integrative way of thinking because it reflects not only the mundane observations about basic utilities functioning efficiently, but that the whole infrastructure is intelligently planned with a long-range vision in mind.

A number of examples can be given from different sectors. The Provident Fund as a forced savings scheme to which both employee and employer automatically contribute provides the government cash flow and an account against which employees can borrow to finance home ownership. The designation of different city zones, the issuance of permits to car owners for access to those zones, and the designation of times of the week and day when access is allowed keeps traffic moving smoothly in a potentially very congested city. The tying of financial incentives and tax breaks to the number of children in a family allows the government to change the policy as it diagnoses the need for more or fewer children.

The development of the growth triangle and the concept of regionalization allows Singapore to expand available land for manufacturing, housing, and tourism while building up joint ventures with neighbors who provide potential markets, labor sources, and security for a small and vulnerable city-state. The decision to tie their industrial development to foreign multinationals serves a similar function of providing stability and security, though Singaporeans are aware that if the MNCs pull out for any of a number of reasons, Singapore is economically in difficulty. To deal with that issue, they are pushing hard to develop their own industry, to get the MNCs to grow roots in Singapore in the form of regional headquarters, R & D centers, and distribution centers, and to develop joint ventures in ASEAN and China.

And, back to the mundane level, the same commitment to making things work is evident in the zoo, the Jurong bird park, the botanical gardens, and other recreational facilities where the arrangements and facilities are maximally tourist oriented. For example, the bird park can be seen from an overhead air-conditioned monorail, a not-unimportant technical solution in a country located near the equator.

What happens when the problems and needs of an investor or tourist require compromise or a bending of the rules? Apart from situations where the rules are not so central, as in the above case of traffic tickets for inexperienced Westerners, the Chinese cultural legacy of not being contradictory or critical to one's face comes into operation. If the problem requires a solution that would not fit into Singapore's strategy or would violate its more important rules, the EDB will find a creative way to solve it that will fit, or will gently "negotiate," or somehow let the client know that he or she is asking for something that is not possible.

Personal examples of such "negotiation" arose in the interaction around this book, when I asked for feedback on early draft chapters from specific people I thought most likely to be able to judge the accuracy of what I had written. In the short run I received only an acknowledgment that the material had been received, but no feedback. Some time later I received detailed feedback from the project manager. It was up to me to realize that this feedback incorporated the reactions and questions of my original informants, but the method of feedback saved them from having to tell me negative things to my face, a situation that our relative statuses would not have allowed. The problems get solved, but they get solved on the EDB's terms and in line with their strategies, values, and principles.

In the economic development arena it was pointed out to me over and over again that early in its history the EDB wanted "any kind" of investment, but once they had achieved the objective of full employment in the early 1970s, they became much more selective. They then screened potential investors very carefully because they wanted to ensure that even though businesses could be set up quite freely in Singapore if it made commercial sense to the investor, Singapore's limited resources made it essential for the EDB to facilitate only those projects that met their longer-run strategy. The strategic elements to be considered varied somewhat over the years but involved (1) the number and kinds of jobs that would be created, (2) the kind of knowledge or technology that would be brought in, (3) the likelihood of a "multiplier effect" of more projects being created by the original project, (4) the export potential of the industry, (5) the size and prestige of the company in terms of its ability to attract other companies, (6) the range of products and services in related areas that a given company would stimulate, especially in local industries, (7) the degree to which Singapore needed a given technology, (8) the degree to which a given company was connected to other companies whose entry Singapore desired, (9) the potential in the project for building and cementing ties to specific other countries, and (10) the degree to which the company was willing to become a long-range partner with Singapore.

Companies that were in the wrong products, were too short-term oriented, had the wrong kind of technology, would not help Singapore upgrade its population, were environmentally irresponsible, or were just plain "undesirable" were not encouraged. Recall that from the beginning Chairman Hon Sui Sen wanted thirty-year renewable leases because of the possibility that a given company might no longer qualify for such lower-cost industrial land because their business activity had changed substantially.

When one listens to the executives, they emphasize how much Singapore has bent over backward to solve their problems and to communicate how much it wanted them. On the other hand, when one reads the EDB cases one is struck by the degree to which the EDB targeted and selected companies, and only after a company was viewed as fitting into the longer-range strategy did the EDB really go all-out to solve that company's day-to-day problems. The EDB also used its strategic intent as a sales tool, pointing out, for example, to AT&T how advantageous it would be for both Singapore and the company to form a partnership. In those instances the EDB showed itself to be a tough negotiator to get what it wanted.

What I am trying to convey in the label of *strategic pragmatism* is a combination of (1) intelligence based on Singapore's meritocratic selection and promotion policies, (2) a clear long-range vision of wanting to become a fully developed nation, and (3) an extraordinary capacity to identify and solve the immediate problems for themselves, for their local and overseas businesses, and for tourists. This is not to say that they have solved all of their problems. Rather, what strikes one is the commitment to solving them, and to doing so in an intelligent way.

Summary

The contextual paradigm consisting of the assumptions that government can and should be directly involved in economic development, can and should create an absolutely stable political system, must stimulate collaboration among the sectors of the society, must create an efficient and corruption-free government, and must build a meritocracy based on recognizing the importance of people as a resource creates a business-oriented mentality that investors respond to very positively precisely because they sense that "the Singapore government is business oriented and thinks like we do."

The best way to capture the essence of this paradigm is with the awkward image of "strategic pragmatism." Based on my own impressions and reflecting the views of the investors, the EDB is able to project an image of readiness to solve whatever problem comes along, and to do so rapidly and efficiently. But at the same time, one always feels that they have an agenda, a purpose of their own, a set of values and principles that they will not violate.

11

The Cultural Paradigm of the Organization: Assumptions about Organization and Management in the EDB

The operational culture of the EDB is a set of paradoxes and anomalies from a Western point of view, but its tacit assumptions are consistent with each other and enable the organization to function effectively. The paradigm of how the EDB works is shown in figure 11.1.

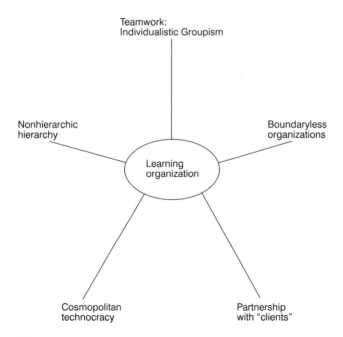

Figure 11.1
The shared tacit assumptions of the EDB's culture

Teamwork: Individualistic Groupism

One of the most striking characteristics of how the EDB works is the seeming comfort of its employees with their challenging individual assignments and their equal comfort and dedication to the work team, the EDB, and to Singapore the nation-state. One sees here a cultural legacy from Confucian principles of concern for family combined with a Western concept of individual achievement leading to an assumption that may be paradoxical in the West, but is clearly workable in Singapore.

The EDB assumes that the best kind of leadership is to build a team, and that the ultimate mission of the team members is to contribute to Singapore becoming a fully developed nation.

Underlying this assumption is the reality that the EDB always had to function as a team because it was a small organization in which members therefore had to help each other. However, this pragmatic reason for teamwork was also supported by a cultural tendency to be comfortable in a team setting, a kind of comfort that is noticeably absent in many Western teams. At the same time, all of the EDB officers were educated in settings where individual achievement was highly valued, were constantly exposed to multinational company managers who lived by individualistic competitive rules, and were encouraged to develop their individual careers within the EDB. How then does this work out?

One regional director who has been with the organization about five years described the EDB as an organization in which "the intellectual level was unbelievable, way beyond expectations." She felt incredibly stimulated by this environment in which there was simultaneously a tremendous individual challenge and a feeling of being part of a family and developing the sense that it is "we" who are in this together.

The organization attracts very strong individualists who do, in fact, compete with each other and notice it when someone is promoted ahead of them, but the competition is mitigated by the fact that they are all kept so busy that in effect "they have no time to compete." If you see yourself falling behind or losing out to the competition, you say to yourself, "If you don't do well now or haven't done well up to now, you can always do better in the future," which, she said, was a direct lesson from Confucianism.

She also pointed out that the intense communication and working with each other forces teamwork in that if you are too individualistic or political, you very quickly lose credibility with your colleagues and find yourself unable to do very much. So the two major distortions that could occur in the communications system—"sitting on information or, at the other extreme, hyping up information and exaggerating what you know, are both mitigated by the need to maintain credibility and trustworthiness." To get anything done you have to build support, and in order to build support you have to maintain your credibility: "Everything in the EDB has to be coordinated."

The EDB's view of itself as a team and virtually a family is partly based on everyone knowing everyone else, even though the organization is today quite large. This level of acquaintance is maintained through the many informal activities such as the weekly Friday afternoon teas, the company functions such as picnics and sports outings that families are encouraged to attend, the monthly newsletter entitled "Network" in which a variety of personal news items, especially awards and individual accomplishments, are given publicity, the general informality in terms of how people address each other and relate to each other, and the encouragement of romantic attachments among employees symbolized by the great pride in the number of married couples who met each other as EDB employees.

One of the more interesting events arranged for me and my wife was a dinner with four EDB couples, who proudly discussed how they met each other at the EDB and were encouraged to get married even though they both continued to work there. Also supportive of this team spirit is a set of personnel policies that are very flexible allowing, for example, part-time assignments or jobs in which one would not be required to travel if family responsibilities made travel difficult. The work of the EDB is, according to most employees, so intrinsically motivating that there is never any question of special arrangements being symptomatic of loss of work motivation. Rather, the EDB tries to accommodate the needs of each employee because each is viewed as being so valuable.

To be a successful performer in this kind of high-pressure family/team requires a complex ability to collaborate with others and be a true team player while, at the same time, exposing one's individual talents and skills for purposes of promotion and career progress. This kind of balancing act was facilitated by the ability to think clearly, articulate clearly, write clearly, and be able to convince others to "join one's team" in support of a project. In other words, individual talent showed up most in the individual's quality of thinking and communicating, and was then tested in the ability to create and work in a team. Individual achievement is recognized with awards and other forms of recognition, but that is above and beyond the baseline of teamwork.

To really get a job done therefore requires not only the formal knowledge of how to analyze what is on paper, but the network of acquaintance to permit identification of who knows what and who is to be consulted about what. To build that network requires a person who is comfortable in the family/team and can use the informal relationships to build an information and support network for him- or herself. Not everyone can perform in this kind of role, so we must look next at the shared tacit assumptions that underlay the recruitment and selection of staff.

Cosmopolitan Technocracy—A Technically and Interpersonally Competent Cosmopolitan Officer Corps

Hunger, tension, conflict—these are the compelling facts of life. Leave the best and brightest to find the solutions.[1]

In the 1969 EDB Annual Report there is a cogent description of the management challenges that the EDB personnel faced then and still face:

All these changes call for imaginative and progressive responses and attitudes, particularly from an entrepreneurial and managerial community attuned to modern needs.

Firstly, they must raise their sights toward wider horizons. Not only manufacturers, but also bankers, traders, transport operators, marketing services, lawyers and accountants, public administrators—especially those concerned with trade, industry, tourism, immigration, utilities and communications—and indeed academics, educators, and the press, must keep up fully with world developments. Sources of information and lines of rapid communication have to be established. Resourcefulness and ingenuity to innovate and seize new opportunities, sensitivity to external and internal changes, the correct response to new requirements and to adapt to new techniques, are essential to developing the capacity of keeping ahead in the highly competitive environment of international operations.

Secondly, to gain such expertise and experience, they must not only themselves travel abroad and develop more contacts, but also ensure that younger members of their staff are similarly exposed whenever possible. . . . Modern business demands a thorough knowledge of the latest sophistication in techniques at all levels. Only the willingness to make such investment will ensure sustained growth and returns.

Thirdly, they must face the growing challenge of social responsibility, for modern management realise they have an identity of interest with and inseparable from the community in which they operate. . . . They will have to take an active and leading role, with foresight and responsiveness, in such matters as improving working environment, pollution control, education and training. They must adjust to the social costs and benefits of having expanded and modernized infrastructure, skilled manpower and other social and economic facilities from which they draw their strength and resources to grow."[2]

If Singapore's fate rested on being able to attract overseas investors, the EDB had to be able to deal with many other cultures and their officers therefore had to be what sociologists have called "cosmopolitan" in their orientation.[3] At the same time, to bring in the right investors and provide good services for them once they were in Singapore, the EDB had to staff itself with a cadre of people who would be both competent marketers/salesmen and entrepreneurs. The EDB officer, therefore, had to be comfortable and knowledgeable in the global multicultural arena and at the same time very much in touch with the situation in Singapore and the potential of synergy between the multinationals and local industry. And within the EDB, officers had to be articulate, individualistic team players. Small wonder that their cartoon version of themselves depicts them as supermen and superwomen.

One can infer the shared underlying assumptions by noting the selection criteria that have operated in the hiring of new senior officers and the criteria for promotion to management.

The EDB assumed that it could only succeed if it recruited:

1. The "best and the brightest" based on scholastic performance;

2. Officers with a "cosmopolitan orientation" based on overseas education and interest in working with and in overseas business settings;

3. Officers who were technically oriented and trained because the kind of businesses that were to be promoted were usually technically based;

4. Officers who had high levels of personal initiative to be able to work in unpredictable and uncharted business and government arenas;

5. Officers and managers who were team oriented and had high levels of interpersonal skill to deal with multiple cultures, multiple hierarchical levels, and across organizational boundaries of all kinds.

It is not clear whether the early EDB leaders were conscious of all of these qualities as criteria or whether they happened to be people with such qualities and were more or less cloning themselves. But one can certainly see the rationale, much of which was explicit. With regard to the decision to hire mostly engineers, not only was Hon Sui Sen a scientist by background and predilection, but, as P. Y. Hwang put it, "a bias toward science and technology has always been in the EDB culture." In the first five-year plan for education launched in 1960, not only was equal treatment for the Malay, Tamil, Chinese, and English educational streams mandated, but emphasis was to be put on "the study of Mathematics, Science, and technical subjects."[4]

It is only in recent times that employees with a broader range of business, marketing, and financial skills have been explicitly recruited; earlier the governing assumption was that it would be easier for engineers to learn finance and marketing than for economists to learn the technical skills needed to work with investors. Note also, however, the strategic bias toward the technically based companies who would make a longer-range investment in Singapore, and the rejection of the "cowboy" who would come just to make "a fast buck."

One of the more interesting recruitment decisions was to seek graduates who had chosen to go overseas for their education. Singapore's leaders, like Lee Kuan Yew and Goh Keng Swee, represented this model and had learned from their own experience the importance of being in touch with other cultures. One can speculate that this kind of life experience made Singaporeans more able to appreciate the mentality of Western managers and therefore to build an infrastructure that would be more appealing to the multinationals. Cosmopolitanism of this sort could also have been the result of Singapore's leaders finding themselves to be sophisticated traders in an island with no potential for growth unless a manufacturing base was developed, and, given that there was no internal market, to build that manufacturing base on an export model. The EDB officers, then, had to become familiar with the economics and sociology of internationalization.

Although it was rarely mentioned as a specific criterion in the selection of people, it appears that Singaporeans who came to work for the EDB were skillful in working across cultural divides because they had all grown up in a multicultural environment—British, Chinese, Malay, and Indian. Singapore has had to integrate four major ethnic groups and many different religions, leading perhaps to a level of cultural sophistication that made it easier to work with Westerners. This cultural sophistication (at least in the educated elite) and their knowledge of and comfort with English differentiates them somewhat from their counterparts in Hong Kong.

Much of the cultural sophistication of young Singaporeans resulted from the availability of government scholarships for university education in the Commonwealth countries, in Japan, in Europe, and in the United States. If young Singaporeans passed their Cambridge A-level exams at a sufficiently high level, they became eligible for one of these overseas scholarships. If they were going to a non-English-speaking country, they would spend a year or so learning the language and then complete their university education in that country.[5] Acceptance of the scholarship "bonded" the graduate to five or more years of government service, thereby creating a good pool from which the EDB could recruit its officers. In that process it appeared that the EDB carefully targeted certain individuals for later recruitment and followed their career outside the EDB until such time as they were needed or until their skills and attitudes became known. This point is important because it reflected an elitist attitude in the EDB that not only helped in convincing young people to come to work there, but also served as an immediate source of motivation. Several interviewees noted that when they realized that the EDB had had its eye on them for some time, this increased their motivation greatly and made them feel immediately like they were part of a special elite if they got a post in the EDB.

The creation of such a "cosmopolitan technocracy" is illustrated by the career history of Chong Lit-Cheong, whom I first met when he was the center director at the EDB's San Francisco office. Chong is a Singaporean whose father was a trader in the leather business; his mother was a housewife. He went to a prestigious high school in Singapore called the Raffles Institution, was skilled in mathematics and science, and so decided on a career in electrical engineering. A good student, he chose to seek a scholarship to a prestigious university and applied to various places including the University of Tokyo. He did win a scholarship to that university as well as to an Australian university, but chose to go to Tokyo because it was a better institution even though that meant taking a full year to learn Japanese. In seeking his education overseas he also launched a pattern of working outside of Singapore, which characterized his later career as well.

Following the successful completion of his engineering degree in four years, he returned to Singapore and entered the national service for the required two and one-half years. One is assigned to a service based on one's background and knowledge, so Chong was put into the officers cadet school and ended up in the army signal corps. Following his military service, he joined the ministry of defense in the air logistics department's electronics group. He ended up in that particular ministry because that was where he was most needed. He says he could have refused that assignment, but there was fairly strong pressure to go into the ministry in which one was needed. (His own aspirations at that time had been to go to the National University and become a teacher, but somewhere along the line he gave up that idea.)

Chong was then twenty-six and, at the end of a year in the ministry of defense, he decided he wanted to do something different. He applied to several places, including the EDB and the Schlumberger Company, to get some exposure outside of Singapore. He learned about Schlumberger through a Japanese friend and, upon receiving an offer from them, decided to join their oil exploration division in Italy.

His general plan had been to work for one year and then return to school to obtain his MBA at the University of Toronto. However, the work in oil exploration as a test engineer using his electronics skill to determine how deep wells should be drilled was so exciting that he decided to stay in Italy for three more years and give up on the Toronto MBA; he had in the meantime also applied to the business school at Manchester University. After his three-year stint, Schlumberger sent him back to Singapore where he had to decide what to do next, a decision influenced by two factors. The EDB, which had kept his records from his previous application and had tracked his career because he was the kind of cosmopolitan who fitted their employee model, offered him a job. He had also met Adelaine Lim, his future wife, who was then employed by the EDB in Singapore.

Chong again gave up his MBA aspirations and joined the EDB as a senior industry officer (SIO) for electro-optics in the electronic systems group. This job required him to promote the electro-optics industry by locating companies and figuring out how to get them to become involved in various ways with Singapore. Chong's next job was to be the western regional director of U.S. operations, based in San Francisco. His wife quit the EDB and took a job in the United States so that they could live together. However, when the international manpower division was set up, the EDB recruited her back to become a center director and assigned her to the San Francisco office as well. This arrangement was considered desirable because it kept them together but working in different divisions, each as a center director.

The concern with recruiting and developing high-talent individuals can be traced to Lee Kuan Yew himself, who not only told the story of "giving his best man (Hon Sui Sen) to Dr. Goh" when the EDB was formed, but who subsequently became concerned that the civil service needed to learn from the private sector how companies attracted and developed their managerial talent. He said he canvassed a number of companies that were operating in Singapore and was very attracted to the system that had been developed by psychologists for the Royal Dutch Shell Company, bearing the acronym HAIR. The H stood for "helicopter quality" or the ability to rise above the immediate scene and see it from a total and overall perspective. The A stood for analytical ability. The I stood for imagination, the ability to see things from new and creative perspectives, and the R stood for realism, having one's feet firmly planted on the ground. Senior Minister Lee pointed out that he wanted all four qualities in the people whom he selected. To achieve this he mandated that the entire civil service adopt the Shell program, distributed the booklet describing the system in detail to everyone, and asked Shell to train people in the use of the system. Though the EDB does not use the system explicitly, these qualities are sought in their recruits. And one can see a connection between this system and strategic pragmatism in that all four qualities are necessary to be both a visionary and an effective immediate problem solver.

One of the most salient characteristics of the EDB officers is their ability to communicate orally and in writing. So much of the work is in being able to think things out, articulate one's conclusions, and sell them to others, that a lack of any one of these three qualities immediately puts the person at a disadvantage. And because everyone is very bright, ideas have to be good ones or they won't sell. The candidate for a position is not only interviewed by members of the personnel department and senior management, but he or she is given one or two standardized psychological tests (e.g., the California Psychological Profile) to determine an overall personality profile. All the information is then evaluated globally rather than in terms of specific trait scores or profiles.

"Best and brightest" in the EDB context thus means good ideas, articulately expressed. It is not just that they express their ideas well and persuasively, but that the ideas themselves are creative and make good sense. Implicit in the concept of the meritocracy is the assumption that the leaders are smart, know what they are doing, and do the right thing for the society. One gets the sense that this commitment to intelligent problem solving and planning is deeply embedded in the EDB officers and managers. "Win-win" for the clients and Singapore is not a cliché or a low-level compromise, but the invention of a new way of solving the problem that will genuinely benefit all.

At the political level a great deal of emphasis is given to *logical explanations* for the various social policies that are promulgated, and when those policies are changed, major campaigns of explanation accompany the changes. Leaders see themselves as rational actors who make sense, not powerful dictators who must be arbitrarily obeyed. When they do exercise power, they always justify it with logic, and, if the logic does not hold water or fails to get results, they look for a better solution. *In Singapore leaders must be able to outthink their subordinates and earn the respect of subordinates through their superior logic and articulation.*

Boundaryless Organization—Modulated Openness

The EDB from its beginnings has emphasized timely, accurate, and widely dispersed information as essential to decision making, often captured in conversation by the concept of a boundaryless organization. Two shared tacit assumptions operate behind this principle, one referring to internal operations and one linking back to the contextual assumption about sector collaboration.

The EDB assumed that the only way it could fulfill its function effectively was for all managers, officers, and other relevant employees of the organization to be fully informed about all projects at all times.

The EDB assumed that the only way it could fulfill its function was to develop and maintain open channels to the other sectors of the government as well as to private and labor sectors.

Though this is somewhat overstated, it captures the spirit. For the EDB to make quick and valid decisions about investments and investors, it believed that it was necessary for all relevant information for any given project to be available to all members of the organizations who might have an input to the decision, and certainly to the higher-level decision makers. This assumption underlies the extensive global communication system that the EDB has set up, the willingness to spend money on communications, travel, and meetings, the standardized reporting system that allows information to be efficiently centralized and filed, the requirement that everything be written down, the training provided to employees in written communication, and perhaps most important of all, the norm that *"one must pass on all relevant information truthfully and not use information as a personal source of control or power."*

We see here the strong interdependence with the teamwork assumption. The abuse of "information power" through withholding or falsifying information is, in most organizations, the product of the assumption that competition among individuals and groups is the best way to build and manage organizations. When one hears references in the EDB to people not being enough of a team player or being *too* individualistic, it is invariably exemplified by noting that the person "sits on information" or fails to pass it on accurately.

Why then do I refer to *modulated* openness? In working with many clients simultaneously, highly confidential plans are often revealed and it is not always clear even within the EDB whose interests could be hurt by too much exposure of such plans. In my group interview with senior officers, all my questions were answered with generalities; requests for specific examples were systematically evaded. In probing for the reasons, I was told that it would be too risky to talk about individual companies in a group context and in front of an outsider, even one who had been requested to learn how the EDB operated.[6] I was also told some stories of internal dissent about the pros and cons of pursuing certain projects, and in that context an EDB officer was advised to withhold some information that would have jeopardized the project. In other words, EDBers learn to be open but with judgment, and to pass on confidential information only to key people by phone or in person "in the hallway."

A second form of modulation occurs around internal relationships where openness about performance or being critical of someone higher in the hierarchy is the issue. Asian and particularly Chinese sensitivity to issues of "face" and the need to preserve group harmony both require judgment and care in revealing what one really thinks about another person and their ideas or performance. EDB officers have to learn early in their career how to appear to be "totally open" without revealing client confidences or offending others, especially those higher in the hierarchy. As many analyses of Chinese culture have affirmed, the necessary sensitivity is learned early in life, so the natural tendency to be more closed and cautious has to be unlearned.[7] Learning how to be more open and how much to reveal is then an iterative process of making mistakes and getting gentle coaching on how not to make the same mistakes again.

In this whole arena we see a combination of a Western rational principle of how to solve problems by full exposure of relevant information even if individual sensitivities are involved, with an Asian tradition of being highly protective of face even if one might have to conceal relevant information or find very subtle ways of getting it across. The *espoused* value is very clear—the EDB is to be as much as possible and organization without internal boundaries, and by implication, Singapore likewise should be without boundaries across its various organizations, but the cultural background makes the full implementation of that espoused value somewhat problematic. And with growing size, age, and success, interorganizational boundaries and internal boundaries will tend to become stronger so it will become harder to maintain openness, trust, and the "boundaryless organization."

Nonhierarchic Hierarchy—The Boss as Patron, Coach, and Colleague

The element in the paradigm that is most paradoxical was called participatory autocracy in chapter 1, but is perhaps better described as a "nonhierarchic hierarchy" based on the following shared tacit assumptions. It will be noted that these assumptions are closely allied to those pertaining to teamwork and the free flow of information mentioned above.

The EDB implicitly assumed that officers could succeed only if they simultaneously had two potentially opposing sets of abilities.

1. A strong sense of autonomy in performing their task, a willingness to initiate decisions through formal proposals up the hierarchy, a willingness to be open and frank in revealing information up the hierarchy, a willingness to go around the hierarchy when tasks require it, and the ability to work with higher levels of management in the client organizations.

And, at the same time, officers had to show:

2. Suitable deference to superiors when appropriate (particularly in public), a willingness to seek and accept guidance from above in revising proposals and in the making of decisions, good judgment in keeping their superiors fully informed when going around the hierarchy, and appropriate humility when being coached and guided by superiors and when dealing with higher-ranking managers in client companies.

The best way to characterize this set of relationships is to note that EDBers are expected to perform as one would in a boundaryless Western organization in which hierarchy is downplayed and, at the same time, to perform as one would in an Asian (Chinese) organization in which deference and hierarchy are dominant. What the young senior officer had to learn in entering this organization was how to do that— how to develop the judgment and interpersonal skills to perform according to both sets of norms.

It is in this arena that the potential conflict with traditional Chinese post-Confucian assumptions would be most visible, in that filial piety extended to family, clan, and the larger community is ostensibly still very much in force in Chinese overseas communities. Studies of Chinese overseas businesses in Hong Kong, Taiwan, and Singapore appear to find a consistent pattern of very strongly enforced hierarchy with only the entrepreneur-owner making the important decisions, and all trust relations limited to family and personal connections, thereby limiting the size of such enterprises.[8]

When one encounters the EDB, one finds a very different kind of organization. First, the EDB is a multiracial mix rather than an all-Chinese ethnic group. One finds few overt deference rituals except in public appearances, and the EDB espouses the value of speaking up—even to your boss. The description of the decision-making process in the EDB suggests much more bottom-up than top-down decision making, and yet at the same time one finds a tremendous respect for the chairman, the managing director, and other directors, and a sense that one cannot or should not act on one's own without consultation and approval from above. Teamwork is espoused and practiced, leaders are not to be put on pedestals, and leaders are very self-effacing; yet at the same time leaders are revered, respected, and given credit for much of the success of the enterprise. The former chairmen who were some of my informants all said that they did not want this book to glorify them or their accomplishments, yet when they talked about the EDB's history, they all credited each other as individuals for various accomplishments. And, as was pointed out in the historical chapters, they had very different styles of asserting authority, thereby training the organization to be flexible in the handling of authority.

Lee Kuan Yew sometimes tested his people severely and thereby got a message across about openness across hierarchical boundaries. One former EDB senior officer told me he was once called to Lee's suite at the hotel in the city where Lee was visiting and was asked whether a particular plan for a joint venture that Singapore was considering would be feasible. The EDB officer said that the country in which he was working (whose culture he understood very well from his several years of experience there) would not agree to go into the venture, and it was therefore not feasible. At this point Lee pulled out a thick book, bound with a red ribbon, thrust it at the EDB officer and said: "You are wrong! This consulting report has looked very carefully at the possibility and they have concluded that the project is entirely feasible. What do you say to that?" The EDB officer swallowed hard and reiterated his point that the country in which he was working would not go for it. Mr. Lee stared hard at him, suddenly broke into a big smile, threw the book down on the bed and said: "You are right; that report is all rubbish!"

Ability to influence upward was illustrated in another story. Prime Minister Lee Kuan Yew was invited to give the keynote speech to the EDB-sponsored 1988 Global Strategies Conference. Lee accepted and asked the EDB to make some suggestions as to what issues he should address. Tan Chin Nam passed the request on to the EDB's planning department, where an officer below the director was asked to come up with some concrete ideas for Lee's speech and to share these with the speech committee consisting of the director and five or six committee members. The basic topic was to be, "What makes a nation competitive?"

The officer assigned to come up with ideas looked for material and asked Chan Chin Bock, who happened to be in town, for suggestions. Chan mentioned George Lodge and Ezra Vogel's book on ideology and national competitiveness, which focused on individualism versus "communitarianism," collective responsibility versus individual rights. She thought the idea was good and worked on several drafts with the director of planning. It was then passed to Philip Yeo and the idea appealed enough to him to be passed to Lee, who redrafted it and sent it back to the EDB for further comments. The EDB officer was especially impressed and considered it a special privilege to be asked to comment on the prime minister's ideas.

She and the director then drafted a reply that presented some different points of view and nervously passed it back to the prime minister, whom she perceived as the much more experienced "thinker" in Singapore. He accepted a number of the modifications, gave the speech, and obviously was taken with the idea of communitarianism sufficiently to pass it on to Goh Chok Tong (his successor as prime minister) who, in turn, used the idea in formulating some ideas about Singapore's future vision. The EDB officer was amazed that "this little idea" that she, as a relatively junior officer, had worked on had gotten so far. It was hard for her to believe that she could influence people so many levels above her, that they would actually listen and engage in discourse with her.

One of the major functions of hierarchy is to be a mechanism of coordination, and here also the system works in a nonhierarchical way. In the process of obtaining coordination and getting people to work on a given project, the initial inquiries are primarily on a professional peer level. If ranks in the hierarchy have to be crossed, officers tend to involve their directors and have them clear with each other before a final decision is made. If there is an overload and people do not have time to work on all ongoing projects, they sometimes have to go to a higher level for "guidance" on priorities. I asked whether guidance meant that the boss now made the decision on who would work on which project. I was told fairly firmly that the boss would not, in fact, make the decision but would "bring up various other points that might have to be considered." The officer learns to use the hierarchy without the hierarchy becoming a dominant controlling force.

Interpersonal skills are especially relevant in the hierarchical situation because, on the one hand, boundaries are nonexistent in the sense that one can always walk into Philip Yeo's office and talk very frankly to him but, on the other hand, EDB officers know that department heads may feel at a disadvantage when their subordinates go around them. Consequently, one of the important interpersonal skills is knowing how to keep the department heads feeling sufficiently secure so that they are not threatened should an officer go around them. The same is true downward in the organization. If one goes around one or more levels, one must sensitively keep the intermediate levels informed so that they will not feel threatened. The implication is that one of the most important aspects of being socialized into the EDB is to learn the rules and develop the skills of being open and nonhierarchical without threatening the hierarchy.

One of the key questions in this regard is how the organization manages performance appraisal. Here again we find a mix of Asian and Western styles. Since most proposals and ideas have to be written down, EDB officers get immediate feedback in the form of written questions and comments on their written products. Beyond this level of feedback, officers learn from their ability to enlist the help of peers whether or not their ideas or proposals are good ones. For guidance on more subtle issues, supervisors will provide feedback in an oblique and sensitive manager, so as to preserve face. Finally, for project or annual reviews, some form of management by objectives is used, wherein each officer is asked to set performance targets and then reviews with his or her manager how well the targets were met. All of these methods used together provide fairly strong and clear signals on how a given person is doing in the organization.

For example, one of the regional directors said she received two forms of feedback. In the annual appraisal she was rated on a series of dimensions after being given the form and asked to evaluate herself. For each dimension there is a five-point scale, and she had to give herself a rating and make some comments. She then got feedback from her boss on the phone. He would give her a very general positive message and then suggest a few areas where "it had been pointed out by others" that maybe there were some weaknesses and she needed to improve herself. The other method of getting feedback is that he might privately say that a presentation she made or some area she was working on could be done a little differently or more effectively.

The point is that employees will not criticize each other in public and will even be careful in a face-to-face situation. The EDB is, however, a cosmopolitan organization that is trying to work by some Western standards so that, in fact, employees do get a fair amount of direct feedback. These more formal and informal feedback processes are of course supplementary to the feedback one gets from successfully winning over others, getting projects started, and getting proposals accepted. Although it was not mentioned directly, the Chinese cultural tendency toward self-criticism undoubtedly plays an important role as well.

Extended Trust Relationships—Clients as Partners and Friends

One of the important distinguishing features of the EDB is its conception that the overseas investor was to become a friend and partner, that the relationship was to be a long-term one that would be of mutual benefit to the company and to Singapore. Implicit in this notion is not only the long-range strategic goal, but an extension of the Chinese philosophy of *guanxi,* or building trusted connections, that can be used in the future. Whereas in the old Chinese system such connections were limited by personal acquaintance and patterns of mutual obligation that extended out from the family and clan, the EDB concept is a much more Western notion of forging strategic alliances and partnerships with investing companies to create the kind of industrial system that the strategy envisions.

The EDB has set aside considerable investment funds to make such partnerships real by allowing the EDB to be an equity partner as well, but the purpose is not to invest to make more money, but to ensure that the enterprise will succeed. Once a business is a going concern, the EDB always intends to sell off its share to make the money available for the next project. This general philosophy rests on two shared tacit assumptions.

The EDB assumed that it could succeed only if it fully understood the needs of its clients (potential and present investors) and collaborated with them in solving their problems efficiently but without compromising its own basic goals, plans, or rules (strategic pragmatism).

The EDB assumed that Singapore's long-range mission could only be fulfilled if initial investors continued to invest and became committed to transferring technology and training Singapore's labor force. Such continued investment could only be achieved if the EDB became friends and partners with its initial investors.

It was never enough just to bring the investor in. Once they were in, they developed new needs and problems, and the EDB officer was usually the one they would call when they needed help. Such help often laid the groundwork for further investment and an expanded relationships with Singapore. In that regard, possibly one of the most important dimensions of the EDB/Singapore culture has to do with their *time horizons* and their *attitude toward time.* On the one hand, there is a lot of emphasis on long-range planning and figuring out how to create a set of incentives and activities that will encourage the investor, who is thinking about the long haul. On the other hand, there is tremendous pride in being a good host and doing whatever it takes to help a foreign investor succeed in Singapore in the short run.

Evidence of the long-range point of view comes in the form of frequent references to human capital and the willingness to spend large amounts of money on training and education. The educational establishment was charged with offering the kinds of curricula that would fit the long-range needs of the country, and generally Singapore seemed to take an integrated view of education, human development, and social progress. Evidence for the short-run pragmatism comes from the frequent changes in social policy that the government was willing to undertake when a given policy did not accomplish what was intended. Singapore as a state and the EDB as an organization both displayed the ability to change course rapidly if their analysis indicated a need.

Singapore is neither a long-range planner like Japan nor a short-range pragmatist like Hong Kong or many Western countries driven by a monthly or quarterly business model. It is both, and it manages somehow to combine the two by having clear long-range goals and visions that are widely circulated throughout he nation-state and, at the same time, a sense that those goals and visions cannot be achieved if the daily problems of helping the industrial establishment are not met and solved creatively and immediately. And the key to this combination is the building of relationships with investors so that their long-range interests will coincide with Singapore's. The day-to-day solving of problems ensures the solidity of the long-range partnership and friendship.

Commitment to Learning and Innovation

Just as strategic pragmatism serves as a kind of integrative assumption around the contextual paradigm, the commitment to learning and innovation serves to tie together the assumptions of the organizational paradigm. In a sense this commitment is paradoxical as well because so much cultural analysis of Asian societies emphasizes fatalism, acceptance of harmony with nature, and commitment to stability and harmony within the social structure. Clearly Singapore has blended whatever Asian legacy it has with a more Western proactive stance that anything is possible, symbolized in Singapore by the often-heard phrase "Dare to Dream." In assumption form this can be stated as follows:

The EDB (and the government of Singapore) assumed that the only way it could fulfill its vision of development was to learn from others and its own experience, and to continuously innovate in dealing with whatever problems were discovered to stand in the way of achieving the vision.

This attitude goes back to the early leaders, to Lee Kuan Yew's and Dr. Goh's willingness to learn from other countries and from various non-Singaporean advisers, and is most clearly demonstrated in the continuous changing and refining of social policy. It is true that the policies are viewed by many as excessively controlling and a real restriction on the freedom of the individual, but in that perception one may miss the equally important point that the policies are constantly changing in response to new data. One of the important roles that the EDB has played in this regard is to be one of Singapore's most important windows to the outside world, and thereby to be a source of data for the government to fashion the appropriate economic policies. Thus the EDB is a source of policy, an adviser to the ministries, and an implementation arm for policies once they are agreed on.

The EDB's role as a source of feedback to the government puts an additional burden on it to stay well connected with what is going on in the world and to reinforce its own capacity to learn and innovate.

The various corporate seminars on marketing and strategic planning are visible manifestations of that desire to stay open and learn, and in the last two years the EDB has openly embraced the concept of itself as a "learning organization," invited speakers on this topic to hold a corporate seminar in early 1994, and conducted a major event in early 1995 using Peter Senge's *The Fifth Discipline* and concepts of systems thinking.[9]

The manner in which this decision was arrived at is illustrative of a number of the cultural elements that have been reviewed in this chapter. Because of their cosmopolitan orientation and their commitment to training and development, EDB officers and managers try to stay in touch with relevant management theories and technologies. Shirley Chen, currently the director of corporate services for the EDB and formerly its legal officer and secretary, has been involved in executive education and the Singapore Institute of Management. She is one of the "sponsors" of this culture project and has kept abreast of relevant management literature.

In one of our discussions she volunteered that she had run across Senge's book, found it interesting and exciting, and gave it to managing director Tan Chin Nam to read. He also found it relevant and obviously saw connections between how the EDB tried to operate and what Senge was articulating, particularly the importance of systems dynamics in an increasingly complex world. That year Tan Chin Nam and Senior Minister Lee Kuan Yew also went to the annual Business Forum at Davos, Switzerland, where they had an opportunity to attend talks by Peter Senge and Bill Isaacs from the MIT Organizational Learning Center.

Senior management then decided to make organizational learning the main theme of the 1994 corporate meeting and to involve all the senior officers in the project to study the Fifth Discipline concepts and examine their applicability in the EDB's context. Ten teams were formed, with two teams examining each discipline. One of the senior officers in charge of preparing for the annual meeting had been assigned the task of inviting someone from the MIT Organizational Learning Center to be the keynote speaker. The invitation came too late to get anyone from MIT, but a speaker was procured from Innovation Associates, a consulting firm active in organizational learning. The speaker was to address the entire seminar proper and also meet with the teams to see if they had understood the disciplines and to help them in preparing the presentations of their findings to the plenary. The whole program was perceived to have been very successful in that EDB officers responded to the challenges to be open in examining the organization's current practices and to identify areas where changes would be needed.

After the January corporate meeting the "learning organization" was officially chosen as one of the major corporate "programs," and the director of special projects, along with Shirley Chen, was assigned to develop the program and a work plan that would cover not just the learning organization but the whole organization development effort for the EDB. The five directors who had been involved in the various teams for the annual meeting and the chairmen of the ten study teams, along with other resource people (a cross-organizational group of about fifteen people), decided to meet weekly to develop a framework that would encompass all the development issues and create the concrete work plans.

This group, under director of special projects Khoo Seok Lin, developed the model shown in figure 11.2. The model emphasizes the four "levels" of the organization: (1) the self, where the corresponding training program is Senge's "personal mastery;" (2) people and interpersonal relationships, where the relevant training program is "team learning" and "dialogue;" (3) style and skills, where issues of intergroup relations and organizational culture have to be explored; and (4) shared vision, where shared "mental models" and "systems thinking" become the relevant training components.

For the first year, the EDB chose to focus on personal mastery and selected the program from Covey Leadership called "The Seven Habits of Highly Effective People" as the vehicle for every officer to focus on himself or herself and get his or her life and career in appropriate balance.[10] Tan Chin Nam's major address at the 1994 annual staff conference focused entirely on the need for everyone in the EDB to find an appropriate "balance" and manage jobs, families, and selves to achieve this. They decided to use the external Covey program for directors and above, and to train internal staff to administer the program to all the officers and staff in-house. In the end they integrated the five disciplines, the Covey model, and other ideas of organization development into a single concept or vision to tie the

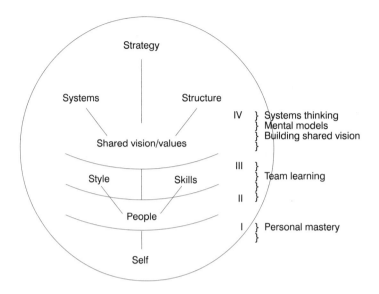

Figure 11.2
The EDB model for planning the organizational development and organizational learning program

whole program together. In talking about this program, the concept has even been escalated to a study of Singapore as "the learning nation."

What is notable about this program is that it grew out of a set of ideas that started in the EDB, combining an inside need for organization development with academic ideas from various books. The concept evolved through many task forces and teams, drew in outside resources, and eventually was shaped into a coherent vision for the EDB as a whole. It is being further shaped for the future by the director of special projects with the help of various members from human resources, planning, and corporate services management. It has become an organization development program that is widely understood, accepted, and supported, which will ensure that the organization makes the most of it.

This book project is itself an interesting manifestation of the assumption that learning and innovation is the key to continued growth. Although cultural sensitivities have at times kept me from learning some of the "secrets" and "dirty linen" of the organization, what is remarkable is how open the organization has been to self-analysis and how anxious the sponsors of this research are to find out what the problems and weaknesses of the EDB culture might be.

Summary

The operational paradigm of the EDB culture is a combination of: (1) commitment to teamwork in support of the basic mission of developing the nation, which, however, does not prevent individuals from feeling that they can contribute as individuals; (2) a sense that to succeed, the EDB officers and managers have to be bright, articulate, cosmopolitan, technically oriented, highly motivated, and interpersonally competent; (3) a commitment to openness across internal and external boundaries modulated by good judgment of how open to be and when and how to express information, especially across hierarchical boundaries; (4) an effort to operate with a nonhierarchic hierarchy in which decisions are the result of broad involvement of all levels and task-related communication is free of hierarchic concern, while at the same time preserving respect for status, especially in public, and accepting guidance and coaching from superiors; (5) a commitment to long-range friendships and partnerships with client companies based on the development of mutual trust; and (6) an overarching commitment to learning and innovation based on a sense of being able to influence one's own fate.

Figure 11.3 shows the combination of this paradigm with the contextual paradigm. It is my basic argument that in order to really understand why Singapore and the EDB work the way they do, one must consider all twelve elements shown and must treat the culture as a system of interrelated parts, not isolated elements. It is Singapore's ability to put all the pieces together that helps to explain the success of their economic development effort thus far.

The twelve elements discussed are part of the essence of the lily pond, the underlying nutrients that feed the surface manifestations. Culture is ubiquitous, so there will be other shared assumptions that I was not able to surface that also play a role. However, these twelve elements are critical, especially as they operate together. One should also note that such a cultural pattern can only evolve over time as various overt behaviors based on the underlying assumptions succeed and gradually come to be shared. If parts of the pattern become

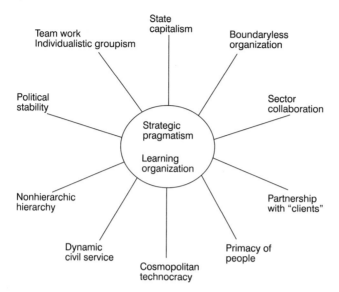

Figure 11.3
The cultural paradigm of the EDB

dysfunctional, a new evolutionary process can be started in a new direction, but that inevitably takes time and usually involves a painful process of replacing the people who are the key culture carriers. Culture cannot be manipulated or controlled in the short run, but it can be evolved in systematic ways. When managers announce a "new culture of quality," they are espousing new values but are not really changing the underlying assumptions. All of these thoughts become relevant as one contemplates an analysis of the strength and weaknesses of the EDB's and Singapore's cultural assumptions. Such an analysis will be undertaken in the remaining chapters.

IV

Problems, Issues, and Lessons

This part pulls together the various problems and issues that the interviews, questionnaires, and my own observations revealed. These problems and issues are of obvious relevance to the EDB and to Singapore itself inasmuch as they may reveal some things that are difficult for insiders to perceive. One of the purposes of this book was to find out not only how the various organizational partners perceive Singapore, but also how the EDB culture looks to an outside analyst. What are the strengths and weaknesses of a culture such as I have described, and what lessons can be learned from Singapore?

Many of the problems and issues that will be reviewed in these chapters are well known to the EDB, and there are already initiatives and schemes in place that are intended to deal with them. But it is important to pull all of the critical comments together in one place and sort them in terms of what they tell us about the EDB culture and what elements of that culture will aid or hinder Singapore's future evolution.

Many countries have watched Singapore with considerable interest and have asked Singapore to help them with their own developmental problems. What can they actually learn from Singapore? The next three chapters will attempt to answer these questions.

12

Problems and Issues: The Contextual Culture

A Note on Culture Analysis and Change

Any given culture is not good or bad, strong or weak, right or wrong in some absolute sense. However, the whole cultural paradigm or some of its elements can be functional or not in terms of what the society or organization is trying to do and in terms of the environmental realities that the society or organization faces at any given moment in its history. The *outsider* looking at the culture can make judgments based on his or her preferences or on assessments of how well adapted a given cultural element is to environmental realities. From the point of view of the *insider,* for example, the members of the EDB, such judgments are more difficult both because it is harder to see the culture objectively if one is in the culture, and because changing what may be perceived to be dysfunctional elements may not be possible anyway.[1]

If culture represents the accumulated learning of a group, one cannot simply shed some of that learning. For this reason the focus of the insider should be on cultural *strengths* and *functional* elements. Organizations evolve and change more by enhancing and building on their strengths than by trying to change those elements that are perceived to be liabilities. Culture change is in general a slow, difficult, and painful process. Organizations that have tried to change the dysfunctional elements of their cultures have learned that this is difficult if not impossible to do without destroying the organization itself. A better strategy is to identify those elements of the culture that help to achieve the strategic goals and build on those elements. It often turns out to be the case that the dysfunctional elements of a culture can be ameliorated or neutralized if the functional elements are strengthened. Some effort to identify such positive initiatives will be made in this chapter. The basic data to be presented come from both insiders and outsiders and are organized in terms of the six elements of the contextual culture identified in chapter 10.

State Capitalism/Government Intervention

Singapore's central assumption that the government can and should play an active role in economic development has been validated by thirty-five years of economic success but, as a number of comments below indicate, government has become both a friend and a problem, and the role of the EDB has therefore become more complicated.

Dealing with the Loss of "Competitiveness"

The government today is too distant, they don't have the feel of the road, the pressure of the marketplace is not felt sufficiently, all of which makes it easier for government to subtly undermine programs or fail to respond to what is needed. (former EDB chairman, 1994 interview)

Singapore is not facing the problem of wages outrunning productivity for the last few years. The problem is clearly there and no decisive action is being taken to deal with it either by the EDB or the government. There seems to be no sense of urgency even though the problems are now getting more difficult with rising costs, less control when you try to go abroad, more checks and balances with other agencies, more competition from other countries. The EDB has to bring in money, remove impediments, and be a window to the outside. What is lacking these days is removing the impediments. (executive, MNC)

Singapore is now the most expensive place to do business, ten times more than Malaysia and twenty times more than China, but the infrastructure is so good that if they can make it financially viable, we will be happy to stay in Singapore. (executive, MNC)

It is getting harder and harder to decide to invest in Singapore because of:

• Rising labor costs
• New taxes such as value-added tax (VAT)
• Increasing cost of doing business
• More and more can be done at a distance, so the need to locate engineers in Singapore is getting less and less.

(U.S. entrepreneur)

The general problem of the rising cost of doing business has certainly been well recognized by the EDB, and any number of strategic initiatives have been launched to deal with it: regionalization, the growth triangle, industry clusters, and most important, the continual upgrading of Singapore's own labor force to enable it to capture the higher-value-added kinds of activities. One central strategic element is the development of entrepreneurship and the evolution of Singaporean MNCs. In this regard some of the comments were discouraging.

Maintaining the Technical Edge through Entrepreneurship

What Singapore lacks that has helped other smaller economies like Switzerland, the Netherlands, and Sweden is active entrepreneurs and the development of world-class MNCs like Nestlé, Hoffman LaRoche, Ciba Geigy, Philips, Unilever, Shell, Volvo, Saab, and Asea Brown-Boveri to stabilize the economy. And the fact that they have been so good at what they are doing (referring to the EDB) will make it hard for them to change to a different mode. (U.S. economics and finance professor)

First of all, there are not enough entrepreneurs in the limited population. The MNCs and the government scoop away too many people and makes them less available for business. The environment is so good for regular organizations, why take the risk? Singaporeans are afraid to make mistakes, to lose face; they prefer to be safe in a group where you are likely to be less scared. (executive, local manufacturing company)

Private local entrepreneurship in Singapore is lacking not so much in terms of absolute numbers but in scale and contributions to the economy. . . . The "lack of local entrepreneurship" in Singapore is mainly the result of the country's deliberate and highly successful policy of attracting MNCs to the country. While the presence of MNCs has in many ways stifled the growth of private local entrepreneurs, it has helped Singapore build up an infrastructure that today supports the growth of specific industries. The timing is now right to take greater steps to encourage potential local entrepreneurs to come forward and existing ones to take on even greater challenges. . . .

Promoting local entrepreneurship is a slow process requiring not only financial and technical resources. The government and Singaporeans in general should pay greater attention to what can be done to change perceptions and attitudes. . . . Singapore needs to create an environment where mistakes are not viewed so harshly, where learning from mistakes is encouraged, where success is more broadly defined to include nonacademic areas. In this respect educational institutions have an important role to play. . . .

In response to suggestions by some Singaporeans that CPF funds (the mandatory savings program) be used to invest in the region, Singapore's

Prime Minister, Goh Chok Tong said, "I would discourage that because it is in the nature of these investments, these new projects, that there will be risks. I would keep CPF investments in Singapore where there's control over the quality of investments" (*Straits Times,* 7 February 1994). Herein lies the biggest obstacle in the government's attempt at promoting local entrepreneurship. On the one hand, while it is encouraging local companies to venture abroad, it is unwilling to let the people fend for themselves. With the government still adopting an approach frequently described as "paternalistic," it is unlikely that the entrepreneurial spirit of the nation will be fully realized. (Tan Chee Keon, 1994)[2]

Stimulating entrepreneurship is acknowledged to be necessary for Singapore's future, but it is not clear whether the kind of culture Singapore has evolved is capable of creating the climate and incentives necessary to stimulate and encourage entrepreneurs. In the discussion of entrepreneurship two major questions arise, and both remain unresolved. First, does "entrepreneurship" in the Singapore context imply *technical* entrepreneurship based on high levels of technical competence, or any kind of entrepreneurship based on financial and business competence?[3] Second, does "entrepreneurship" imply the building of large Singaporean multinational companies, or the creation of a large number of ancillary local companies that work in a symbiotic relationship with the large foreign MNCs?

The encouragement of local industry to become the parts and components supplier of the MNCs has certainly maintained the technical bias with which Singapore started, and seems to encourage the model of the small technical entrepreneur working with the existing MNCs. However, entrepreneurship requires a willingness to try risky ventures and make many mistakes along the way. Singapore has a strong tradition of favoring technical education and has all kinds of incentives for people to get higher degrees, but the general emphasis on higher education also increasingly leads many of the best students to go for less risky careers as civil servants, scholars, doctors, and lawyers. Such careers are seen as not only safer but more prestigious than business. Because the government has been such a desirable employer over the decades, there is perceived to be a growing tendency for young people to avoid the more risky careers.

Many comments suggested that such a trend is culturally supported by the norm that even a single failure in the Singapore environment is viewed as a permanent mark against the person.[4] In a small society in which it is possible to track every citizen very carefully, one can see how such a norm could be devastating to any kind of real adventuresome risk taking, especially when it is fairly well known that in the careers of successful entrepreneurs there are usually many failures before a successful enterprise is launched.

In other words, the flourishing of local entrepreneurship may require changes far beyond what the EDB can stimulate—real changes in Singaporean attitudes toward education and achievement, and far greater tolerance of risk taking and mistakes. The lesson for the EDB would appear to be that a clarification is needed of what kind of entrepreneurship is really desired, and a set of policies must be designed that would create an economic and social climate for such specific entrepreneurship to flourish.

Maintaining the Technical Edge through R & D

Singapore being more of a government-type economy using government money might not be as willing to engage in high up-front investment in risky research even though there might be high payoff." (U.S. executive regarding basic R & D in Singapore)

Overall the competitiveness of Singapore is changing very fast and the influence of the growing neighbor countries is expanding. Although such general evolution cannot be challenged, the EDB has to provide clear visibility of how to support today's business in Singapore. Many companies worldwide are facing financial difficulties and some time before deciding to shift their investments (manufacturing, for example), they have to generate profitable operations in Singapore. For example, EDB is promoting the development of R & D facilities and new technologies, but for our business, this evolution requires a competitive manufacturing environment in Singapore. (executive, large Asian MNC)

In order to undertake higher value-added activities such as R & D that requires huge and risky investments, besides EDB's valuable advice and comments on our activities, we would also need their financial support. Furthermore, through the assistance of EDB, we may also be able to seek technological support from a relevant body such as the NSTB (National Science and Technology Board). (executive, large Asian MNC)

Singapore needs to continue and accelerate efforts to build a pool of R & D talents in Singapore. (executive, large U.S. MNC)

Several of the comments connect the issue of maintaining a technical edge with specific ideas for the role the EDB should play in "fixing" the problem.

EDB should play a more active role in shaping workers' attitudes, helping industry to overcome manpower shortages, and lobbying for infrastructural developments to support industry, e.g., for third-shift workers. (executive, MNC)

The EDB needs to train more technical talent to support manufacturing. With the tight labor market in Singapore, especially of talented engineers for manufacturing industry, suitable educational programs would be required to help bring up this pool of people. And, if this industry is to be considered a key industry in the country, it may be necessary to educate the younger generation, insisting on its importance to the economy. (executive, large U. S. MNC)

We require talented and dedicated engineers who would also *stay on the job* in order that technological know-how and new breakthroughs can be safeguarded within the organization. With the high turnover of such labor in Singapore, to help build up more confidence for the industries to engage deeply in R & D activities, the EDB may be able to help by introducing programs or schemes to assure industries of technological proprietorship. (local manager of large MNC)

One of the key points to support this evolution is to generate on a national basis a clear knowledge that moving to high technology takes time to develop the adequate know-how. Cycle time of changes is expanding rapidly when we are moving to new technologies.
  A key factor is that the companies are committed to developing the right resources to generate stability of the workforce and skilled employees. A major burden today in our R & D in Singapore is the impatient attitude of the staff in climbing up the corporate ladder and job hopping. It takes many years to train and develop skilled engineers and managers in key areas. With EDB's help, the company can develop the retention program, action and knowledge of what needs to be achieved for the next step in Singapore's economy. (executive, large European MNC)

  Building up a viable R & D environment requires large risky investments and an appropriate pool of talent. As the comments indicate, there is a question about the feasibility of making such investments if the government does not provide more support for the manufacturing sector and there is a question about the availability and retainability of technical talent. In particular, the strategy upon which Singapore has embarked to become "the intelligent island" through sophisticated nationwide information technology, to form industry clusters built around key manufacturing sectors, and to become an R & D center—virtually a "technocratic meritocracy"—will require levels of technical talent that Singapore may not be able to produce locally.[5] For this reason the EDB launched its International Manpower Program to locate and recruit not only Singaporeans studying overseas, but to liberalize immigration and foreign worker policies to permit non-Singaporeans to fill those jobs if needed.

There were virtually no negative comments from insiders or outsiders about Singapore's overall longer-range strategy and programs in this regard. But there were many problems identified that reflect the perception that the EDB is providing insufficient support for companies who are trying to remain and grow in Singapore with ever-increasing costs. Particularly in relation to the desire on Singapore's part to become an important player in the R & D arena, there was not only the critique that the environment is not conducive to the kind of risk taking and investment that R & D requires, but that more specific financial support will be needed to make the risky R & D investments possible. And beneath this wish lies a suspicion that the EDB is so enamored of and used to working with large foreign MNCs that it cannot really empathize with local enterprises and do what is right for them (as some of the comments in the next section will indicate).

The unresolved dilemmas around both entrepreneurship and R & D can then be stated as follows: (1) Can and should Singapore stick with a de facto technical emphasis that is clearly one of its strengths? (2) How can a viable R & D environment be created without large and risky investments? and (3) What changes in educational and social policy will be needed to make risk taking more attractive to Singaporeans?

Helping Local Companies

The same kinds of issues from a slightly different perspective focus specifically on how the local companies can be helped more. As the reader will note, these comments are linked to the kinds of issues raised above, but are more focused on the local company issue.

We still have not broken through the internal enterprise barrier, and maybe the situation for the small businessman and entrepreneur is even worse than it used to be. The EDB used to be more pro-business in its early days when it opened four factories a week and took virtually anyone. Now all sorts of criteria have to be met.

When we were all guerrilla fighters, we trusted each other more. Now we have become more questioning of our own companies. We seem to trust the foreign companies not to cheat us more than we trust our own companies, so we are much more careful in examining their loan requests. We ask too many questions and only want the right kind of business. We only want flagship investments. (former EDB chairman)

The incentive system that was in place tended to favor working with the big MNCs in that *individual officers' performance was measured by total dollar investment you brought in rather than the number of companies,* and working with the local investors would always lead to only small dollars. So the basic incentives favored the large company. The qualifying criteria for tax incentives also favored the large MNCs in that you wouldn't get any tax breaks unless you were investing more than a million dollars. A lot of the small companies didn't reach this cutoff point.

Furthermore, the EDB attracted the best and the brightest Singaporeans from overseas universities, and these cosmopolitans would naturally gravitate to looking after the multinationals where they could project themselves better and where they felt most comfortable. Most of the officers were fresh out of school so they had little empathy for the local companies where the managers or entrepreneurs might have been much less educated. There is one story of a local entrepreneur who became extremely successful and revealed late in his career that he had been initially rejected by the EDB when he had applied for a job there. (EDB alumnus)

EDB should play a more effective role in providing feedback on all new government policies, cost increases, the labor situation, levy, COE on lorries, transportation, dormitory for the foreign workers, etc.

EDB should not only provide the above feedback, she should also study its impact on the competitiveness of doing business in Singapore and feed back the results to us. (manager, local technical company)

As the main government body promoting investments in Singapore, EDB should, besides wooing new investors, continue to service existing investors and assist them to remain competitive so as to encourage them not only to maintain but hopefully to expand their operations here as long as it is viable to do so. In this respect, it should continually review the incentive schemes available to ensure competitiveness of businesses operating in Singapore vis-à-vis our competitors located elsewhere. (local division manager of a large European technically based MNC)

We need stronger representation of investors' concerns in response to government policies that impact the cost of doing business in Singapore, the industrial relations climate, etc. (manager, large MNC)

The manufacturing cost in Singapore is getting higher and higher. EDB should liaise and provide feedback to the various government departments on the steps to be taken to retain the MNCs still staying in Singapore. She should study the impact on us of the MNCs setting up plants in the low-cost neighboring countries to compete with us. It becomes the common practice for the MNCs in Singapore to ask for "cost down" every now and then. If we wish to continue to do business with them, we have no choice but to respond to them. Then how long can we continue to service them with the continuing rise in cost? (managing director, local technical company)

EDB should be commended for their present standard of helpfulness. In addition to that, they should maintain good rapport with industries in the local scene and continue their support in the growth and development of local industries.

Towards the future development of high-tech industries, support from local small and medium-size industries is essential. These local industries can provide services to the MNCs so that these MNCs can in turn be more competitive in the larger global market. Perhaps the EDB can consider further support to the development of such local industries, such as proposing some incentive schemes for them. (manager, local technical company)

The local companies that are intended to become Singapore's own future MNCs are progressing, but, in their own view, not fast enough. From their point of view, they are caught in several dilemmas in relation to the large MNCs and feel that the EDB should play a stronger role in helping them:

1. The most severe dilemma appears to be that if the MNCs are to maintain some manufacturing base in Singapore, they must be given cost advantages, and those often result in the local suppliers being asked to lower their prices to the point where they question their own viability.

2. The local companies need better information on the potential impact of new government policies, and if that impact is negative, they need the EDB to provide strong feedback to the other government agencies to get them to change those policies.

3. The local companies need direct financial help and one-stop service.

4. The local companies need assurance through EDB-sponsored incentive schemes that enough technical talent is available and will remain with their companies.

This is a tall order for the EDB and may not be appropriate anyway, because some of the EDB alumni and other observers saw the basic problem quite differently. They view Singapore as having been such a paternalistic society for so long that local companies have lost their entrepreneurial spirit and have become much too dependent on the government. They feel that the government should *decrease* its role, to stimulate more free enterprise forces rather than increasing its own support and thereby continuing to foster complacency and dependency on the part of local business.

Officially the government agrees with this position. Nevertheless, companies see the Singapore government as a powerful helpful force and continue to expect support of various kinds, in part because they believe that the mentality of the government is itself pro-business and that the government truly understands the needs of business. Apart from what may be desirable from the perspective of the government, the question arises of what the government can do. Can it let go, having had so many years of success in managing the economic affairs? Is there enough entrepreneurial spirit in Singapore to overcome the difficulties identified? Is there a systemic interaction with the needs of the MNCs that will continue to undermine the needs of the local companies? Or will the EDB and the rest of the government find some new hybrid form or free enterprise that will work in that particular cultural nexus?

Dealing with Government Complexity (Bureaucratization?)— What Can and Should the EDB Do?

With success and age, all the segments of the government are getting more powerful and potentially diverse in their goals and strategies. Many interviewees felt that these circumstances placed a specific set of demands on the EDB.

Another new area where life will be a bit more difficult has to do with the growing strength of the environmental agency in the Singapore government and the involvement of the public in environmental affairs. Back when we first created the petrochemical industry, which is a "dirty, land-hungry industry," we had to decide whether to encourage it or not, to decide to invest money to fill in land to create some of the space, and to risk some of the environmental problems. At that time we clearly made the commitment, but today it is increasingly difficult to override environmental concerns.

For example, the Public Utilities Board owns a great deal of land and was proposing to build an additional golf course on some of this land. This was strongly fought by academics and various citizens groups who created a very effective public relations movement against the golf course and forced the Public Utilities Board to abandon the idea. If an industry project ran afoul of environmental concerns you could always use the EDB to plead industry's case, but increasingly the popular element in the other government agencies are more difficult to sell.

Another new issue is the fact that with changing leadership it is not clear how deeply embedded some of the "good" elements of Singapore really are. A colleague from an MNC who had observed this for a long time said that some of the cleanliness, lack of crime, etc., were ethics that were really only a few years old and therefore only a few years deep. The green ethic is very recent and not yet very internalized. If the next leader is not as strong as Lee Kuan Yew, we might very well revert to looking more like a Hong Kong or a Bangkok. (EDB alumnus, now an executive)

The EDB should act as a catalyst to whittle away at those government statutory boards' rules/regulations/procedures that tend to stifle businesses and prevent them from conducting their operations in the most efficient manner.

It could also consider conducting regular briefings to keep investors better informed on new or proposed government policies and decisions affecting the business community either through forums or newsletters. And perhaps EDB could act as a feedback mechanism to solicit information/reactions on the impact of such policies on the cost of operating in Singapore and discuss ways to mitigate its adverse effects. EDB could then forward these views to the relevant authorities for their consideration and report back to the participants upon receipt of the reply. (manager, local division of MNC)

To maximize coordination within the government, the same person should chair both the EDB and the Trade Development Board or the Permanent Secretary of Trade and Industry should be the chairman of the EDB. (former EDB chairman)

The various government departments involved in education, social policy, environmental concerns, land management, defense, finance, trade, tourism, and foreign relations are today mature organizations in their own right. Though the EDB has seeded many of these organizations and the EDB culture is characteristic of many of them, inevitably as organizations age they develop their own subcultures and, to varying degrees, will begin to work at cross purposes with one another. Such strong subcultures are the predictable result of years of success; whether one calls them "bureaucracy," and whether one chooses to view bureaucracy as a good or bad thing, *it is an inevitable result of social evolution.* To develop a common economic philosophy is therefore much more difficult in a successful thirty-five-year-old country than it was when Singapore was just getting started.

Diversity among the subcultures can be either a strength or a weakness depending on how it is managed. In a rapidly changing world, it is not always clear which subculture will develop the coping mechanisms best adapted to some unknown future problem. *Diversity is therefore inherently an advantage during periods of rapid change.* The dilemma is how to maintain coherent economic, political, and social policy as subcultural diversity increases and as the subcultures become stronger. The suggestion that the EDB be made an economic czar, as some advocate, would probably not be possible, however desirable it might seem. But the EDB as the "animator" of the government might be a sustainable role.

Political Stability

Political stability has clearly been one of Singapore's strengths. It is stability that attracted foreign investment in the first place, and it is a continuing sense of stability that allows a longer-range technocratic strategy to flourish, in that companies are willing to invest in very long-range, capital-intensive projects such as petrochemical complexes. The price of such stability has of course been the heavy social control that the government has exercised over the decades. Some of the comments from my interviews dealt with that issue.

Some people found freedom of expression lacking. Some Westerners were invited to leave if they had made indiscreet remarks. (U.S. executive)

It's a Chinese country and will go out of its way to keep it that way; it's officially integrated, but the Malays will not be allowed to get an advantage. (U.S. executive)

I loved living in Singapore and even considered retiring there, but one negative factor was that I felt I was being watched all the time. Whenever I left Singapore I always felt somewhat freer. Because they were very tough in enforcing rules and the government was very repressive I, for example, did not report it when my wife once stumbled on an unfinished sidewalk and broke her foot. When a friend asked me, "Are you going to sue the government?" I said, "No, I wouldn't do that because the government would probably blame my wife for not being careful enough." (U.S. executive)

He noted Singapore's very strong crime deterrence, mentioning that they hanged a mother of five children because they found enough drugs in her possession to assume that she was a dealer, and for dealers they have the death penalty. In other words, you knew they were going to enforce all rules. He was also somewhat uncomfortable with the bonding system, under which a person would have to pay off the cost of his training over three years or more on a sliding scale, but got used to it. He pointed out that this also applied to his American friend who flies for Singapore airlines. When he was trained on the 747-400s, he had to sign a multiyear bond.

He noted that the younger people today are somewhat more vocal, but that they still fear Lee Kuan Yew, so it is a question of what will happen when Lee Kuan Yew is no longer there and a new government comes in that may not be quite so feared. People might in fact become more vocal and critical. They are becoming more challenging partly because they have become more Westernized.

These and other comments made by various interviewees are well summarized by Bellows in his 1989 analysis:

Singapore's elected officials now face the task of reconciling a regime that has long been accustomed to managing a unified society through a Mandarinate (top civil servants) with growing demands for more individual autonomy, political pluralism, and a leadership more willing to accommodate popular feelings on important issues.[6]

The issue of political stability interacts with the previously identified issue of the growth of diverse subcultures and a new issue, that of the growth of individualism. There is some empirical evidence to suggest that one of the *consequences* of economic development is the growth of individualism.[7] To the extent that Singaporean society is becoming more affluent, it is becoming more individualistic because affluence provides people more choices quite apart from their loyalty and nationalism.

For example, it was pointed out that with the increasing standard of living, families are not as dependent on government scholarships. They have enough income to send their children overseas and allow them to concentrate in whatever fields they desire. Even if they then go into technical careers, they are not bonded or in any other way obligated to return to Singapore, creating the possibility of a brain drain. Such a brain drain is, in turn, going to depend on the degree to which Singapore continues to be perceived as an environment in which the social and political controls are accepted as still necessary or, alternatively, perceived as excessive at this stage in Singapore's evolution.

If political stability is so important to continued economic development, it behooves the EDB to become very analytical about the ultimate bases of such stability. For example, one provocative analysis of Singapore examines it as a prototype of a commercially based city-state of the sort that have existed throughout history such as Athens, Venice, the Hanseatic cities, and Hong Kong.[8] It has always been difficult for such city-states to remain stable because of the inherent tension between them and their land-rich neighbors. Furthermore, even a very successful city-state built on trade does not secure stability because the trading partners can always take their business elsewhere, or the neighboring countries can overrun them whenever they choose to do so. Hence the "island mentality" and sense of vulnerability that Singapore has always had.

If ownership of land is not available as a basis of stability, what can function in its place? Money won't really do it, because it can be moved easily. It would appear in Singapore's case that the functional equivalent of land is "knowledge and skill." Singapore appears to be trying to become the place where critical knowledge resides and where the technical base for implementing the knowledge is located, that is, the concept of an information hub or R & D center, the repository of what Lee Kuan Yew has labeled Singapore's "software," its knowledge of *how* to do things.

Singapore quite rightly has recognized that being a trading hub is not enough; that the various investors in Singapore must become dependent on what Singapore knows and can implement. In that regard, manufacturing is necessary but not sufficient, because manufacturing can also be moved elsewhere unless it involves large amounts of capital investment. From that point of view, the long-range strategy of going for the high-tech industries becomes a better stabilizing force. Being a financial center is another possibility but that may not be enough either, so Singapore is clearly pushing toward the notion of an information and knowledge infrastructure center. If enough headquarters and R & D organizations can be located in Singapore, so that Singapore truly becomes the economic "software" center—the place where the knowledge of how to do things is developed and resides, and where information is centralized and coordinated—that may provide the stability and economic viability that Singapore needs.

That scenario requires special attention to the development of a technically sophisticated population, which in turn has implications for the educational system and raises questions about the balance between technology and the arts. On the one hand, can Singapore survive without becoming even more of a technocracy? On the other hand, is there a risk in becoming too technocratic and losing touch with other aspects of life? As one analyst puts it:

Mulford Sibley's warning some time ago is still applicable today. Sibley (1971, pp. 21–2) maintained that an overemphasis on scientific and technological development will make social and political values completely subordinate to the needs of the machines and constrain freedom and equality to the planning and co-ordination made imperative with the infinitely complex division of labour that accompanies industrial-age technology."[9]

Sector Collaboration

One of Singapore's greatest strengths is the cultural assumption that the sectors of society (i.e., government, employers, and labor) can and must work together, backed by the network of trusting relationships that has been built up and nurtured over the decades. The fact that most senior executives, both in the public and private sector, have multiple positions ensures that the level of acquaintance among them will remain high. Level of acquaintance is of course a prerequisite to maintaining the high level of trust that makes efficient coordinated action possible.

Are there enough processes in place to ensure the continuation of a high level of acquaintanceship and mutual trust? Can such collaboration sustain itself with growing size and complexity, or do the subcultures that form in the different sectors inevitably create communication breakdowns and diversity among goals and agendas? Or, to put it another way, how does one maintain consensus in an increasingly diverse affluent society in which individualism is growing?

Western political processes, built on advocacy and majority rule, have not been all that successful in dealing with diversity of interests, as can be witnessed today in the U.S. efforts to reform the health care system or to deal with any of a number of other major social problems. Can Singapore, with its technocratic meritocracy built on its definition of the "best and the brightest" and on its Asian roots, invent its way to some better form of reaching consensus? In this arena the West probably has much to learn from watching how Singapore will cope with increasing diversity and growing affluence.

The Danger of Elitism

Two potential problems were identified in relation to this issue: (1) Are the new generations developing the same levels of trust, or is this a characteristic of an "old boys' network" that will fade away as the old boys do? and (2) Are these levels of acquaintance and trust limited to the elite, or are they being fostered as well in the middle- and lower-income strata of the society and across ethnic and religious lines? What influence do the lower-income and lower-status segments of Singapore's society have, and how important is their active participation? Some comments from my informants suggest that the elitism is sensed by them and causes some concern.

The "Mandarins" of Singapore, which includes the EDB, take too much for granted. For example, when you are invited to participate in activities or attend events, it is taken for granted that you will agree to come. The message comes "please be there tomorrow," delivered in a way that makes it awkward to refuse. The organization or the cause is always assumed to be more important than your needs, and the thought that you might wish to decline is not even considered. The fact that they might involve you in a conflict of interest is not considered because of their own strong sense of integrity, and it is not considered that one might have an agenda other than serving Singapore. (local CEO of large MNC)

I trust the EDB and can share with them, but my brother is completely unwilling to talk to anyone in the government. He doesn't think they understand him and he certainly would not trust them. (manager of a medium-size local company)

Singaporeans lack an "inner smile." They are a little bit too self-centered, a little bit too driven. (former manager from large MNC)

They are a very aggressive group and often asked me to make some retrospective testimonial comments that could be used in relation to promoting other companies. You get coopted into selling Singapore. Frequently when I met senior EDB people it was in connection with photo opportunities at times when the company had signed a new contract or had given a grant or done something for Singapore, at which time the press was always called in. They would show up to shake hands with the executives and a great deal of publicity would be given to the event. (former CEO from large U.S. MNC)

A number of people expressed concern about another aspect of elitism—the tendency to become arrogant and the danger that one becomes blind to one's own areas of incompetence. Several comments along these lines were made.

The EDB is very sharp and hard working but lacks maturity in a certain sense and has a rather narrow sense of the complexity of business, particularly business overseas; and possibly they are somewhat overspecialized. (former local manager of U.S. MNC)

They are quite limited in their experience and knowledge of what it is like to work in various foreign countries, and so at this point to get involved in a lot of overseas projects and to send people out into them may not be all that practical. They have a very clear concept and idea and maybe even a plan, but too little appreciation of the problems of middle management, of creating an infrastructure and making it all work together. They are too driven by "we can do it here, just imagine what we could do elsewhere," but they should not confuse the outside world with the good infrastructure that they have in Singapore.

They have much too little experience in more corrupt environments and in dealing in messy foreign situations. When feedback of this sort was provided to them on various projects that they proposed in various executive breakfasts, they really did not like it, especially the feedback "that it may be more difficult to do those things than you think." (former executive of local division of large U.S. MNC)

The EDB officers are too naive and idealistic about how the decision process in the multinationals really works and how complicated and multifaceted it is. EDB officers need more of a sense of realism. (alumnus who is now with a large foreign MNC)

The EDB has been too perfectionistic, and that will be a problem since they have so much on their plate. (EDB director)

From arrogance we have to develop more humility. From impatient action orientation we have to learn to be patient and make a steady effort. (EDB director)

Ultimately the real danger of elitism, when looked at from a cultural point of view, is that the members of the elite get caught up in their own mental models to such a degree that they cease to observe accurately what is going on around them. Success breeds a worldview and thought process that comes to be taken for granted.

Another force toward such homogenization of thinking can come from the narrow definition of "the best and the brightest" in terms of scholastic achievement. Valuing ethnic and religious diversity while maintaining narrow educational and intellectual standards can become rapidly self-defeating as the world demands more different kinds of skills. The EDB and the Singapore elites may then have to invent ways to surmount their own biases.

An Incorruptible, Competent Civil Service

In spite of the risks of elitism, having "the best and the brightest" in government is probably one of Singapore's major strengths in that they are potentially the most able to invent what the country needs to survive and grow and to overcome the kinds of biases and blind spots alluded to above. Singapore may be one of the few models existing in the world of how a society can progress with a government that attempts to maximize intelligence, skill, and honesty. What is easily misunderstood by Western observers is that Lee Kuan Yew's autocracy was used to create a meritocracy, a concept that is consistent with Chinese concepts of a responsible and respected government, and is very alien to Western concepts of minimal government intervention and government in an adversarial rather than integrative role. In a recent speech, the new head of the EDB consulting group mentioned the tripartite wage negotiations between government, employers, and labor and was told by the Canadian delegates that this was a radical idea that they had never heard of or considered as a possibility.

Primacy of People

The recognition that Singapore's future depends on the education and development of its people is perhaps the single most important cultural assumption in the whole paradigm. People are the only resource Singapore has, but people cannot create a modern developed nation-state without education, opportunity, and a sense of pride that will encourage them to stay and continue the building process. The various efforts on the part of the EDB to stimulate and further technical education are, from this point of view, crucial elements in bringing Singapore to where it is. But, as the various comments above have implied, there is much more to be done. The technical levels needed by companies, especially in the R & D arena, are escalating rapidly and Singapore faces the need to import some of this talent. The strategies that the EDB sees for Singapore's future all hinge on having the human talent available to fulfill them, which would suggest that the EDB needs to focus on its linkages to Singapore's educational system.

The EDB is in a good position to assess whether the educational system inherited from the British and evolved by Lee Kuan Yew and others is optimally adapted to the needs of the future, and if not, how to influence it. As noted above, one of the dangers of a meritocracy is that it creates an inbred elite without realizing it, because curricula, examination systems, and scholarly standards are simply taken for granted. As Singapore's situation evolves, its educational system will need reexamination, and the standards by which "the best and the brightest" are selected will have to be carefully reviewed. Singapore's system of sending its scholars to universities in many different countries is, from this point of view, a critical strength to be preserved.

The EDB should also ensure that Singapore's educational system evolves quickly enough to train citizens *at all levels* for the modern city-state that is forecast. There is some evidence that the gap between the affluent and the poor is not being closed in spite of various schemes to help the poor.[10] Perhaps those schemes do not take sufficient account of what is actually going on with the poor population. From that point of view, feedback from local companies becomes especially important. What strikes one as most troubling in that feedback is the perception that EDBers really only want to deal with the big, glamorous, flagship companies and have neither the ability nor the inclination to deal with small and medium-size enterprises. It would pay the EDB to look into this matter to ensure that all Singaporeans have the opportunity to advance.

An implicit concern that should be faced explicitly in this regard is whether the assumption that "the government and even Singapore, the nation, must be a technocratic meritocracy" can become a weakness if that government loses touch with the less able parts of its population. The very success of that assumption can lead to mental models of how society works that subtly disenfranchise the less technically oriented or able, not in a political sense, but in a social sense of being seen as less relevant. As one analyst puts it: "The major objective in promoting scientific and technical education is the promotion of economic prosperity. By promoting scientific and technological education, people expect their society to become more modernised and industrialised, and the corollary is to have greater economic growth. However, other aspects of social development such as social equality or cultural enrichment do not seem to fall within this understanding of development."[11]

Strategic Pragmatism

The mentality that allows the EDB to think both long run and short run, both globally and locally, both generally and specifically is clearly a strength that should be acknowledged and nurtured. It is implicit in everything Singapore does, so one finds little comment about it, but its manifestations are clearly visible and commented upon. If there is any problem at all, it is the one already mentioned that the short-run fixes are pursued with more enthusiasm and vigor when large MNCs are involved. If the EDB could marshal the same energy and enthusiasm for the small and medium-size enterprises, both local and foreign, this might go a long way toward stimulating the local economy further. Officially this is clearly part of the EDB strategy, but I am suggesting that there are subtle biases that favor the large MNCs and that these have to be brought to the surface, assessed, and dealt with.

In concluding this section, one should note that the problems and issues identified are interconnected and reflect the basic complexity of economic development in a complex world. The challenge to the EDB is to make an accurate diagnosis of what the situation is and invent solutions to deal with that reality. If the EDB's history is any kind of indicator, one may anticipate that they will invent new strategies rather than falling back on traditional solutions. Is their organizational culture adapted to dealing with the levels of complexity that they are encountering? That is the basic question for the next chapter.

13

Problems, Issues, and Opportunities in the EDB's Operational and Managerial Culture

In the last chapter I focused on the cultural element that characterize Singapore's government as a whole, including the EDB. In this chapter the focus shifts specifically to those cultural elements that characterize how the EDB operates and manages itself. This operational and managerial culture is a fairly tight-knit system of assumptions around a shared vision, teamwork, individualistic groupism, boundarylessness, modulated openness, nonhierarchic hierarchy, cosmopolitan localness, partnerships with clients, and a commitment to organizational learning. The comments made about this culture did not easily sort themselves into these categories, however, so they will be presented in terms of the broader issues they reflect.

Strategy and Shared Vision Issues

Many interviewees noted that Singapore's vision of its own future is becoming much more complex and may require a more fundamental rethinking of how the EDB operates and what its core competencies need to be. This transformational trend was started with Philip Yeo's arrival as chairman and has continued as the competitive pressures from other developing countries are forcing more substantial changes. A former minister for finance put the matter quite bluntly, and his sentiments were echoed by an EDB staffer:

Maybe the EDB has branched off into too many directions. Should it be involved in the performing arts or banking? Is it losing focus? Other government agencies should be taking more of a hand in the various things the EDB was doing. The EDB has become a dumping ground for all government problems such as regionalization, but the EDB is being dragged into it and it may not be wise to take investments abroad. Is it tempting companies, especially the GLCs, to go beyond what their own judgment would recommend?

We are stressed out to death with overload and multitasking. Is the EDB doing too many of the tasks that other organizations should be doing? (EDB officer)

Senior EDB directors saw less need for a change in mission, but noted the need for many internal changes:

Changes that will happen in Singapore that need to be dealt with are considerable. We will have to move:

1. From more to less hierarchy;
2. From a more Asian to a more Western value system;
3. From a low-income to a middle-income society;
4. From being the "one damsel at the party" to being "one of many damsels who are just as pretty" (the "minidragons" and "tiger cubs" such as Vietnam).

Hence the 1990s will be a period of major restructuring economically, which will force the EDB to think much more broadly than it has done before. Few agencies in Singapore are in a mode of economic proactivity. Only the EDB forges new ways of doing things and is at the forefront of driving economic growth. In a way it is too much for the EDB to do. Is the EDB sufficiently broad in its thinking and action to do real competitor analysis and positioning?

The challenge is to go after everything that is attractive and learn how to manage limited resources. The broadening has to come internally; the EDB has to learn to be more reflective and analytical. It has always been very good at action ("the Commandos") but not always good at figuring out what to act on, what to do. Singapore needs more visionaries and the EDB needs more visionaries. It has only a few at the top. (EDB director)

From a commando mentality suitable to troop movement and action we have to develop a more strategic overview. (EDB director)

From having a common mission and being able to be a team because we were event driven, we now have to recognize that we are perpetually interdependent. We have to institutionalize teamwork, we have to enhance the level of openness among all the members and build much higher levels of trust. (EDB director)

From individual autonomy and freedom we have to move to more commitment to a mutually developed vision. (EDB manager)

Part of what made the EDB so successful was the clarity of its vision and focus. It is much easier to be a team when there is a clear shared goal than when the goal is multifaceted and unclear. A big question facing the EDB is how to maintain this unity of purpose as the strategic imperatives themselves become less clear and more complex.

Systems Thinking and Causal Complexity Issues

Most of the interviewees acknowledged in one way or another that new learning will be needed in dealing with complexity of all kinds. Philip Yeo and Tan Chin Nam recognize this need in focusing on the "learning organization" and "The Fifth Discipline" systems thinking.[1] The issue was spelled out by several of the former chairmen in noting that "deals" with potential investors are no longer straightforward, but may involve multiple geographic sites, multiple investing companies getting into joint ventures, and complicated multifaceted financial elements.

The EDB must become more relevant to the current world. The matter of development is becoming very complex, requiring new kinds of financial packages, even involving complex trades of goods instead of money, and the ability to put together packages that involve several companies and even several countries. The Trade Development Board should really be under the EDB so that they could work things out together, since trade and manufacturing and services increasingly will go together. There will be a need to look into banking, insurance, and various new ways to raise very large sums of capital by going to multiple partners. EDB has little skill in inventing such innovative financial packages. (former EDB chairman)

The EDB does not have enough broad business types to deal with the new complex opportunities in financial service, multiple ventures, multiple regions. (former EDB chairman)

We have to move from linear thinking to systems thinking to understand and deal with the many interdependencies. (EDB director)

The pace is now much faster than it used to be partly because the environment is so much more complex and there is so much more to do. (EDB director)

The recognition that the EDB will have to develop more competence in systems thinking and develop more capacity to develop complex shared visions correlates with the observations of U.S. managers that the EDB officers sometimes come across as "naive." I would add my own observation that the high pace and intensity of their work sometimes seems to lead to superficiality of thinking and a falling back on routines and slogans. This superficiality obviously does not extend throughout the organization. Its strategic thrusts are deep and well thought out. But under time pressure, pragmatism can sometimes overwhelm clear strategic thinking.

A number of managers interviewed wondered how the EDB would be able to relate to the complex political scenarios that will evolve when more projects are done in the various Chinese provinces. For example, how will they deal with corruption of various sorts? As one U.S. executive put it: "International companies who rush into China will be burned because they don't know how to deal with the Chinese, so partnering with the EDB will help, but the EDB and Singapore companies themselves will have some difficulty in dealing with China because of the corruption and Singapore's own rules."

One implication is that the tasks may become so complex that "rookies" can no longer perform them. Though it is obviously a great developmental experience to come into the EDB without too much prior work experience, perhaps the EDB will have to hire more experienced people as tasks get more complex. That might require a more fundamental review of how the EDB is structured, how it recruits people, the kinds of people it needs, and the fundamental reward system in place at this time.

Teamwork and Hierarchy Issues

As the EDB's work becomes more complex and demanding, and as more people are multitasked across a lot of projects, it will become more difficult to remain coordinated and to sustain open, collaborative, trusting relationships.

The EDB's information technology system is obsolete. There is conflict between increasingly sophisticated senior officers and the IT group over length of time to log on and off, lack of responsiveness, and availability of new programs. (internal survey result)

We are too hierarchical, and too many decisions are made at the top and consensus is then engineered. We are a very paternalistic system with supermotivated enthusiastic children. (EDB director)

The EDB will have the same problems as the Singapore government. As it matures, it will inevitably develop subcultures, and the coordination problems among them may become greater. The strong tradition of boundarylessness may become harder and harder to implement as multitasking and complexity increase. On the other side of the equation, however, is the motivation and cleverness of the EDB itself and the probability that they will invent new coordination mechanisms to deal with the situation.

Elitism and Arrogance Issues

What was noted in chapter 12 as a potential problem for Singapore as a whole certainly has its counterpart within the EDB. With growing self-confidence sometimes comes insensitivity, as the following quote notes:

During negotiations I was interrogated and pressured by one of the assistant heads until I got angry and told him that if he did not believe my figures, I would walk out. He backed off and later apologized, but it was a most unpleasant experience. They were trying to get me to commit to more than I could do, and they did not believe in the integrity of my position. It was most unpleasant. (local manager of U.S. company)

There is a narrow line between the self-confidence born of experience and success, and the illusion that one knows more than others. Very few managers had experiences like the one described above, but it may be symptomatic of a problem that will creep in more and more—success corrupts, humility is lost. To repeat the point made above, the danger in this trend is not that one may offend someone by coming across as arrogant, but, more important, arrogance creates blind spots and one ceases to see reality for what it is.

My own experience with EDBers would confirm the concern. I sometimes felt that they were so anxious to tell me the things that *they* wanted to talk about that they did not really hear my questions or deal with my particular needs for certain kinds of information. Their pride in their success and their need to maintain face biased them toward reporting things that have worked well over the years, making it very difficult to diagnose where they were vulnerable or in need of new learning.

Some Actual Mistakes

Because of the EDB's strong positive self-image, it was not easy to elicit stories of mistakes made over the years. One group of alumni, however, got into the spirit of reminiscing and was able to remember some of the mistakes and fiascoes along the way. For example, one Hong Kong company proposed a deal in which it would bring a lot of sophisticated new machinery to build various kinds of equipment into Singapore; it turned out, however, that this was mostly second-hand machinery that was being palmed off and was not very useful for anything. This illustrated one type of danger that the EDB faces, namely being fooled by an investor. Since the EDB officers were young and inexperienced, the possibility of that happening was considerable.

At one time the Japanese wanted to do a lot of ship repair in Singapore, with the implication that if they came in they would be using a lot of local resources for their supplies. In the end the Japanese used only 5 percent local content, leading to strong complaints from local industry that they had been misled and were being exploited. The EDB treated that not as a mistake but as part of the learning process, and eventually created a policy of letting investors decide whether to buy locally or not, that is, not even promising locals that their labor and materials would be bought. Instead, the EDB decided to try to be more supportive to locals to make them more competitive.

Another kind of miscalculation was simply not understanding the economics of an industry such as ship building, so there were various false starts and finally the abandonment of it. In a number of these instances the mistake, if it was a mistake, was to give insufficient attention to local companies and to get too tied up with the multinationals.

The "rig-building fiasco" occurred when Singapore went overboard in building rigs for the oil industry and grossly overestimated the market and underestimated the impact of changes in world oil prices. In these instances the EDB had recommended more investment than the bank was willing to put up, so they did not lose too much money—but the EDB judgments had clearly been wrong.

Another failure occurred when the EDB went into a three-way venture on building liquid-crystal displays for computers. The idea was to do the unusual, especially in high tech, and since one of the investors, an American, was pouring his own money into the venture, they figured it must be sound. Suspicions about the whole thing began to grow when it was learned that one of the production principles was to "rub the glass with cat fur to make minute grooves that would help line up the electrons underneath appropriately." This venture failed completely, but the EDB person who had promulgated it was not punished. The same investment group had also gone into a color picture-tube project, which was making lots of money through a joint venture with Hitachi.

Mistakes clearly occur and they serve as a source of internal learning, but one gets the distinct impression that the public image of the organization must convey a sense of success and knowing what one is doing. Mistakes are not likely to be made very public for this reason, or if they do become public, they tend to be rationalized away.

Specific Career Development Issues

Many of the EDB's internal problems have to do with recruitment and career development. The EDB was highly conscious of these as the following comments from various insiders illustrate. The first issue has to do with bringing people on board faster and then retaining them long enough to create a stable core for the organization.

The EDB needs a better induction program, short internships of three to six months, because what newcomers need is more of a hands-on feel of an industry. In the present system it is very hard to get the pulse of the industry. The EDB employs "rookies" because they are cheaper, are bonded, and are willing to do paperwork. Starting salaries are okay but advancement is very slow; the first two years are a probationary period and you only get an annual review. (EDB director)

New people don't know the culture; we are not roping them in fast enough; we need new programs to teach them much faster. (EDB manager)

The career development system is not working, and it is unclear what the EDB should provide. Why are so many people leaving at mid-career, and is this okay? The concept of EDB giving people experience to enhance their further career growth (but not necessarily within the EDB) is operational, but is it keeping people long enough to be productive? People may be moving on too soon, so no stable core develops. Age and length of service are out of balance with too many young and too many old, not enough in the middle. (EDB manager)

The EDB has been too preoccupied with the customer and has neglected internal staff development needs. The EDB gets excellent people but exploits them. It needs to define a core group and make sure that they stay on. The organization is spread too thin and the core group is being eroded. The stress level at the officer level is very high and many good people are leaving. (EDB director)

Another set of issues has to do with the integration of local and overseas returnees. Going overseas initially is seen as a step up the career ladder and a broadening of responsibilities, but evidently the return to Singapore can be fraught with difficulties. As one person put it:

It is very hard to come back from overseas. It is hard to integrate and you feel left out relative to headquarters people who have gotten promoted while you were away in your overseas posting. (EDB director)

The EDB is also conscious of the fact that changing external requirements will eventually require new kinds of talent.

The EDB should be getting better officers, better educated, and they must have animal energy, be activists. EDB should be given more authority and freedom. The chairman of EDB should be the economic "king pin" and the directing mind for economic development. Other ministries like those for environment are getting too strong. (former EDB chairman)

EDB could improve in the future by being proactive in revising its administrative procedures as well as being actively involved with the industry in meeting the changing needs of the business environment.

Also the officers being assigned need to understand the situation of each organization and follow up closely with the dialogue on the changing business environment that the organization is facing. (manager, local engineering company)

Philip Yeo commented on these issues both in his interviews and in his speech at the 1994 annual staff day and noted that the educational level of EDB officers needs to increase to meet some of the future challenges. To this end, he proposed that one should liberalize the scholars policy to allow people to stay on for a master's degree or give sabbaticals to get a master's. He also reinforced the point that the EDB should remain a young and innovative organization and should not therefore expect to hold people for their entire career. In fact, it is more important for people to learn the EDB philosophy, make their contribution to the EDB, and then move on to other jobs where they can proliferate this philosophy in other organizations. However, he confirmed that people are leaving too early, before they have made their best contribution, and there is indeed a problem of developing the stable core.

Everyone appears to be feeling the competitive pressures and senses that not only is there more work to be done, but that the nature of the work is changing in fundamental ways toward more complex projects that will require higher levels of teamwork and coordination. As Tan Chin Nam pointed out in his annual staff day speech, this situation will require more careful alignment with the vision and will put an even greater burden on individual officers and managers to figure out how to balance their lives and careers. In all of this there is a strong message that each person must take charge of him- or herself and learn how to achieve an appropriate balance. To this end the EDB is currently supporting programs on "personal mastery" such as the Covey Leadership program and in 1993 had also run many officers through Ned Herrman's "Whole Brain" program.[2]

In spite of these efforts, there are several dangers in the situation as it is developing in the EDB:

1. The demands of the jobs and the multitasking will cause levels of overload that will result in more and more superficial work, resulting in potentially bigger mistakes.

2. Careers in the EDB will increasingly be seen as too stressful and people will leave early, as they apparently have been doing, or will fail to come to the EDB in the first place.

3. First- and second-level line management will continue to over-emphasize technical performance and fail to provide the developmental climate necessary to encourage high-talent officers to remain in the EDB.

4. The high level of pride and self-confidence of the organization will blind it to its own weaknesses, or worse, cause it to defensively deny that any weaknesses exist.

As of this writing, there are a number of efforts in place to deal with these problems, but it remains to be seen whether the organizational development and learning program will achieve their goals. When one asks leaders of the MNCs that are continuing to invest in Singapore about these issues, they have a common response that reflects the learning organization theme. They acknowledge most of the problems that have been reviewed in the last two chapters and then state confidently that somehow Singapore will invent its way to solutions. I asked several of them what specifically they thought Singapore should do and got the clear answer: "I don't know, but somehow the EDB will figure something out."

From an outsider perspective I would argue that the EDB culture is, in principle, well geared to solving its own and Singapore's problems if it can maintain a learning orientation under increased work pressure and stress. Learning and innovation are not possible without some organizational slack. If everyone is stretched too thin, the organization will inevitably fall back on old routines and superficial solutions. The emphasis on staying open to the environment and maximizing learning opportunities is valuable, provided the organization can make the internal transformations that may be necessary to adapt to the changing environment.

14

Lessons and Conclusions

In contemplating the lessons of the EDB, I want first to reiterate why this book was undertaken. One of the major purposes was to illustrate the role of a particular organization in the economic development of a nation. Economic development does not occur without the active generation and implementation of specific policies. The EDB has from the beginning been an exemplar of how a small government statutory board can organize itself to have a major impact on the development of a country. The way it was created, the kind of leadership it had, the management structure it evolved, and the human resource policies it pursued created, over time, a culture that not only guaranteed its own success for several decades, but set an example for other organizations within the Singapore government. An important conclusion to be drawn is that in one form or another a country embarking on a development program must create an organization that can animate this process and carry it through. The form of this kind of organization will vary with the particular culture and circumstances of the country in which it is created, but it is fair to say that unless such an organization is created in some form, and unless such an organization becomes effective in its own right, economic development will be slowed down.

What then are the factors that made the EDB so effective?

Lesson 1: The EDB Culture Is an Integrated System

The Singapore government and the EDB work because the various elements of the culture are all integrated into a coherent system. An error we have made repeatedly when we have analyzed organizational or national cultures is to overlook how the various elements work together to form a pattern that works. Instead we pick out one or two elements, apply them somewhere else, and are disappointed when they do not produce the expected result. As one reviews the EDB story, what is striking is how much effort went into thinking through how to make it all fit together, and how Singapore's experience reinforced the pattern, not the isolated elements.

One can describe this cultural pattern by analyzing it in a sequential way:

The initial leadership team assumed that (1) the government had to play a lead role and be business oriented. It realized that economic development would not be possible without (2) political stability and (3) collaboration among all the sectors of the society. If the government was to be effective, it had to create (4) a dynamic, competent civil service made up of the best and brightest talents available.

If economic development was to succeed, the key resource would be (5) Singapore's own people, who had to be trained and educated to fill the jobs that would improve their own standard of living. That could only be accomplished by (6) a strategy of attracting foreign investments and working closely with investors to meet their ongoing needs (strategic pragmatism).

If this process was to work, the government needed a somewhat independent agency (statutory board) that would have the power to create and implement an economic strategy for Singapore.

That agency, the EDB, in turn realized that if it was to function effectively, it would have to (7) operate as a team focused on a clear vision to build the country, (8) maximize the flow of information within the organization, (9) staff itself with highly cosmopolitan, technically and interpersonally competent people, and (10) empower the staff to be innovative and self-motivated while retaining a hierarchy necessary for coordinated action. It also realized that economic development built around technology, large capital projects, and knowledge was a long-range proposition that would work best if Singapore (11) created partnerships and friendships with investors. And, finally, since the world was changing rapidly, the EDB had to (12) become a learning organization that would be alert to what was happening and nimble in its ability to change course and adapt as needed.

Are all the elements in this cultural paradigm of equal importance? Having said that they all work together and form a pattern, one can nevertheless distinguish some elements that are almost prerequisites to the others. What one often feels when talking to Singaporeans is that they seem so sensible and smart. They seem to have figured out how to make everything work. I suspect that this is not due to historical accident, but to several of the cultural elements that set them apart.

The two elements that I consider to be prerequisites are "primacy of people" and a "dynamic, competent civil service." Singapore decided to be a meritocracy and to recruit its best talent into the government. The mission of the government was to create the economic circumstances that would provide jobs, housing, and an increasing standard of living for its people. A strong and talented government was thus created to provide benefits for the people, who were recognized from the beginning as the key to development.

When people first become acquainted with Singapore, they observe its one-party rule and the fact that it was ruled for thirty years by one person, a condition that Western democracies tend to view negatively. What is missed in that observation is the task that this autocratic regime set for itself—to develop its people and to become a modern nation with a high standard of living. There are lots of examples of autocracies in the world, but relatively few, if any, that had such a clear goal of valuing its people as its critical resource and that chose to populate its government with the best talent available. It is perhaps the high level of talent in the government that produced such insights as the need to get the sectors working together and figuring out mechanisms for making it happen. These leaders saw the need for a strong Economic Development Board that proved to be not only a creator and implementer of economic strategy, but "Singapore's first business school"—a training ground for future bureaucrats and executives who took the EDB culture into their own organizations. And it is this "seeding" of other organizations in Singapore that created and now maintains the high mutual trust levels that make sector collaboration and one-stop investing possible.

What are the implications of all this for economic development and organization theory? First, one should realize that economic development results not from one or two structural conditions or leadership insights, but from a combination of (1) favorable external circumstances (e.g., Singapore's favorable location as a trading hub), (2) a careful diagnosis by the leadership of how to take advantage of those circumstances, and (3) a whole series of specific processes and mechanisms such as those that have been described, but (4) always with an overarching attitude of trying to continue to learn from experience.

Nor can one explain economic development with simplistic cultural explanations such as Confucianism or a strong work ethic.

Rather it is the combination of many circumstances and an active trial-and-error learning process by a highly motivated government that seems to make the difference. The focus of analysis must shift from conditions or variables or "root causes" to processes. It is how things are done that seems to make a difference, because the actual circumstances and conditions that a given country will find itself in will vary greatly.

The lesson for economic development, then, is for each country to figure out its own cultural legacy and build development processes on the strengths of that legacy. The likelihood that some other country can reproduce the paradigm that worked for Singapore is very small, but that should not prevent a country from trying to figure out what its own situation is and build its own processes based on those insights. What Singaporean helpers, that is, EDB Consulting, can do internationally is to help diagnose the situation and to help a government develop strategies and tactics (i.e., processes) that will work for it in its own situation. For example, Singapore was able to go for high-tech manufacturing because of the ability to develop the necessary infrastructure very rapidly. In many developing countries the lack of such an infrastructure or the means to create it rapidly would argue for an entirely different approach based, for example, on tourism, joint venture hotels, etc.

Lesson 2: Theory Y Leadership Is a Prerequisite

The EDB has been able to create both a strong hierarchy and a group of officers and managers who are self-motivated, high-achieving team players. It is, from some points of view, a management theorist's dream organization, something that is written about but rarely observed in practice. How can this work? I believe we need to go back once again to that much misunderstood concept of leadership that McGregor called "Theory Y."[1] McGregor observed that effective managers assumed that people were willing and able to work and to mesh their own goals with those of the organization. If a person was found to be lazy or took advantage, the manager dealt with it, but he or she did not start out with cynical assumptions (Theory X) that all people are basically lazy and therefore have to be given organizational incentives and be controlled. Theory Y managers assumed that people are capable of self-control and that if they are provided adequate feedback on their performance, they will be motivated to improve.

McGregor also argued that whether one behaved in a very autocratic or delegating manner had less to do with Theory X or Y assumptions and was determined more by the task at hand. Some tasks require tight coordination and autocracy, others are performed better by distributing authority more widely in the organization. So Theory Y managers will often behave autocratically because the task demands it. The Theory Y manager could give crisp orders and they would be obeyed because the subordinates knew that the task demanded it and therefore did not feel demeaned by following the orders.

But the impact of autocratic management coming from a Theory X manager is completely different from that of a Theory Y manager. The Theory X manager always conveys the hidden message that "unless I tell you what to do, I know deep down that you will not do anything." And as McGregor pointed out, eventually subordinates will respond to this hidden message, cease to be motivated contributing members, and thereby tragically confirm what the Theory X manager feared in the first place. Theory X managers in high places inevitably become victims of this self-fulfilling prophecy. They end up proving to themselves that people are lazy and need to be controlled because they have trained people to behave that way. Once an organization has fallen into that mode of operation, it is very difficult to change.

What has never been understood in organization theory is that if you have a leadership that is Theory Y—one that basically believes in and trusts people—it is perfectly possible to run the organization as a formal hierarchy because subordinates know they are valued and are therefore not going to hide information or attempt to subvert the organization. A hierarchy can work perfectly well as an open, boundaryless system when people feel valued and trusted, so when they are asked to become involved, work as a team, and share information, they do so freely and openly.

It is my observation that EDB managers, especially at the higher levels, strongly hold Theory Y assumptions. In other words, they believe in people, treat them as motivated adults, and create the expectation that everyone will contribute to his or her own maximum. The communication system of written proposals, presentations, and having to recruit others into one's own team provided more than enough feedback, so that people could tell when they were off track. The willingness to plunge young officers into the executive suites of big international companies sent a strong message of "we expect you to learn from your own experience and we know you can do it." If the person was not able to respond to this kind of challenge, he or she left on their own or were guided to other kinds of careers. But the expectation was never compromised. As Philip Yeo put it when answering a question about how to do something, "If I knew how, I would do it myself; I expect you to figure it out." Or, as he put it on another occasion, "I don't want any passengers; I only want people who will help to drive the train."

Although I have less data, I would speculate that the same Theory Y assumptions function in Lee Kuan Yew, and his charisma partly derives from his powerful challenge to people. It is reputed that people were very intimidated when they were around him because he made quick judgments and you could quickly fall out of favor. That may be true, but quickness of judgment is not the same thing as Theory X. Rather it suggests a person with very high expectations of others and relatively little patience for certain kinds of "incompetence." That kind of impatience creates tension, but is entirely consistent with Theory Y and leads to both fear and high levels of motivation.

If one were to extrapolate this to countries working on their own economic development, one could argue that finding leaders and managers who are committed to the development of people might be a minimum prerequisite for a successful development program. All the elaborate programs and schemes in the world won't work if there is not an underlying concern for and faith in people.

Lesson 3: The Power of a Shared Vision

Singapore's small size made it possible to think of the entire nation as a community and to demand of everyone in the nation a commitment to teamwork and joint effort by articulating a vision of Singapore's future that everyone could identify with. Lee Kuan Yew's intellectual strength and articulateness were sufficient to convince the population that various kinds of controlling policies were essential to rapid economic development and that everyone should commit to a brighter future.

This point also has implication for leadership theory. I referred above to the necessity to embrace Theory Y, but that may not be enough. In observing Lee Kuan Yew and his team, it is also obvious that leadership in Singapore was based on being bright enough to figure out what to do, articulate enough to sell it to others and get them on your team, and patient enough to implement it no matter how long it took or how difficult it was. This kind of leader is not an intellectual autocrat. He or she listens intensely to others, seeks ideas, forms teams and task forces, and is committed to learning from others. But once convinced, this kind of leader is unrelenting in his or her efforts to convince others. I can recall many a meeting where one or another EDB director articulately and meticulously laid out for me all the elements of Singapore's vision and all of the strategies and tactics that would go into making it a reality. If I did not understand something, it would be patiently explained to me over and over again until I understood.

What Singapore illustrates that is missing in much recent leadership theory is a focus on the importance of the power of intellect and articulation, of having and spelling out powerful ideas, of involving a wide population in the development of those ideas, of "daring to dream," of exciting others with bold initiatives, and of valuing ideas wherever they come from.[2] Getting ahead in the EDB is clearly related to this power to think clearly and to articulate convincingly. Managers appear to be willing to take whatever time is necessary to convince subordinates of the logic of what is being asked of them, so that subordinates are always clear on what they are doing and why. Similarly, we heard over and over again that though Lee Kuan Yew imposed many tough controls, there were always major communication efforts to spell out the logic behind those controls.

The implication for economic development is clear. If the programs require the support of the people, the people must be brought on board and must understand what is being done and why. The Singapore story implies that blind faith in leadership is not the way to go, but rather, a well-informed population that is collectively working around a well-articulated vision is more likely to be successful.

Lesson 4: Successful Implementation Is in the Details

One cannot understand social or organizational processes without going into detail on how they actually work. One cannot understand a culture without seeing it in operation on a daily basis. The important and deep meanings are embedded in the detailed daily rituals, and one cannot understand those meanings without observing and participating in those daily rituals. Where one cannot participate, one can attempt to reconstruct historically by eliciting detailed stories of how things happened. For example, Singapore is given great credit for its innovative joint training institutes with various governments. But without knowing the detailed history of how the EDB first figured out what its needs were, how it studied countries and companies that could meet those needs, how it created the relationships and incentives to attract companies from those countries, and how in the end it set up these joint ventures, one has not really learned anything useful. How the EDB was created, how it set up its international function, the kinds of leaders it had and how they operated must be understood if one is to learn from Singapore's experience. I provided as much detail as I could gather, but if one is trying to extrapolate to other situations, it would pay to go even deeper into detailed historical reconstruction before drawing conclusions about how things actually worked.

Most of the stories one reads about economic development describe some broad strategies and their outcomes, but one does not have a clue as to how those strategies were actually derived in the first place, how they were implemented, and what might have been involved in their implementation. For me the most valuable aspect of this research has been the discovery of some of the details, the personalities, the schemes, the trials and tribulations, the team efforts, the enthusiasms of the "worker bees," and so on. We need in this domain the equivalent of what the anthropologists call "thick description" because it is ultimately in the details of the processes that the real lessons reside.

To give one example, the decision to hire technically competent, overseas-educated university graduates as the front-line officers of the EDB, to expose them as quickly as possible to senior managers in the investor companies, to send them out to open offices in the major capitals of the world, and to create an information system that linked them all and that provided constant feedback to them on the quality of their work were all essential details in making the broad strategy of "attracting foreign investment" a workable reality. Similarly the EDB as a one-stop agency hinged on all the detailed processes of building relationships among government agencies.

Lesson 5: Culture as a Constraint

A cultural analysis of the EDB reveals the complexity of how culture in an organization is actually built and, more important, how what has been built ultimately has to be reckoned with. As I have tried to show, Singapore embarked on a course of action that produced a powerful and successful technocratic meritocracy. The success of that course of action not only reinforced the basic assumptions upon which it was built, *but has created its own cultural infrastructure that may make it very hard to change direction.*

In other words, if we were now to conclude that Singapore is, from a long-range point of view, on the wrong track, it is not clear that Singapore could get off that track. A successful culture is very hard to change because its assumptions have become so embedded in the mental models of the leadership and in the organizational structures and routines of the society.

Cultural explanations may have very little value in trying to explain the *origins* of things, but they may have great value in explaining why and how things *persist.* In an age where change and learning have become very fashionable, it becomes all the more important to understand the constraints to change that result from shared cultural assumptions, especially under conditions of success and satisfaction. Of particular interest in that regard is the decision to go for high technology, a direction that Singapore may now be committed to for better or worse. Even though the EDB has a track record of adaptation and learning, it is not clear to what extent three decades of success with a technocratic strategy have created mental models that are now so taken for granted that they will function as filters or blinders with respect to new data that might challenge such a strategy in the future.

The implication of this line of reasoning is that one must build on and evolve the culture one has, rather than wishing for some dramatic changes or some other cultural forms. Management has often perverted the concept of culture by calling for "cultures of quality" or "cultures of customer focus," as if culture was something one could order like a new office building or product. Yet everything we know about culture from a century or more of anthropology and current studies of organizational cultures shows that culture is one of the most stable elements of a social system. Culture is probably the *last* thing in the system that will change.

When leaders really do change organizational cultures, it is invariably by destroying the present organization first, starting with new people and gradually building up over a long time a new set of assumptions.[3] This kind of starting over is clearly not possible at the level of a society. Even with major revolutions, a society's culture persists. Cultures change through slow, incremental, evolutionary steps, and those steps inevitably have to build on what is already there. For better or worse, the EDB and Singapore as a whole will have to build on the culture that is there and slowly evolve it to enable whatever future strategies may require.

One of the EDB's slogans is "Dare to Dream." What has to be recognized, however, is that culture even infiltrates our dreams, and we can only dream in terms of the categories of thought and the values that our culture has embedded in us. This situation is different in a nation that is culturally more diverse, where subcultures are themselves in adversarial relation to one another. But Singapore, in spite of its multicultural origins, has a very strong and consistent national culture at this stage in its development, and that culture must be given its due. It will only succeed with further strategies that are consistent with the cultural strengths already there.

What are the implications? If one wants to prepare for culture change that may be dictated by an unknown future, one has to foster subcultural diversity so that one has created within one's society the cultural variants that may be needed in the future. Bureaucratization and the evolution of strong subcultures in different government departments and sectors of society can, from this point of view, be a strength because the different mental models evolved in the different subcultures provide more possible solutions to whatever new problems may arise from environmental changes. Many organizations that have created strong cultures by destroying such diversity have found that they have become very vulnerable when the environment shifted. In a rapidly changing environment, diversity is valuable and should be nurtured rather than suppressed, while at the same time keeping the subcultures in good communication with each other. The task of leadership then becomes a difficult balancing act of how to achieve real consensus without destroying diversity.

Lesson 6: The EDB as Singapore's First Business School

One of the prime motivators for studying the culture of the EDB was the recognition by the alumni in the EDB Society that their years in the EDB had been so developmental for them. They had learned a point of view toward the world that they carried into other organizations and tried to teach those organizations. When asked specifically, "What did the EDB do for you?" a variety of comments were given:

- It trained me to look more macro, to take a broader perspective;
- I developed a sense of importance in everything we do;
- I learned how to execute;
- It stimulated creativity;
- It taught me to become more resourceful;
- I learned how to get around overseas;
- I learned how to package a deal, how to be a hell of a good salesman, ready with answers for whatever negatives the other person might have;
- It taught me to move back and forth between being very practical and very theoretical;
- I learned how to handle multitasking; we all had multiple jobs to do and learned how to do several things at once;
- I developed enthusiasm, learning by doing; you have to react to whatever happens, you have to prepare for the unknown;
- It brought us closer to the marketplace, we were always on the same side of the table as the investor;
- We became more pro-Singapore and learned that we are different;
- We learned to be proactive—go and get things done.

One of the former chairmen, Ngiam Tong Dow, noted that the EDB was in effect Singapore's first business school in that it taught not only some of the necessary business skills but, more important, developed in its people self-confidence and the ability to think. The building of this kind of self-confidence in a cadre of leaders of a society is a consequence of the basic belief in people that I have been trying to describe, and it suggests that *whatever else a developing nation does, it must start with a belief in its people and a program to build their skills and self-confidence.* Other developing nations may not be able to reproduce all of the factors that helped Singapore, but a program for building on people as the prime resource is within the power of any government, and if Singapore has anything to teach us, it is that this is the essential starting point.

Lesson 7: Asian and Western Managerial Styles Can Mix

Singapore's assumptions about the role of government intervention in economic affairs, sector collaboration, benign autocracy, individualistic groupism, modulated openness, and nonhierarchic hierarchy seemed at first to be anomalies, but only because I was judging them from a Western perspective. The lesson is that management theory is not culture-free at all, and that there are very few principles of management that apply across all cultures. What Singapore illustrates is how various managerial processes that it inherited, evolved, and imitated can be put together into a management system that works but that is neither Asian nor Western—it is Singaporean.

One can find all kinds of connections to and legacies from the British civil service, from Confucianism, from being expatriate Chinese, from cosmopolitan educations, and so on. And one can seek all kinds of comparisons between Singapore and Hong Kong, but in the end, Singapore built on its own unique strengths and succeeded in that effort.[4]

The Final Lesson: Problems or Opportunities

One of the most striking things about Singapore and the EDB is their "proactive optimism." The EDB wants criticism so that it can become more perfect. Every mistake is an opportunity to improve. This attitude was well captured in my interview with Khoo Seok Lin, then the director of special projects and currently the director of human resources, who is charged with promoting the organization development and organization learning initiative upon which the EDB has embarked. Her career illustrates many of the themes discussed, in that she is a working mother who requested a move from an operational job that would have required her to travel a great deal to a more project-based job that permits her to remain fully committed but with minimal travel. Khoo talks rapidly and intensely and conveys the high level of commitment and energy characteristic of so many EDB officers.

We were discussing her model for organization development and focusing on the kinds of skill and style that EDB managers will need as the EDB moves into its own more complex tasks. The interview is quoted at length to get across the point that a self-criticism by EDBers is invariably couched in highly optimistic terms and reflects the EDB's strong positive self-image. I quote it at length in the spirit that without some specific detail, the general point does not get across.

EHS What problems is the organization development program trying to solve?

Director I am not here to try and solve problems. Of course there are always problems—this isn't optimal or that isn't optimal—but that is not the issue. The issue is being innovative and talking about enhanced performance. So it's not about looking back at history and talking about improving here or there, but to look ahead and see where Singapore needs to be, to figure out where the EDB can contribute, and what must we be as an organization in order to meet the challenges.

EHS So even though you don't know what those challenges will be . . .

Director We cannot foresee everything, but we do know where we want to go and we have in place some of the strategies relatively clear-cut. And one thing we know is that the environment will be more complex and the competition will be fiercer for sure because we already feel it now.

EHS So when you earlier said, "Let's look at skill and style," for example, you are relating that to currently known strategies?

Director For example in style, we said we need two things—we need a style of management where every officer, every manager is a *people empowerer.* Many middle managers still look at their job as a technical thing—they look at your memos and correct them—and not enough in the area of being a builder of people, motivating them and cheering them on instead. You have to be a model, not a judge and a critic saying "wrong, wrong" all the time.

EHS Historically is that what they have been, technical supervisors, critics?

Director Not critics, but the focus at the middle-management level, assistant heads, the bulk of their focus has been there, because, as I told you, to be promoted you had to be technically very competent, excellent in what you are doing. It is easier to talk about the job than to sit and say, "What is your aspiration? Where does the EDB fit it?" Our officers are very confident individuals, so we must have very confident managers.

EHS What is puzzling about this is that if I talk to alumni of the EDB of the 1960s and 1970s, they talk about it as an organization where they got a lot of power and could take initiative. So where did this middle-management technical supervision attitude develop, because it wasn't apparently true of the early organization. Hasn't it always been a people-enhancing organization?

Director It is, but we are saying that there is a lot more that can be done.

EHS even more.

Director *Oh yes* [said with great emphasis]. The moment we start thinking that we have done all that can be done, that's the time we start going downhill. We have to think about how we can improve ourselves. Put it this way: there is a lot of opportunity for bottom-up ideas to flow; that's true of EDB. But there is also a lot of opportunity for middle managers to enthuse the younger officers. There is a lot of potential. The moment we think EDB has it, that's when we don't have it. That's why we do benchmarking of EDB . . .

EHS [Interrupts] But do you see problem cases? If you were asked, would you be able to point to supervisors and heads who are too technical, who are not good enhancers of people, who need this kind of training?

Director Of course I can [laughs]. Don't quote me [laughs].

EHS But that's the thing that is interesting, that this has crept into the organization. Or has it always been there?

Director Put it this way. The same people, if put into another organization, would probably be among the top people. That's the unique thing we have here, both a strength of EDB and a question. Everyone is, because of the recruitment system which is so stringent, MD [Managing Director Tan Chin Nam] himself interviews everyone that comes in, so there is tight quality control at recruitment. Everyone who comes in is excellent on paper and in their interaction.

Then you are competing among excellent people, and among excellent people, you know, if you look at the bell-shaped thing, there will always be some who are more excellent than others. So we do have a cohort of people who, when they are viewed among the excellent ones, do not appear to be as excellent as the others. But if you put the same people into another organization, they will be among the top 20 percent of that organization. That is where the EDB has to feed back into our career development system. If we have these individuals here in EDB—but we have to be very careful that we don't label people—we have to give them the best opportunity there is, because again this is part of modeling.

That's why we do give them opportunities to go to other places, that's why some of them have gone to other companies where you can grow faster, that's why we have alumni, you know, you can grow faster in other places . . . [pauses]

EHS Do you have a plan for how to teach a technical supervisor the people enhancement skills?

Director Yes, training and development, either in-house or we bring a program in, like even on a skill like empathic listening, there are programs on it, and we just have to evaluate whether they are good enough and some of the evaluations have already been done . . . and role modeling and role playing, both formalized and nonformalized programs; I mean on the job there is so much opportunity but, you know, they have to have the skill first, so we will do it formalized as well.

EHS And that will typically be by finding a good external program and then either putting everyone through it or bringing it in?

Director Yes . . . and that's where it feeds back into the training and development module.

EHS So are you going to be involved with this for some years?

Director Yes, a minimum of three to five years, but if you think of it being over in five years, no, of course, it's an ongoing thing . . . if you are building an organization or enhancing it you cannot say you are finished, we have arrived. But the first two years are really the most critical.

EHS And you see it really, the bottom line, as building an organization?

Director Well, the organization is built, and I always tell Chin Nam, actually, when I took on this program, that we have such a fantastic foundation, and my own vision is, "If we think we are excellent, you ain't seen nothing yet" [laughs].

I really feel that because we have such a talented pool of people, and people with experience from all over, like we have got people who have spent eight years in the U.S. in an international environment, in Germany, and in Japan, you know, bringing them all together, and because we are so busy doing so many things, I feel we are not tapping the latent expertise that we have in the EDB.

And so my own vision, that's why I am so excited about it, is that if we think we have done brilliantly—which we have, you know—I think we can do even more brilliantly because we are going to tap all the synergies of the different people. So that's why the whole program of organization development, and that's how I position it because that's how I see it, is talking about bringing EDB into a whole new level of performance that is beyond our imagination of what we have done. It's not just more of what we have done . . . but really an organization in which ideas are bubbling up from all over . . . even the clerk can come up with an idea, but it must be aligned. I mean, we don't want to have a crazy system where there is chaos . . . that's why the key to it is balance and alignment.

Concluding Note

All organizations tend to have the same weaknesses—communication failures across functional, hierarchical, or inclusionary boundaries, failure to define their goals, their products, and their customers, inability to get the resources they need to fulfill their plans and aspirations. The EDB has all of these organizational problems in some measure—occasional lack of coordination between departments, individuals hiding or harboring information that is needed in other parts of the organization, supervisors who are too technocratic or autocratic, overloaded and stressed out employees, turnover at certain levels of officers whom the organization wishes it could retain, career development problems, especially in moving people back from the field into headquarters, and so on.

The important point to recognize is that real organizational effectiveness is *not* just the inverse of these symptoms of failure. These kinds of problems have to be perpetually attended to and fixed, but paradoxically fixing them does not automatically create a more effective organization. Effectiveness has more to do with the alignment and integration of the various cultural components. As with a chain, a single weak link can be fatal. From that point of view the EDB is a very effective organization. The various elements of its culture align with each other and produce a whole that is greater than the sum of its parts.

The biggest lesson to learn from all of this is that overall sustained success such as Singapore and the EDB has had depends upon many factors working in concert with one another. Singling out individual factors such as leadership or favorable geography clearly is not sufficient, but even if we go beyond this into the inner cultural workings of the society, it is not enough to single out political stability or teamwork or strong government intervention, or the choice of a particular economic strategy. It was the combination of all of them that made Singapore's growth possible.

The culture of the EDB is full of strengths. There are no obvious dysfunctional elements. The problem will be how to sustain such a culture since it depends very much on a common task that the organization is very committed to. Singapore as a whole will have the same problem. Can it sustain the work ethic, the level of motivation, and the level of sacrifice that its people have displayed so far? Can it make the transition from a very benign, paternalistic regime to one where higher levels of individualism and diversity will require much more complicated governance structures and conflict resolution methods? Singapore is now contemplating whether to escalate the concept of a learning organization to itself as a learning nation. This image seems very appropriate. Perhaps as Singapore continues to learn, the world can also learn something more from Singapore.

Appendix: List of People Interviewed

Anthony Ang, Armstrong Industries
Charles Atkinson, Whole Brain Corporation
Frank Cassidy, DEC
Chan Chin Bock, EDB
Peter Chen, Shell
Shirley Chen, EDB
Chia Teck Swee, DBS Bank
B. C. Chong, DuPont
Chong Lit-Cheong, EDB
Kevin Chua, EDB
Clyde Coombs, Hewlett-Packard
S. Dhanabalan, former Minister of Trade and Industry
Robert England, Texas Instruments
Eric Goh, EDB Alumnus
Dr. Goh Keng Swee, Former Minister of Finance
Penny Goh, EDB
T. K. Goh, SGS Thomson
Barry Goldstein, DEC/Modular
Bud Green, Polysar
Paul Henessey, The Bay Group
Roger Hsu, Lubrizol
Willian Hui, Asian Environmental Improvement Project
P. Y. Hwang, Temasek Holdings
Hisashi Isozaki, Hitachi Electronic Devices
Marc Jean, Thomson Consumer Electronics
Khoo Seok Lin, EDB

Lawrence Khor, Mobil

Koh Tat Liang, Apple

Lam Yeen Lan, EDB

Bonite Lee, EDB

BG Lee Hsien Loong, Deputy Prime Minister

Lee Kuan Yew, Senior Minister

Lee Suan Hiang, EDB

Lee Yock Suan, Minister of Education

Dr. Lien Ying Chow, Overseas Union Bank

Adelaine Lim, EDB

Lim Chiang Peng, EPAN Cable & Wire

Grace Lim, EDB

Lim Swee-Say, EDB

Loh Leok Yeen, EDB

Loh Wai Kiew, EDB

Bernard Lim, Apple

A. V. Liventals, Mobil

E. J. Mayer, C/O Meda, Israel

Ed McDonough, DEC

Donald Michael, formerly of University of Michigan

John Miller, AT&T

Jaya Mohideen, EDB Consulting

Allen Murray, Mobil

S. Natarajan, EDB

James Ng, EDB

Ng Pock Too, Sunstrand Corp., formerly with Sembawang Group

Ngiam Tong Dow, DBS Bank, Permanent Secretary Ministry of Finance

Vicki Novak, EDB

Mel O'Donnel, Fisher Rosemount Systems

Felix Ong, Seksun Precision Engineering

Lucian Pye, MIT

Gordon Redding, University of Hong Kong

John Sanders, Apple

M. Saravanamuthu, Shell

Peter Seah, Overseas Union Bank

Timothy Sebastian, EDB
Masanobu Sekiya, SONY
Daniel Selvaretnam, EDB
Shum Sze Keong, EDB
Renato Sirtori, SGS Thomson Micrelectronics
Tan Chin Nam, EDB
Lana Tan, EDB
Peter Tan, Apple
Sonny Tan, EDB
I. F. Tang, Wearne Bros. Ltd.
Rei Torres, Shell
G. Urschel, Thomson Consumer Electronics, Video Group
Gary Weitz, CoActive
Alan White, MIT
Garland Williamson, Eastman Chemicals
Wong Choon Fei, International Video Products
Ernest Wong, United Overseas Bank
M. Q. Wong, EDB Alumnus
Edgar Woolard, DuPont
Yeo Chow Tong, Minister of Trade and Industry
Philip Yeo, EDB
Yeo Seng Teck, Trade Development Board
Patrick Yeo, DBS Bank

Notes

Chapter 2

1. Toh Mun Heng, "Partnership with Multinational Corporations," in Linda Low et al., *Challenge and Response* (Singapore: *Times Academic Press,* 1993), p. 152.

2. The data are based on interviews conducted in 1993 and 1994 with Senior Minister Lee Kuan Yew, Minister S. Dhanabalan, Dr. Goh Keng Swee, Mr. Chan Chin Bock, Mr. I. F. Tang, Mr. Ngiam Tong Dow, Mr. P. Y. Hwang, Mrs. Shirley Chen, Mr. Ng Pock Too, Mr. Daniel Selvaretnam, and correspondence with Mr. E. J. Mayer and Dr. A. Winsemius.

3. T. J. Bellows, "Bridging Tradition and Modernization: The Singapore Bureaucracy," in Hung-chao Tai, ed., *Confucianism and Economic Development: An Oriental Alternative?* (Washington, D.C.: Washington Institute Press, 1989), p. 195.

4. These historical comments are based partly on D. Bloodworth's account of the history of communism in Singapore, reported in his book *The Tiger and the Trojan Horse* (Singapore: Times Books International, 1986), and on comments made by Senior Minister Lee, Dr. Goh, and the three former EDB chairmen.

5. Quoted from a letter Dr. Winsemius sent to correct a number of points in my draft chapter, 1 August 1994.

6. United Nations *Expectation and Reality,* 1961. Part 3, "Organization," section 6.2, entitled "Operations."

7. Mr. Mayer's impressions were conveyed to me in a series of letters in response to my 1994 inquiry regarding his role in the EDB.

8. United Nations, 1961.

9. Excerpted from the *Straits Times,* 24 November 1961.

10. Mayer, 1993 correspondence.

11. The Colombo Plan was the result of a meeting of the Commonwealth ministers in Colombo, Sri Lanka, in 1950; a fund was created to support

various efforts by the less developed countries to launch programs of financial and technical aid for economic development. Among its provisions was a scholarship program under which qualified applicants could attend Commonwealth universities.

Chapter 3

1. L. Low, "The Economic Development Board," in Linda Low et al., *Challenge and Response,* p. 63.

2. Ibid.; EDB, *Thirty Years of Economic Development,* 1992.

3. *Strategic Economic Plan,* 1991, pp. 2–5.

4. *Strategic Economic Plan,* 1991, pp. 7, 8.

Chapter 4

1. Information about the late Mr. Hon Sui Sen is based primarily on interview data from former colleagues and subordinates. In addition, I have read all available biographical material and have integrated that wherever possible.

2. *The Shell Endeavor: First Hundred Years in Singapore,* 1991, p. 16.

Chapter 5

1. Information about Mr. I. F. Tang is based primarily on interview data from former subordinates, the other former chairmen, and several long meetings with him during which his own history was covered in some detail.

2. Information about Chan Chin Bock was obtained primarily from several long interviews with him, his colleagues, the other former chairmen and his subordinates.

3. EDB, *Thirty Years of Economic Development,* p. 34.

Chapter 6

1. EDB, *Thirty Years of Economic Development,* p. 37.

2. Information on Mr. Ngiam Tong Dow is based on interviews with him and comments from former subordinates, the other former chairmen, and colleagues.

3. EDB, *Thirty Years of Economic Development,* p. 45.

4. Information on Mr. P. Y. Hwang is based on interviews with him and comments from former subordinates, the other former chairmen, and colleagues.

Chapter 7

1. EDB, *Thirty Years of Economic Development,* 1992, p. 48.

2. *Singapore Sunday Times,* 19 June 1994.

3. Information about Philip Yeo was obtained from subordinates, colleagues, former chairmen, and alumni, as well as from direct observation and several long interviews with him.

4. *Singapore Business,* August 1991, p. 24.

5. *10th Anniversary Report of the National Computer Board,* 1991, p. 12.

6. *Singapore Sunday Times,* 19 June 1994.

7. It is interesting to note that the earlier system that Hon Sui Sen had simply taken over from the British civil service was now asserted by Philip Yeo and Tan Chin Nam, his managing director, as a contemporary principle of organization. Yeo's stated theory was that *the organization had to be completely open with respect to information* and Tan frequently referred to the "*boundaryless organization.*"

8. Philip Yeo was recently given an award by the government of Indonesia for his regionalization efforts.

9. The need to have real insight and entrepreneurial energy on the Tourist Board led to the recent decision to ask Mr. Tan Chin Nam to become the chief executive of the Tourist Promotion Board and to work closely with the EDB in furthering the concept of tourism as one of the pillars of economic development strategy.

Chapter 8

1. The details of that story are found in chapter 1.

2. *Singapore Investment News,* Singapore: EDB, July 1995, p. 4.

3. Ibid., p. 4.

Chapter 10

1. This model of "culture" is based on my book *Organizational Culture and Leadership,* 2d ed. (San Francisco: Jossey-Bass, 1992). What I call a "basic assumption" often contains both a component of what one *believes to be true* and a component of how one thinks things *ought to be.* Both elements, however, have come to be *taken for granted* to the point where they are more or less non-negotiable and non-discussable. Whereas such assumptions might be argued about early in the history of an organization, once they become operational and "work" in the sense of producing actions that solve the organization's problems of how to survive and thrive in its particular

environment, they come to be viewed increasingly as how things actually are.

2. Ibid., chapters 8 and 9.

3. This issue becomes especially relevant if the Singapore "model" of economic development is being viewed by other countries as a model for their development. It would be easy to mistakenly take one or two elements of the EDB culture, try to build those into the workings of another economic development organization and yet fail completely in attracting foreign investment or stimulating internal growth. The EDB culture needs to be understood in its entirety before one can try to extrapolate to other countries how the lessons of Singapore might or might not apply. Members of the EDB who have become involved in helping other countries are acutely aware of these differences and do *not* try to advocate their model; rather they work on helping each country work within its own cultural boundaries.

4. R. McVey, "The Materialization of the Southeast Asian Entrepreneur," in R. McVey, ed., *Southeast Asian Capitalists* (Ithaca: Cornell University Press, 1992).

5. "The intimate relationship between the statutory boards and private companies has considerably enhanced the influence of the civil service, since Division I officers are placed in charge of the statutory boards. Many top civil servants also sit on the boards of directors of private companies to oversee government investments, loans, and interests. Through these arrangements, the influence of civil servants is effectively diffused throughout the entire economy." T. J. Bellows, "Bridging Tradition and Modernization: The Singapore Bureaucracy," in Hung-chao Tai, ed., *Confucianism and Economic Development: An Oriental Alternative?* p. 207.

6. "At the top of the Singapore government stand the political elite and the Administrative Service of the bureaucracy. . . . The pre-eminence of the Administrative Service dates back to the colonial days when Singapore was governed by the Malayan Civil Service; the Administrative Officers, known as AO ever since, were once dubbed 'the heaven born' or the 'mandarinate.' The elite status of the Administrative Service continues to this day. The 'new Singapore mandarin,' as a cabinet minister once described, is more interested in being right than in being popular. He must tell the people the truth—which is that progress, peace, and prosperity can be achieved only if people are prepared to pay the price." (S. Rajaratnam, 1970 speech, quoted in Bellows, "Bridging Tradition and Modernization," p. 204). Technical expertise and administrative orientation in the Singapore cabinet encourage a close, professional working relationship between the highest level of the civil service hierarchy and the PAP leadership. This working relationship helps promote top civil servants to cabinet membership. See also L. Pye, *Asian Power and Politics* (Cambridge, MA: Harvard University Press, 1985), p. 40.

7. Bellows, "Bridging Tradition and Modernization," pp. 196–1197.

8. Ibid., p. 210.

9. Excerpts from *The Next Lap,* 1991, pp. 15, 16, 33, 41, 49.

10. The *Straits Times,* 28 April 1971, p. 3.

Chapter 11

1. Philip Yeo, *Singapore, The Sunday Times,* 19 June 1994.

2. EDB Annual Report, 1969, pp. 19–20.

3. R. K. Merton, *Social Theory and Social Structure* (New York: Free Press, 1968).

4. Soon Teck Wong. "Education and Human Resource Development," in L. Low et al., *Challenge and Response,* p. 245.

5. Among the countries offering such scholarships were the United Kingdom, Australia, New Zealand, Canada, Japan, Germany, France, and the United States.

6. Details pertaining to potential or present investors are guarded closely and each EDB officer is required to sign a nondisclosure agreement to guarantee the confidentiality of information pertaining to particular companies.

7. Pye, *Asian Power and Politics;* S. G. Redding, *The Spirit of Chinese Capitalism* (New York: de Gruyter, 1993).

8. Ibid.

9. P. Senge, *The Fifth Discipline: The Art and Practice of the Learning Organization* (New York: Doubleday, 1990).

10. S. Covey, *The Seven Habits of Highly Effective People* (New York: Simon and Schuster, 1989). Covey runs open seminars on this topic regularly. Several people from the EDB attended one of them in order to assess it and decided it was the appropriate learning vehicle.

Chapter 12

1. Schein, *Organizational Culture and Leadership.*

2. Tan Chee Keon, "Promoting Entrepreneurship in Singapore," MIT Sloan School of Management, Master's Thesis, 1994, pp. 122–126.

3. E. B. Roberts, *Entrepreneurs in High Technology* (New York: Oxford University Press, 1991).

4. Tan Chee Keon, "Promoting Entrepreneurship in Singapore."

5. Mr. Chan Chin Bock commented that if Singapore is to get ahead, it must leverage its defense technology. The EDB's current chairman, Philip Yeo, was in fact originally from the ministry of defense, and his appointment first to the Computer Board and then the EDB was apparently intentional. An-

other comment that suggests that the technology issue is critical was made in response to my questioning what their attitude toward Taiwan was. The comment was made that Taiwan is a bigger country with its own home market, and that the only relevance of Taiwan to Singapore would be to watch carefully what role government there played in the development of science and technology.

6. Bellows, "Bridging Tradition and Modernization," p. 198.

7. G. Hofstede and M. H. Bond, "The Confucius Connection: From Cultural Roots to Economic Growth," *Organizational Dynamics* 16, 4 (1988): 4–21.

8. The best analysis along these lines is provided by Philippe Regnier in *Singapore: City-State in South East Asia* (Honolulu: University of Hawaii Press, 1987).

9. M. Q. Sibley, *Technology and Utopian Thought* (Minneapolis: Burgess, 1971). Quoted in W. O. Lee *Social Change and Educational Problems in Japan, Singapore, and Hong Kong* (New York: St. Martin's Press, 1991), p. 129.

10. J. W. Salaff, *State and Family in Singapore* (Ithaca: Cornell University Press, 1988).

11. Lee, *Social Change and Educational Problems in Japan, Singapore, and Hong Kong,* p. 122.

Chapter 13

1. Senge, *The Fifth Discipline.*

2. Covey, *The Seven Habits of Highly Effective People.* N. Herrman, *The Creative Brain,* 2d ed. (Lake Lure, N.C.: Brain Books, 1990)

Chapter 14

1. D. McGregor, *The Human Side of Enterprise* (New York: McGraw-Hill, 1960). See also E. H. Schein, "In Defense of Theory Y," *Organizational Dynamics* 4, 1 (1975): pp. 17–30.

2 The best statement of these requirements is in W. Bennis and B. Nanus, *Leaders* (New York: Harper and Row, 1985).

3. Schein, *Organizational Culture and Leadership,* chapters 15 to 17.

4. F. C. Deyo, ed., *The Political Economy of the New Asian Industrialism* (Ithaca: Cornell University Press, 1987); R. McVey, (ed.), *Southeast Asian Capitalists;* Pye, *Asian Power and Politics;* Redding, *The Spirit of Chinese Capitalism;* Hung-chao Tai, ed., *Confucianism and Economic Development: An Oriental Alternative?*

References

Most of the references in this list are directly correlated to the readings referred to in the footnotes. However, this list also contains a number of general readings that were critical to an understanding of Singapore but were not specifically referred to in any one place in the text. I have not made specific references to the various newspapers, brochures, and house organs published by the EDB, and a myriad of other materials that provided a general context for the research.

Bellows, T. J. 1989. "Bridging Tradition and Modernization: The Singapore Bureaucracy." In Hung-chao Tai (ed.), *Confucianism and Economic Development: An Oriental Alternative?* Washington, D.C.: Washington Institute press.

Bennis, W., and Nanus, B. 1985. *Leaders.* New York: Harper and Row.

Bloodworth, D. 1986. *The Tiger and the Trojan Horse.* Singapore: Times Books International.

Bond, M. H. (ed.) 1986. *The Psychology of the Chinese People.* New York: Oxford University Press.

Covey, S. 1989. *The Seven Habits of Highly Effective People.* New York: Simon and Schuster.

Deyo, F. C. 1983. "Chinese Management Practices and Work Commitment in Comparative Perspective." In L. A. P. Gosling and L. Y. C. Lim (eds.), *The Chinese in Southeast Asia. Vol. 2: Identity, Culture, and Politics.* Singapore: Maruzen Asia.

Deyo, F. C. (ed.) 1987. *The Political Economy of the New Asian Industrialism.* Ithaca: Cornell University Press.

Deyo, F. C. 1989. *Beneath the Miracle.* Berkeley: University of California Press.

Economic Development Board. 1992. *Thirty Years of Economic Development.*

Economic Development Board. 1993. *Growing With Enterprise: A National Report.*

Herrmann, N. 1990. *The Creative Brain* 2d ed. Lake Lure, N.C.: Brain Books.

Hicks, G. L. and Redding S. G. 1992. "The Story of the East Asian 'Economic Miracle': Part One: Economic Theory Be Damned!" *Euro-Asian Business Review* Vol. 2, No. 3, pp. 24–32. "Part Two: The Culture Connection." Vol. 2, No. 4, pp. 18–22.

Hofstede, G. 1980. *Culture's Consequences.* Newbury Park, CA: Sage.

Hofstede, G., and Bond, M. H. 1988. "The Confucius Connection: From Cultural Roots to Economic Growth." *Organizational Dynamics* 16, 4: 4–21.

Hsu, P. S. C. 1987. "Patterns of Work Goal Importance: A Comparison of Singapore and Taiwanese Managers." *Asia-Pacific Journal of Management* 4, 3: 152–166.

Lee, W. O. 1991. *Social Change and Educational Problems in Japan, Singapore, and Hong Kong.* New York: St. Martin's Press.

Lodge, G. C., and Vogel, E. F. (eds.) 1986. *Ideology and National Competitiveness.* Cambridge, MA: Harvard Business School Press.

Low, L. 1993. "The Economic Development Board." In L. Low et al., *Challenge and Response.*

Low, L., Toh Mun Heng, Soon Teck Wong, Tan Kong Yam, and Helen Hughes. 1993. *Challenge and Response.* Singapore: Times Academic Press.

McGregor, D. 1960. *The Human Side of Enterprise.* New York: McGraw-Hill.

McVey, R. 1992. "The Materialization of the Southeast Asian Entrepreneur." In R. McVey (ed.), *Southeast Asian Capitalists.* Ithaca: Cornell University Press.

Merton, R. K. 1968. *Social Theory and Social Structure.* New York: Free Press.

National Computer Board of Singapore. 1991. *10th Anniversary Report of the National Computer Board.*

Pugh, D. S. 1993. "Cultural Differences in Attitudes and Values." In T. D. Weinshall (ed.) *Societal Culture and Management.* New York: de Gruyter.

Pye, L. 1985. *Asian Power and Politics.* Cambridge, MA: Harvard University Press.

Redding, S. G. 1980. "Cognition as an Aspect of Culture and Its Relation to Management Processes: An Exploratory View of the Chinese Case." *Journal of Management Studies* (May): 127–148.

Redding, S. G., and Ng, M. 1982. "The Role of 'Face' in the Organizational Perceptions of Chinese Managers." *Organization Studies* 3/3: 201–219.

Redding, S. G. 1986. "Developing Managers without 'Management Development': The Overseas Chinese Solution." *Management Education and Development* 17, Pt. 3: 271–281.

Redding, S. G. 1991. *Determinant of the Competitive Power of Small Business Networking: The Overseas Chinese Case.* Fontainebleau: Insead.

Redding, S. G. 1991. "Weak Organizations and Strong Linkages: Managerial Ideology and Chinese Family Business Networks." In G. G. Hamilton (ed.), *Business Networks and Economic Development in East and Southeast Asia.* Hong Kong: Centre of Asian Studies.

Redding, S. G. 1993. *The Spirit of Chinese Capitalism.* New York: de Gruyter.

Redding, S. G., Norman A., and Schlander, A. 1991. "The Nature of Individual Attachment to the Organization: A Review of East Asian Variations." In M. D. Dunnette (ed.), *Handbook of Industrial and Organizational Psychology.* Vol. 4. Palo Alto: Consulting Psychologists Press.

Redding, G., and Wong, G. Y. Y. 1986. "The Psychology of Chinese Organizational Behavior." In M. H. Bond (ed.), *The Psychology of the Chinese People.* London: Oxford University Press.

Regnier, P. 1987. *Singapore: City-State in South East Asia.* Honolulu: University of Hawaii Press.

Roberts, E. B. 1991. *Entrepreneurs in High Technology.* New York: Oxford University Press.

Salaff, J. W. 1988. *State and Family in Singapore.* Ithaca: Cornell University Press.

Schein, E. H. 1975. "In Defense of Theory Y." *Organizational Dynamics* 4, 1: 17–30.

Schein, E. H. 1987a. *Process Consultation, Vol. 2.* Reading, MA: Addison-Wesley.

Schein, E. H. 1987b. *The Clinical Perspective in Fieldwork.* Newbury Park, CA: Sage.

Schein, E. H. 1992. *Organizational Culture and Leadership,* 2d ed. San Francisco: Jossey-Bass.

Senge, P. 1990. *The Fifth Discipline: The Art and Practice of the Learning Organization.* New York: Doubleday.

Sibley, M. Q. 1971. *Technology and Utopian Thought.* Minneapolis: Burgess.

Government of Singapore. 1991. *Strategic Economic Plan.*

Government of Singapore. 1991. *The Next Lap.*

Soon Teck Wong. 1993. "Education and Human Resource Development." In L. Low et al., *Challenge and Response.*

Tai, H. C. (ed.) 1989. *Confucianism and Economic Development: An Oriental Alternative?* Washington, D.C.: Washington Institute Press.

Tan Chee Keon. 1994. "Promoting Entrepreneurship in Singapore." MIT Sloan School of Management, Master's Thesis.

Toh Mun Heng. 1993. "Partnership with Multinational Corporations." In L. Low et al., *Challenge and Response.*

Tong, C. K. 1990. "Centripetal Authority, Differentiated Networks: The Social Organization of Chinese Firms in Singapore." In G. G. Hamilton (ed.), *Business Groups and Economic Development in East Asia.* Hong Kong: Centre of Asian Studies.

United Nations. 1961. *Expectation and Reality.* Part 3, "Organization," section 6.2, entitled "Operations."

Van Maanen, J. 1988. *Tales of the Field.* Chicago: University of Chicago Press.

Index

JTC. *See* Jurong Township Corporation
Jurong Industrial Arts, 41
Jurong Industrial Estate, 62, 162
Jurong Industrial Park, 91
Jurong Township Corporation (JTC), 21, 62, 66, 109, 118, 119, 123, 167, 169

Karimun, 111
Khoo Seok Lin, 199
  on career development, 246–249
Korea. *See* South Korea
Kotler, Philip, 107

Labor, 21, 22, 150, 171, 172–173, 206
  and management, 36–37
  shortage of, 48, 77, 210
  skilled, 71, 72, 81–83, 84, 135–136
Land, 108, 119
  management of, 61–62, 65, 167, 175, 214
Leadership, 120–121, 188, 236, 240–241
  sectoral collaboration and, 165–169
  and teamwork, 179–182
  Theory Y, 238–240
Leapfrogging, 35
Learning, 13
  commitment to, 197–201
Lee Hsien Loong, 50
Lee Kuan Yew, 29, 30, 31, 39, 40, 42, 43, 49, 52, 69–70, 108, 121, 138, 165, 169, 173, 174, 184, 187, 197, 198, 215, 218
  on education reform, 35–36
  and hierarchical boundaries, 192–193
  leadership of, 140, 166, 216, 222, 240–241
  and E. J. Mayer, 34–35
Lee Suan Hiang, 107
Lee Yock Suan, 83

LEF scheme. *See* Local Enterprise Finance scheme
Levitt, Ted, 107
Lim, Bernard, 140
Lim Chiang Peng, 151
LIUP scheme. *See* Local Industries Upgrading Program
Liventals, A. V., 118–119, 120, 121–122
Local Enterprise Finance (LEF) scheme, 150
Local Industries Upgrading Program (LIUP), 143, 146, 150, 151–152
Lockheed, 47
Lodge, George, 193
London, 83, 94
Lubrizol Corporation, 126–129

McDonough, Ed, 134–136
McGregor, D., 238–240
Machinists, 81, 82
Malaya, 31–32
Malays, 44, 69
Malaysia, 51, 111, 124, 134, 206
Malaysian Federation, 1, 47, 69, 79
Management, managers, 1, 13, 14, 15, 115, 138–139, 163–164, 246
  Chan Chin Bock's style, 79–81
  Hon Sui Sen's style, 62–63, 68–69
  P. Y. Hwang's style, 95–96
  and labor, 36–37
  Ngiam Tong Dow's style, 88–90
  and officer corps, 182–184
  I. F. Tang's style, 73–76
  Theory Y, 238–240, 241
  Philip Yeo's style, 101–105
Management theory, 8–9
Manpower development, 111
Manufacturing, 11, 19, 32–33, 34, 36, 38, 47, 49, 51, 77, 123, 308
Marketing, 51, 107, 113–114
Marks and Spencer, 35
MAS. *See* Monetary Authority of Singapore
Matsushita (MESA), 53